THIS WOMAN

THIS WOMAN

The Secret Prison Affair and Escape Plot of
Myra Hindley, Britain's Most Notorious Criminal

HOWARD SOUNES

SEVEN DIALS

First published in Great Britain in 2022 by Seven Dials,
this paperback edition published in 2023 by Seven Dials,
an imprint of The Orion Publishing Group Ltd
Carmelite House, 50 Victoria Embankment
London EC4Y 0DZ

An Hachette UK Company

1 3 5 7 9 10 8 6 4 2

A CIP catalogue record for this book is
available from the British Library.

ISBN (Mass Market Paperback) 978 1 8418 8511 7
ISBN (eBook) 978 1 8418 8512 4
ISBN (Audio) 978 1 8418 8513 1

Typeset by Born Group
Printed and bound in Great Britain by Clays Ltd, Elcograf S.p.A.

MIX
Paper from
responsible sources
FSC
www.fsc.org FSC® C104740

www.orionbooks.co.uk

CONTENTS

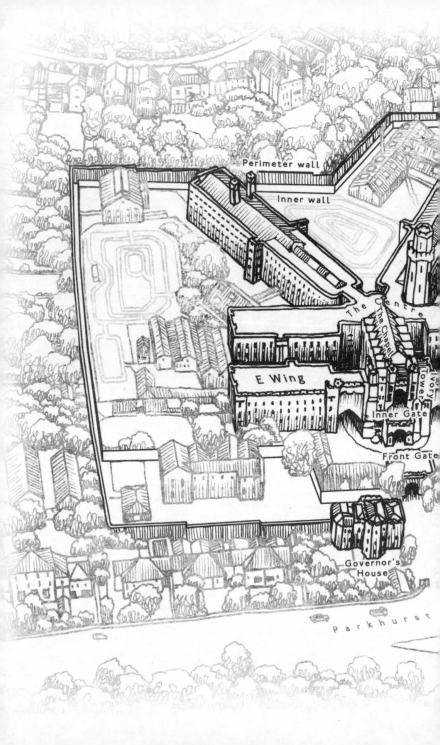

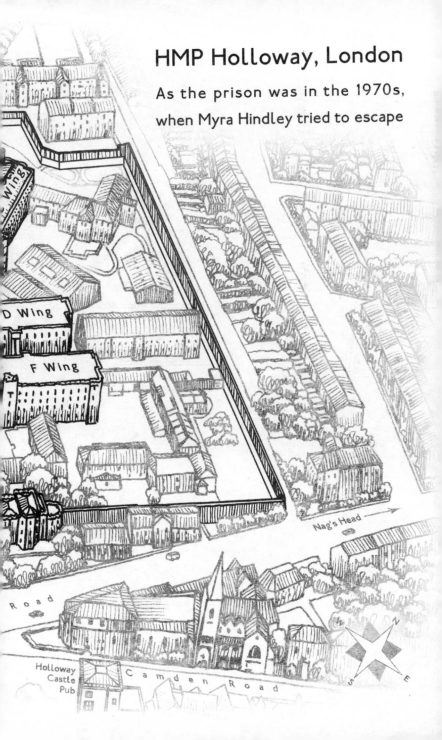

HMP Holloway, London

As the prison was in the 1970s, when Myra Hindley tried to escape

I

MYRA HINDLEY IN LOVE

One evening in 1971, the prisoner Muriel Clarke told one of the guards in Holloway that a fellow inmate, Violet Ali, had left a piece of cannabis wrapped in foil in her cell. She also said that Violet had £15 in cash, which was against prison rules. Muriel was reporting Violet because she was frightened that she might hide drugs and money in her cell.

The following day when Violet was searched by prison staff she was found to be carrying a fountain pen with £5 inside. She was put on report and confined to her cell on E Wing, where Muriel, 'full of remorse for having reported her', brought her tea. 'I poured the tea through the observation hole in the door. She had her cup held to the hole on the other side of the door.' As she drank her tea, Violet said that she was thinking of telling the screws that the money belonged to another inmate.

'I advised her to tell the truth,' said Muriel.

Five days later, Violet told prison officer Miss Browning that she had been passing letters and gifts, including the £5, for a prisoner and her girlfriend who, she claimed, was a prison officer. Having started as a dispute between two inmates, this suddenly became a much more serious matter.

Violet's allegation was reported to Deputy Governor Hildegard Leissner, an East European with a German accent who had been held in an internment camp during World War Two. Wrongly assuming Miss Leissner to have been a Nazi guard, rather than an inmate, the women teased her in Holloway, asking, 'Did you know Hitler, Miss?'

Leissner came to Violet's cell and asked her if she stood by her story. 'You know it is an offence against prison discipline to make false and malicious allegations against an officer,' she warned. If Violet meant to pursue the matter, she would have to make a statement.

'I can't make this statement, as I can't read and write,' said Violet. 'I want help.'

So she dictated her statement. 'About seven months ago I was approached by Myra Hindley and asked if I could keep a secret. She told me she was in love with officer Miss Cairns. She said she would give me letters to carry from her, and I should give [the] letters to Miss Cairns, and she would give me letters to carry back.' Violet carried up to three letters a day for the women, sometimes containing gifts, like the £5 note hidden in the fountain pen. She said that Cairns now wanted to give Hindley a key to the dining room, so they could meet secretly. Violet was speaking out because she didn't want to get into more trouble.

Myra Hindley was the most infamous female criminal in the country, and a Category A inmate held under the highest security in Her Majesty's Prison (HMP) Holloway. The allegation that this notorious, dangerous woman might be conducting a clandestine affair with one of her jailers, someone entrusted to keep her safely locked up, and that this prison officer, Miss Cairns, was trying to give Hindley a key, was alarming.

Hildegard Leissner hurried out of Violet's cell, through the clanging gate at the end of E Wing, and ran upstairs to tell the governor.

2

WE'VE ONLY JUST BEGUN

The Victorians built Holloway prison to look like a castle, with battlements and turrets, topped by a chimney that was crenellated and pierced with arrow loops like a medieval tower. The prison had been built right up to the pavement on Parkhurst Road in north London, along which the life of the city streamed: its black taxis, double-decker buses and pedestrians passing within yards of the inmates, but protected from them by the prison gate and wall; while over the years houses and flats were built up to the prison walls on the other three sides. By the 1970s, Holloway was an antiquated relic of the last century in the midst of the modern metropolis, with a melancholy atmosphere that one former prison governor describes as 'built-in depression'. The 120-year-old jail had become so decrepit that it was scheduled for demolition.

If Holloway was a castle, the governor was its queen. Dorothy Wing was a matronly woman in her sixties who had previously served as an army officer. Divorced, without children, Mrs Wing joined the Prison Service in 1956, becoming the governor of HMP Holloway, Europe's largest female prison, the year after Myra Hindley became its most famous resident. Mrs Wing lived in the governor's house by the front gate, close enough to bustle back into the prison at short notice if the emergency bell rang, or if staff blew long blasts on their whistles to signal an escape. The governor's job was stressful and Mrs Wing drank. She had a drink with lunch, and she liked to invite senior staff into her flat for a sherry. She was sometimes seen to clutch the railings on the landings to steady herself as she toured the prison in the afternoon, checking on 'my girls', and handing out cigarettes to win their trust.

Most women in Holloway smoked, which added to the stench of a smelly place. Inmates were restricted to one bath per week, in nine inches of water, and many women didn't bathe at all, because the dominant prisoners hogged the bath for themselves and their friends, so body odour was rank. Women washed on a daily basis in buckets in their cells, and they relieved themselves in potties which they slopped out each morning, if they hadn't tipped the contents out of the cell window overnight, to dribble down the prison walls into the yard, where the shit was collected by work parties of prisoners. The prison crawled with vermin: cockroaches, mice and rats; while feral pigeons nested in the rafters. Their droppings added to the general pong. 'The place stank,' says former Holloway officer, Veronica Bird. 'It was horrendous walking in through that prison gate.'

Holloway also rang with noise day and night, not just cell doors banging, gates closing and keys jangling in locks, but ungovernable and desperate women fighting, screaming and weeping in despair. The most disturbed inmates were strapped into restrictive dresses known as 'strips', then locked in padded cells under the wings as if they were in Hell.

Even Mrs Wing admitted that Holloway was grim, though it was a model prison when it opened in 1852, built to the new panopticon design, so that an officer standing in the middle of the complex – an iron cage of bars, gates and stairs

4

known as the Centre – could see every cell on the four main radiating wings. There were two more, smaller wings facing Parkhurst Road, including E Wing, where Myra was held with the other long-term prisoners and high-security inmates.

Dorothy Wing was not a harsh governor. She believed that depriving women of their liberty was punishment enough, and she had pushed through a popular reform that allowed the women to wear their own clothes, rather than the uniform Myra wore when she first arrived at Holloway. Mrs Wing believed in rehabilitation, even for Myra, who she had got to know better than most prisoners. It was her statutory duty to check personally on all Category A prisoners every day, and Myra often requested private interviews, so they spoke frequently.

One definition of a Category A inmate was that they were 'highly dangerous'. Myra was never violent in prison, but her crimes were appalling. Together with her boyfriend, Ian Brady, she had picked up children and teenagers to sexually abuse and murder, for their pleasure. Four of the victims were buried on the moors near Manchester, the youngest being just ten years old. Two were twelve years old. The fifth and eldest victim, a youth of seventeen, was found dead in Hindley's bedroom with his head smashed in. The case was bizarre and nightmarish, with Hindley reviled as an unnatural woman for the way she had treated these children. Her brassy appearance in court confirmed her heartless image, and the popular view was that she was lucky not to have ended up swinging by a rope. If she had been convicted a few months earlier, before the law stopped judicial execution for murder, she would have been hanged.

Despite the horror of the case, some of the people who got to know Myra in Holloway found her to be very different to their expectations of a child-killer. Far from behaving like a monster, Myra was an intelligent, calm and personable young woman, and one or two even believed her when she said that she hadn't, in fact, killed anyone. She said that her principal mistake had been to fall in love with Brady, who planned and carried out the Moors murders. She went along with it, to some extent, because she was besotted with her boyfriend, and terrified that he might kill her, too. Although they were both convicted of murder, the trial judge agreed that Myra was primarily Brady's follower. 'Though I believe that Brady is wicked beyond belief without hope of redemption . . . I cannot feel the same is necessarily true of Hindley once she is removed from his influence,' Justice Fenton Atkinson wrote to the Home Secretary after sentencing the couple in 1966. 'At present she is as deeply corrupted as Brady, but it is not so long ago that she was . . . a normal sort of girl.'

In the fifth year of her sentence, and still only twenty-seven years old, Myra no longer resembled the sullen peroxide blonde with dark eyes in her iconic police mug shot, one of the most famous photographs of the 1960s, or the hag in the dock at Chester Assizes. Her hair was naturally brown again, and cut in a more becoming, modern style, though she had the unhealthy pallor of someone who spent all her time inside. 'She looked very pale, what they call "prison grey". Her hair had no shape or bounce,' says Veronica Bird. 'She looked quite transparent.' With the little money she earned working in prison, Myra assembled a small wardrobe of fashionable clothes, including high boots and short skirts, that made her look like any other young woman in 1971. She also read voraciously and took a keen interest in her education, already having taught herself German. As she became better educated, Myra adopted new mannerisms – such as referring to herself or others as 'one' – but she never lost her working–class Manchester accent, speaking slowly and quietly in a flat, joyless voice. She appeared to be a model prisoner, save for the fact that she refused to acknowledge her guilt.

When she met the governor privately, Myra tried to persuade Mrs Wing that she was trustworthy enough to be decategorised, which would give her more freedom in the prison; and she talked longingly of being released on parole. Mrs Wing was sympathetic, though she knew that parole was a distant dream for Myra. She didn't realise how desperate she was to be free. Privately, Myra was consumed with what prisoners call 'gate fever'. She was determined to get out of Holloway, by hook or by crook.

As well as craving freedom, Myra was a woman in the prime of life who wanted love and affection. Separated from Ian Brady, and locked up with three hundred women, her prison life was that of a gay woman.

'Who is that?' Myra asked her friend Carole Callaghan one day in 1970, while standing on her bed to peek through the cell window. A prison officer around their age, smartly dressed in the blue service uniform, which was worn with a tricorn hat, was walking across the courtyard into work. Myra liked the look of this young jailer. 'She's nice.'

Carole was one of Myra's few friends in Holloway. While most inmates shunned her as a 'nonce', a person involved in sex offences against children, and many women were scared of her, Carole developed respect for the way that Myra coped with her life in prison. Carole was a gangster's moll from Cardiff, coming to the end of her sentence for demanding money with menaces, and she wasn't scared of anybody. She was also clever, like Myra. The women made each other laugh, and they worked happily together in the tapestry room.

Although they were heterosexual on the outside (Carole was married, and Myra thought of Ian Brady as her common law husband), both had lesbian relationships in Holloway. 'When you are in prison for a time you must, as a necessity, form a lesbian relationship. You've got to have some outlet for your emotions,' Carole told a man from the BBC, when the corporation filmed in Holloway at this time. 'Most of the women in Holloway have got some lesbian tendencies . . . it's perfectly natural.'

The young prison officer who had caught Myra's eye was Patricia Cairns. Some people called her Pat, but she preferred to be known as Trisha. She was twenty-six years old with a solemn face and short, dark hair, and she tended to wear a scarf to cover her neck. When Trisha Cairns escorted Myra and some other inmates to the prison library one day, not long after Myra had caught a first glimpse of her from her cell window, the women got a closer look at each other. Trisha was as smitten with Myra as the prisoner was with her. 'She stood out, straight-backed and calm, not like the others. They were chatting away. She would think that was beneath her. She was very dignified,' Trisha told Duncan Staff for his book, *The Lost Boy: The Definitive Story of the Moors Murders.* 'And she was very bonny in those days as well.'

Shortly afterwards, Trisha Cairns was walking past Myra's cell when she saw an inmate lounging on her bed, which was against the rules. When she entered the cell, to tell this woman off, she saw that Myra was also in the room, stark naked, moisturising herself after a wash. She made no attempt to cover herself, but looked Trisha boldly in the eye. After this startling encounter, Myra wrote a note to Trisha Cairns, in her distinctive, tiny handwriting, every word perfectly formed and correctly spelt, saying that she hoped they could be friends. She gave the note to Carole to pass to the screw. As a Category A inmate, Myra was watched too closely to pass notes herself. Each time she left the wing she was escorted by two officers.

One evening after 8:00PM lock-up, as the inmates were shouting good night to their friends through the windows, and tapping bedtime messages on the heat pipes, Carole attracted Miss Cairns's attention. 'Open up,' Carole whispered. 'I've got a letter here from Myra.' Trisha Cairns reached through the slit in her smock to her skirt pocket, where warders kept their prison keys, doubly protected in a leather wallet and chained to their belt. She selected the universal cell key from the large key ring, unlocked the heavy, iron-plated door, took the note from Carole, then relocked the door.

A few days later, Trisha joined Myra for a game of ping-pong on E Wing, where staff were playing inmates in a prison tournament. This was the start of their friendship. Myra and Trisha played ping-pong together right through the summer of 1970, the year that the Beatles broke up and Edward Heath became Prime Minister. They played during free association time before evening lock-up, on the 'flat' of the wing, which is what prisoners called the ground floor. Cells rose above them on four levels, with a net strung between the lower floors to catch any woman who was pushed or fell from above. Myra had always been sporty, and she coached Trisha who was a poor player.

As they got to know each other they discovered that they shared an interest in music. Trisha gave Myra a Rachmaninov LP, which they played in the music room. They also played pop music. Myra loved 'Close to You', the new single by the Carpenters. The duo's next release, 'We've Only Just Begun', also spoke to her heart. As romantic music echoed off the hard prison surfaces, inmates began to dance together on the flat and some dared to kiss, though this was forbidden. The ping-pong tournament brought prisoners and screws together in a social setting more like the common room of a girls' boarding school than a prison. Trisha Cairns shouldn't have been there at all. She didn't work on E Wing, and officers were not supposed to hang about the prison after their shift. 'I'm afraid at that particular time, not just Holloway, the female [officers] did abuse the system,' says Veronica Bird. 'They didn't want to go off duty and leave the girlfriend.'

Friendship turned to romance. One night Myra heard a tap on her cell door and found a rosebud had been placed in her spy hole, as reported by Duncan Staff. Trisha Cairns was on the other side of the door. Myra told her to put her ear to the spy hole.

'I love you,' she whispered.

'I love you, too,' said Trisha. 'It's hopeless, but I can't help it.'

3

TENDRILS OF POISON

Carole Callaghan left Holloway in 1971, waving goodbye to Myra as she walked out of the front gate onto Parkhurst Road. Myra continued to use Carole, though, getting her to bring notes and gifts into Holloway on visits, but she needed a new gofer in the prison. Meanwhile, rumours of an illicit relationship between Myra and the prison officer Trisha Cairns spread through Holloway.

Intense friendships between women were not unusual in prison. Sexual contact was classed as 'offending behaviour', and if two women were seen kissing and cuddling they could be broken apart, but staff usually turned a blind eye to prisoners in love. Lesbian relationships between members of prison staff were not unusual, and several Holloway officers lived together as couples. Romantic relationships between staff and inmates were, however, forbidden. 'A prison officer must be in command the whole time and she cannot be if she has a crush on a prisoner,' said the governor Dorothy Wing. 'She lays herself open to blackmail from other prisoners and, possibly, demands from her crush for extra privileges.'

When Deputy Governor Leissner reported Violet Ali's allegation that she was acting as a go-between for Myra Hindley and Trisha Cairns, after the departure of Carole Callaghan,

Mrs Wing summoned Cairns. She told her to have no further contact with Hindley, and not to go back to E Wing, where she had no business being, considering that she worked in the Remand Centre. Cairns was also asked to reply in writing to Violet Ali's allegations.

In her statement, Trisha denied 'all that this woman [Ali] has accused me of', before going on to explain to the governor how she had got to know Myra by volunteering for the table-tennis tournament on E Wing. She had taken part in ping-pong games until the principal officer on the wing 'advised me that she had heard a rumour amongst the women on E Wing that a relationship had grown up between Myra Hindley and myself, and suggested that I drop table tennis for a week or two until the rumours died down.' She did so and had not been back since. 'However, the seed was sown and shoots of suspicion developed to cling like crushing tendrils of poison, my most innocent actions were misconstrued.'

Dorothy Wing may well have paused to reread that peculiar last sentence. 'Crushing tendrils of poison' was an unusually colourful phrase, reminiscent of romantic fiction, giving an insight into the officer's mind.

Trisha Cairns went on to deny exchanging illicit letters and gifts with Myra, or trying to pass her a key to the dining room, while she accused Violet Ali of making up stories to cover her own illegal activities. 'If this were true,' Trisha wrote in summary, 'not only would I be rejected from the [prison] service, but no prospective employer would entertain accepting someone with such a blemish on their character.' Violet Ali's claims that she had carried gifts and love letters between Cairns and Hindley were 'fabricated nonsense'.

The governor sent for Myra, who was also asked to write a statement. She did so on 29 March 1971, which happened to be the day that workmen exhumed the remains of five women who had been executed in Holloway for murder since the start of the twentieth century, their bodies buried in the prison yard. The dead included Ruth Ellis, who was the last woman to be hanged in Britain in 1955. Their bones were being disinterred for reburial as workmen prepared to tear down the old prison, bit by bit, before building a new Holloway on the same site over the next few years, while women continued to occupy the crumbling Victorian wings. Myra could hear the men digging up the bones of past inmates as she wrote in her cell.

Myra's character was revealed in her statement, which like her prison letters was long and verbose, but the expression of a clever woman who was anxious to give a good impression of herself. She admitted that she had asked Violet to pass letters for her, but these were notes for an inmate, not a prison officer. She admitted to being friends with Miss Cairns, though, and described how she had got to know her during the ping-pong tournament. 'It may be irrelevant to add that I won the singles tournament,' Myra boasted. 'Eventually, I began to hear rumours that there was "something going on" between Miss Cairns and I, but during my 5½ years in prison I have been the subject of so many fantastic, slanderous and ludicrous rumours that I took no more notice of this one than I did of the others, for these are things I have to take in my stride.'

When Violet made her allegations, Myra decided that she did so 'to elevate herself' in the prison hierarchy, 'probably thinking it was "big" to say she was carrying letters for Myra Hindley and an officer, instead of for two inmates less "notorious" than myself.' Myra ridiculed the idea that she would ever trust a woman like Violet with a secret. 'I would no more believe she could keep a secret than a bottomless bucket

13

could hold water, for she is known to be one of the most untrustworthy, unscrupulous women in Holloway, and I don't think there is one "fiddle" in the prison that she hasn't been involved in, according to the prison grapevine.' Furthermore, Myra didn't think it credible that she would send Miss Cairns £5, 'if it were true that Miss Cairns and I were in love with each other'. Surely, it would be Cairns who would give her the fiver. Anyway, Myra didn't need money. She earned good wages working in prison, and she was economical.

Indeed, Myra portrayed herself as a model of probity. 'I have always striven as best I can to abide by the prison rules, for although I have little hope of being released on my own merits, due to the press and public opinion etc., nevertheless, with the exception of a couple of innocuous misdemeanours, I can say in all honesty that I have behaved as a reasonable and responsible person, and at the risk of "blowing my own trumpet" I think I can claim some degree of integrity, in spite of allegations to the contrary.'

There was, though, a deeper connection with Trisha Cairns. Myra revealed to the governor that their association had a spiritual dimension. Myra had begun to think about resuming her Catholic faith and Miss Cairns had been of 'considerable spiritual help' in bringing her back to the church. 'I can only hope and pray that these mendacious and wicked allegations made by [Violet Ali] are proved to be the fabricated perpetrations that they are, and that Miss Cairns's good name and integrity can be preserved intact.'

Religion, like education, was promoted in prison as a route to rehabilitation, so nobody could criticise Trisha Cairns for helping Myra with her faith, and Cairns was well-known to be highly religious. Remarkably, before joining the Prison Service, she was a nun.

A nun and a murderer might appear to have nothing in common, but Myra and Trisha had similar backgrounds.

Myra was born in 1942 in working-class Gorton, three and a half miles from the centre of Manchester, the first child of Bob and Nellie Hindley. Originally, the family lived with relatives, including Myra's maternal grandmother, in a little house in Beasley Street, where poor people lived on the brink of squalor. The terraced houses of Gorton, with the corner tick shop, huddled around the vast Beyer, Peacock & Company locomotive factory and foundry on Gorton Lane, where most local men worked. Half a mile down the road stood the equally impressive church of St Francis, designed by Augustus Pugin, where the Catholic families congregated. Factory and church were the dominant landmarks and twin hubs of Gorton life for families like Myra's.

Dad – Bob Hindley – was a hard-faced man who served as a paratrooper in World War Two. After being demobbed, he worked in the Gorton foundry and wasted his pay next door in the Steelworks Tavern, becoming a notorious fighting drunk. The Hindleys moved around the corner to Eaton Street after the war, but when Myra's sister Maureen was born, in 1946, Myra was sent to live with her widowed grandmother, Ellen Maybury, at 22 Beasley Street, and she would live with Granny Maybury until her arrest.

Myra insisted that her childhood was happy and normal, though it wasn't normal to be sent to live away from home as she had been at a young age, and she hated her father. 'I disliked him intensely for his violence, drunkenness, and the tyrannical way he dominated the household.' She said that her father hit her mother, and when Myra intervened he hit her, too. A prison governor who got to know Myra later suspected, though can't prove, that Bob Hindley may have abused Myra's sister. 'You get quite shrewd when you work with prisoners with complicated backgrounds,' says Chris Duffin, who knew Hindley in the 1990s, 'and I got the feeling the reason the grandma was constantly trying to keep Myra away from home was because of her knowledge [that] her sister was abused.' It is natural to look for something untoward in the childhood of a serial killer, but the odd truth about Hindley's early life is that it appears to have been unremarkable. Even if her sister was abused, and there is no proof that she was, Chris Duffin doesn't believe that Myra was molested.

Bob Hindley was a Catholic who loathed priests. He mocked them when they called at his house soliciting donations. But Myra was baptised and received holy communion at St Francis's at sixteen. Her Uncle Bert and Aunt Kath presented her with a white prayer book to mark the occasion. She had left school by now, and was working as a clerk/shorthand-typist. Looking back, Myra considered the three years between leaving school and starting to date Ian Brady to have been the happiest part of her life, when she was a confident girl who had fun and time to contemplate the life she wanted. 'I had a wide circle of friends with whom I went dancing, swimming and roller-skating, and also spent a lot of time in local libraries where I could browse and read in peace and quiet.'

At the same time, Trisha Cairns, almost two years younger than Myra, was growing up only a couple of miles away in working-class Denton. Their Manchester childhoods were almost identical. The girls used the same shops, swam in the same public baths, and as Catholics they both frequented St Francis's church, though they didn't know each other at the time. Trisha was the eldest of four children. Her father, David, served in the Royal Navy, then worked as a fireman before going back to sea as a merchant seaman. 'He was always abroad,' says Cairns's brother-in-law, Stan Ball. 'When he did come home, he would drink.' David Cairns's drinking upset his family, like Bob Hindley's drinking did, which was another common experience that helped bond Myra and Trisha when they met. 'Her childhood was marred by a poor relationship between her parents. Her father [was] a very heavy drinker. Although never violent, his drinking habits were a constant source of conflict,' a probation officer later wrote about Cairns's early life. 'The children tended to support their mother and in particular [Trisha], to whom Mrs Cairns frequently turned for comfort.'

Educated at a convent school, Trisha decided early on that she wanted to be a nun. Her mother Ada persuaded her to go out to work before she made such a momentous decision, so she worked at the Co-op for a couple of years. She didn't change her mind, though. Shortly after turning eighteen, in 1962, Trisha was admitted to a Carmelite monastery at the bottom of a leafy lane near Salford, where she joined a closed order of twenty-five nuns. As a Carmelite sister, she would adopt a new religious name, and it seems that she chose to be known as Sister Therese of St Joseph. The nuns lived an austere, reclusive life of silent prayer. Apart from a couple of 'external nuns' who did the shopping, and ringing monastery bells, neighbours never saw or heard from the sisters. Behind the monastery walls, the nuns wore rough brown habits with their heads shorn and covered. Makeup was forbidden, as was television and newspapers. As a result, Trisha apparently knew next to nothing about the Moors murders, which filled the news from the autumn of 1965, when Hindley and Brady were arrested, until their conviction the following spring. It was a story so sensational that it was reported around the world. 'Sherlock Holmes would have been at home there, and

Dr Watson, too. On the mist-shrouded moors of northern England, men poked sticks into the mushy peat and then held the stick ends to their noses, seeking – and fearing – the smell of death,' reported America's *Life* magazine.

All this passed Sister Therese (Cairns) by in the Salford monastery, where the nuns lived in plainly furnished cells heated just enough to stop them catching pneumonia, and ate meagre meals, growing their own produce, and baking their own bread. As well as being enclosed, this was of course an exclusively female world, save for the fact that a Servite priest came in each morning to give the sisters communion. 'There would be a grille between the altar and the sanctuary and them,' recalls Father Vincent Coyne, one of the priests who said mass. 'They had communal time, when they would be allowed to speak [to each other]. They might have an hour recreation, [but] the rest of the time it would be silence.'

After a period of postulancy, Trisha became a noviciate nun. After several more months, she would be expected to take perpetual vows, that included chastity, poverty and obedience, at which time she would don a black veil and could only be released by Papal dispensation. Before that happened, Trisha suffered a crisis. She fell ill and underwent a thyroid operation, which left a prominent scar on her neck. She decided to leave the Carmelites, resigning from the order in 1966. 'I was never sure why she stopped being a nun, except that she had been very depressed,' says prison colleague Margaret Middlemiss. 'I would have thought if she was ill in the convent they would have cared for her.'

The church remained central to Trisha's life, though. 'A true Christian through and though is Trisha,' says Stan Ball, who describes his sister-in-law as a caring woman who would want to help anybody – even a murderer. After leaving the monastery Trisha applied to join the Prison Service, another enclosed female world, where she met the woman who changed her life; and when Myra Hindley told Trisha that she wanted her spiritual guidance she believed that Myra was genuine, where others might have questioned her motive in making up to a jailer. Faith was Trisha's strength and it was her weakness. 'Trisha, she loved Myra Hindley [and] she would do anything for Myra Hindley,' says Stan Ball. 'We all told her, *You are going down the wrong road here.*'

4

THE VISITING COMMITTEE

Violet Ali was a 'red-band trusty', which meant that she was allowed to move about Holloway freely in order to clean up and make tea for the staff. This made her an ideal go-between for Myra and Trisha after the release of Myra's friend Carole Callaghan, plus the fact that Violet was illiterate – meaning that she couldn't read their love notes.

Violet said that Trisha approached her first. 'She was a pretty little thing, an ex-nun, and someone who you would think wouldn't even let butter melt in her mouth. But she was absolutely head over heels about Myra Hindley.' She said she smuggled letters and gifts between Myra and Trisha in little boxes, referring to boxes of fountain pen cartridges; picking up from Myra and delivering to Miss Cairns on a daily basis, in passageways or in the workroom she cleaned. 'I used to pretend to sweep the step and give [the message] to her [Cairns] when we were passing.' Violet said that the affair between Myra and Trisha was common knowledge. 'It's known all over the prison.'

When the governor Dorothy Wing summoned Violet Ali to her office and demanded to see these notes, after Violet told staff that she was running errands for Hindley and Cairns, Violet said that she didn't have any with her. But friends of hers outside the prison had got hold of some of the notes. 'I think you must get them sent in, don't you, and we will not make any decision until then,' said Mrs Wing, warning Violet that she would be punished if she couldn't prove her allegation. 'It will mean a great deal of remission to you.'

'If I lose remission then I may go to the press.'

'If you have these letters, you must produce them, and you will prove that this is not a false and malicious allegation, won't you?'

'I know it's not false.'

'You may know. I am not psychic,' said the governor. 'I am doing my best to find out the truth, and if you show me a letter in Miss Cairns's handwriting then you have proved it.'

While Violet could be exasperating, she was not untypical of Holloway inmates. She was a heavyset woman with the lugubrious face of someone who had known little comfort or happiness, and seemed old beyond her years. (She was about forty at the time, but her exact age was uncertain.) With virtually no formal education, Violet came from a barge family in the Midlands and she had a long criminal history. She was currently in Holloway for having made a false insurance claim on a car she had reported stolen but had sold for scrap.

Women like Violet who had committed fraud, or failed to pay their fines, were among the most common types of Holloway inmates, along with the sex workers and drunks, who were held together on C Wing. The latter group included the meth drinkers of no fixed abode, who shuffled around London talking to themselves most of the year but got arrested near Christmas so they could come into the warm. 'They came in to be cared for, and when they died it was Holloway that buried them,' says former prison officer Monica Carden.

'They knew which room was theirs.' There were also a lot of women simply held on remand in Holloway prior to a court appearance. Most women passed through Holloway within a few months. Long-sentence prisoners were rarer. Few women were in Holloway for crimes of violence, and only a handful were in jail for killing somebody. As a multiple murderer, Myra Hindley was in a class of her own. She was different to most prisoners for other reasons, too. Her intelligence, the interest she took in education, and her superior manner, carrying herself as a woman of unimpeachable integrity who found herself incarcerated with common criminals, marked her out from inmates like Violet Ali.

Kindly Mrs Wing went out of her way to help Violet, in case she *was* telling the truth. The illiterate woman was given assistance in sending letters to ex-prisoners who might be able to corroborate her story. But it wasn't easy to contact women once they had left Holloway, especially the sort of women Violet knew. The best contact address she had for one pal, who had just been released, was a billiard hall in Soho. One or two women responded to her appeals, but the letters that dribbled back were not very helpful, and some were barely intelligible. This is one such reply, with its original spelling and grammar:

> Dear Governor,
>   all I kown that [Violet] Ali use to hang behind to meet the officer in question and at one time she did have a box off [pen] cartridges which see show me and letters which she use to tack to the wing and give to the girl on the E wing . . . I hope this will help you with the enquiry.
> [Signed]

Ultimately, Violet's allegations against Hindley and Cairns had to be tested by the Visiting Committee (VC), a prison court that heard serious disciplinary cases, and had the power to punish prisoners more severely than the governor did. Holloway had historical links with the City of London, and the chairman of the VC was a City of London Alderman, George B. Graham, QC. On 11 May 1971, Violet Ali and Myra Hindley were brought before this Visiting Committee, which also included Mrs Wing and a magistrate, the inmates flanked by prison officers who stood facing them during the hearing in case they turned nasty. Trisha Cairns was also marched into the room.

The women were questioned by members of the Visiting Committee and allowed to question each other in front of the VC. 'Do you remember when I come to the workroom and passed letters to you?' Violet asked Trisha at the start of the hearing.

'No, there is no truth in it.'

'It is true,' insisted Violet. 'I did pass letters to you, and you passed them to me.' Turning to the committee, she added, 'Miss Cairns said in her statement she was ordered off the wing through this.'

Trisha corrected her. 'I said the principal officer advised me that she had heard a rumour amongst the women, and suggested that I should drop table tennis.'

Part of Violet's story was that Hindley and Cairns had been canoodling in the music room, near to where they played ping-pong. This was the room where they played Carpenters records. Alderman Graham asked Trisha: 'Did you go to the record room with Myra Hindley?'

'Yes, choosing records for people to put on, but never just with Myra Hindley.'

'It's not true,' Violet interjected, saying that other inmates had seen Cairns and Hindley 'making love' in the room. She named one witness, Mary Scorse, who was serving life for stabbing her lover to death. 'Didn't Mary Scorse, Pat Clarke and others go in [the music room] one night, and you were sitting in the corner making love?' she asked Myra.

'I deny it absolutely.'

Violet said that her friends watched the door while Hindley and Cairns were in the music room together, but the women she named weren't available to back her up.

In contrast to Myra, who kept her answers brief, Violet made rambling and inexact statements to the VC; her story was also inconsistent, and she made mistakes. She said that Cairns wanted to pass Hindley a Yale key to the dining room, for example, but the VC heard that there was no Yale lock to that door. She stuck like glue to her central allegation, however.

'May I tell you how it really happened?' she asked the chairman, Alderman Graham. 'Miss Cairns used to come to E Wing and play table tennis nearly every night, very late. It was not just rumours, it was true about Myra Hindley and Miss Cairns.' There was a note of jealousy in her evidence as she referred to Myra receiving favourable treatment from prison staff, some of whom treated her as a celebrity. 'We were ashamed that we could not play records, or table tennis, [but] they were always there being nice to each other . . . I like Miss Cairns . . . I bear her no malice, as she did nothing wrong to me. I have got nothing to gain by telling lies, and no reason to make false statements. It would not get me out before my time . . . everything I put in the statement is true, and I cannot take it back in any way . . . When these rumours got round, Myra became very upset because Miss Cairns stopped coming to the wing and [she] could not get in touch with her any more.'

Violet said that one day Myra asked her: 'You know about me and Miss Cairns?'

'Everybody knows about it.'

'She is not here any more and she cannot come on the wing. I want someone to carry letters for us.'

Violet said she hid their love letters in 'terrible places' (probably no more terrible than in her underwear, which was the normal place for hiding contraband). She told other prisoners what was going on, and almost got into a fight about helping Myra. 'Lots of people are against her, although I am not – I quite like her . . . They [the other women] said they were disgusted that one of the officers, who was in charge of us prisoners, should be risking another girl's freedom to make love to Myra Hindley. [So] they would take them [the letters] out and give them to the newspapers.'

When all had been said, it was Violet Ali's word against Myra and Miss Cairns. Violet had failed to produce examples of the letters, and she didn't have any witnesses. Violet and Myra were taken outside while the Visiting Committee considered its verdict. Dorothy Wing deferred to Alderman Graham during the deliberations. Violet was soon called back.

'We find you guilty of this offence,' the chairman told her. 'It was a very, very unpleasant act which you committed. You will lose 180 days remission, and be on cellular confinement for fourteen days.'

Seven days later, while Violet was being punished in solitary confinement, Myra applied for permission for 'holy pictures' to be sent in to her in prison, as part of her return to the Catholic church under Trisha Cairns's guidance. The day after that, Myra booked a private interview with the governor. She asked Mrs Wing to give her more freedom in Holloway, and Mrs Wing agreed to do what she could to help this well-behaved and pious prisoner, who, she believed, was a reformed woman.

5

THIS WOMAN

Two months later, there was another complaint about Trisha Cairns and a prisoner. This time the inmate was Gail Payne, a young woman from Derbyshire who was serving life for murdering her husband. A former club singer, Gail had battered her husband Walter with a hammer at home in bed, in 1968, then strangled him with a belt, after a quarrel over money. One Tuesday morning in July 1971, after Gail had been shovelling coal into the Holloway furnace for her prison work, she bumped into Miss Cairns on her way to the toilet. The women were observed by prison officer Mrs Briggs, who suspected that they had collided on purpose, which was how contraband was sometimes passed. Briggs asked Gail Payne where she was going.

'To wash my hands.'

Briggs watched Cairns walk past again, and this time Cairns 'gave her [Gail Payne] a note, which I saw in her left hand'.

When work was finished, and Gail had been brought back to E Wing for lunch, Briggs and two fellow officers, Clinch and Watson, took her into their office and told her to hand over the note. 'What note?' asked Gail, who was told to empty her pockets. Gail tried to run for it. 'We restrained her and we pulled her back into the office,' reported Watson. In the scuffle, Gail appeared to take the note out of her bra and put it in her mouth. 'We attempted to open Gail's mouth, but she swallowed the note before we could unclench her teeth.' The officers reported the incident to the governor.

Once again, Dorothy Wing was faced with an allegation concerning her officer, Trisha Cairns, passing illicit notes to a prisoner, only this time a fellow officer was accusing her of wrongdoing, which made it more serious. In a statement, Gail admitted that she'd had a letter, which she ate, but she said that it was from a fellow prisoner, not Cairns. 'I was shocked when [Mrs Briggs] said another officer was involved.' Gail was confined to E Wing while Trisha was questioned. She denied the allegation, as she had denied what Violet Ali said about her and Myra, telling Mrs Wing: 'I can only suggest that officer Mrs Briggs was mistaken.' Without the note, which was travelling through Gail's guts, the governor gave Trisha the benefit of the doubt. When it later emerged that Trisha used a series of women to pass notes for her and Myra, Mrs Wing would regret letting her get away with it. 'I know she [Cairns] was always under suspicion,' Mrs Wing confessed to a colleague, 'but after that searching VC enquiry, with a QC in the chair, I inclined to think it was a case of giving a dog a bad name!'

There was growing disquiet among staff that security on E Wing was lax, and there was too much fraternising between officers and prisoners, especially Myra Hindley, who divided opinion among staff. Many officers abhorred the Moors murderer for the same reasons as most members of the public hated her. They referred to Myra coldly in their reports as 'this woman', a phrase sometimes used to anonymise inmates, but also a prison insult for a contemptible woman. These officers argued that Hindley was a devious, manipulative and dangerous prisoner who had to be watched carefully. Then there were other members of staff, like Trisha Cairns, and the governor, who showed sympathy for Myra, and even seemed to like her; while Myra was skilled at identifying prisoners who would run errands for her.

Kath Moores was one of those prison officers who were concerned that some colleagues were being manipulated by Myra. Kath usually worked with remand prisoners in Holloway, and on the mother and baby unit, but on one occasion she was asked to fill in on E Wing where Myra was held with the other hard nuts. 'I was sat at the desk in the office and I could just sense something, or someone, behind me, and I turned round and it was her. The hairs on the back of my neck went up.'

'Can you stand outside and then knock on the door, please?' Kath asked Myra, who said that she only wanted to borrow a pair of scissors. Told again to go outside and knock, Myra said, 'Do you know who I am?'

'You are no different to any other prisoner on this wing. You will follow the rules while I'm here,' replied the officer. Although new to the job, and only twenty-four years old, Kath prided herself on working by the book. Prisoners had to knock before they entered the office, and if Hindley wanted to borrow scissors she would have to sign for them.

Myra went outside and knocked, but she didn't want to sign the register. Then a regular E Wing officer came and backed her up, telling Kath that it was all right: Myra could have the scissors.

'No, she can't, and she won't sign for them.'

'She doesn't have to.'

'Yes, she does.'

'Yeah, but it's *Myra*.'

Kath was flabbergasted, by Myra's entitlement ('Do you know who I am?'), and by a workmate's willingness to show *that woman* favours. 'People on her wing treated her totally differently. She was like top dog,' she says. 'Hindley was a great manipulator. That was one of the biggest dangers. Lots of people couldn't see it . . . It's like they say, familiarity breeds contempt. After a while [colleagues] weren't aware of what was going on. They weren't alert.'

Yet Kath liked and respected Trisha Cairns, as an experienced officer in a prison where a lot of the younger members of staff hadn't been in the service long at all. In fact, Trisha had only been a prison officer for three years, but that was more time than women like Kath had under her belt. 'She trained us. She was efficient. I thought she was a good officer . . . She was caring and she helped people, [although] there were times when she could be a little bit sharp.'

Trisha was rejected by the Prison Service on her first job application, after abandoning her life as a nun. She was only accepted on her second attempt. After training in Wakefield, she was posted initially, in 1968, to Bullwood Hall borstal. Built around an old manor house on the edge of Hockley Wood, seven miles from Southend-on-Sea, Bullwood Hall was the only enclosed female borstal in England and Wales at the time, meaning that girls were locked in. It held just over a hundred teenagers, and they were a handful. 'We probably had the naughtiest teenage girls in the whole of England and Wales,' says former staff member, Margaret Middlemiss. 'A lot more sinned against then sinning, to be honest, but they could be quite volatile, and quite difficult.' Many of the inmates came from broken homes, and had spent some or all of their childhood in care. Often no family members visited. Many girls had been abused. Psychiatric issues were common, with girls frequently self-harming. Girls were also often simply scared. The idea of being sent to Bullwood Hall was enough to terrify an Essex girl. Its reputation preceded it locally as an animal house for the most delinquent local teenagers, many of whom were essentially vulnerable, frightened children who put on a front. 'I saw people just stand there and wet themselves as they were getting in the van, because they were so scared,' says one former inmate. 'I saw people try and slash their wrists so they didn't have to go. I saw people try to hang themselves.'

Girls locked up together in Bullwood Hall often developed crushes on each other, and on members of staff. Close relationships also developed between the female staff, most of whom shared on-site accommodation. 'There was a gay community, if you like,' says Margaret Middlemiss. 'I moved in different circles . . . I always had boyfriends.'

As in Holloway, some officers were suspicious of lesbian colleagues, and of women they suspected of being gay, thinking that their sexuality affected the way outsiders perceived them all. There was prejudice, and a concern that security might be compromised if officers became emotionally involved with prisoners. 'We had one or two quite notorious customers – women at Bullwood, on the staff – who caused all sorts of problems. We had Cairns, and we had a particular officer who befriended her,' recalls Monica Carden, who was a young Assistant Governor Grade II (the lowest of the governor grades, which were akin to officer ranks in the army). 'She [Cairns] arrived as a very young, innocent ex-nun . . . but I think very quickly the governor and I realised that she wasn't as innocent as she tried to make herself out to be.'

Trisha formed a close friendship with a slightly older, exceedingly shy Bullwood Hall colleague named Janet Harber, who

like many prison officers came from a background almost as
difficult as some of the inmates. Originally from Kent, Janet
and her twin brother Ivor grew up in an orphanage after their
mother died young. Janet developed into an intensely private,
close-mouthed woman who told her family next to nothing
about her adult life. 'She kept herself to herself, really . . . she
used to visit, but she never spoke about her actual life [with]
Cairns,' recalls sister-in-law, Maureen Harber. Prison staff and
inmates saw Trisha and Janet as a couple, and some of them
didn't approve of this relationship. 'The governor tried to let
it be known to the department that [Cairns] wasn't exactly
the best of officers, but at that moment wasn't believed, and
she was allowed to continue, and obviously went on to create
havoc,' recalls Carden, who felt uncomfortable in the company
of lesbians, a word she claimed not to have known before she
joined the Prison Service at twenty-one, when she says that she
felt herself being eyed-up. 'The hawks were out to get you.'

Carden wasn't alone in thinking that Trisha was unsuitable
to work as a prison officer, partly due to her personality. 'I
know a lot of people who have been in the Prison Service
and I don't know any [other] nuns – my impression is that
they are quite unusual people . . . obsessional,' says Margaret
Middlemiss, who remembers Trisha as 'always saying things
that were holier than thou' and alluding to having suffered a
personal crisis at the end of her time in the Salford monastery. 'She was the sort of person I wouldn't have let into
the service . . . One of the things you want officers to do is
help prisoners, but she didn't know where to draw the line.'
Another colleague, Judy Gibbons, agrees. 'I think she was
emotionally very vulnerable.'

After a year working together at Bullwood Hall, Trisha
Cairns and Janet Harber transferred to HMP Holloway and set

up home together in a Prison Service hostel in west London. They appeared to be inseparable, and happy. But then Trisha found a new best friend.

Myra Hindley was only allowed to exchange letters with people whose names were on an approved list. In the summer of 1971, she went to see the governor to ask if she could add a name to her correspondence list: a cousin from Manchester named Glenis. Myra made her application with strings attached. Mrs Wing summarised her conditions in a prison memo:

> *The above named inmate [Hindley] requested a private interview with me at which she stated she has a cousin of about her own age with whom she would like to correspond on certain conditions:*
>
> *a) That no police or probation enquiries were made at the cousin's home address or in the vicinity – i.e. local police or probation.*
> *b) That all correspondence was conducted through [Hindley's] mother's address. The reason which she gives for this request is that gossip has caused her cousin to move on three occasions and that even a letter with a Holloway post mark could cause the same upset.*

Mrs Wing was naturally and plainly suspicious. She referred to the woman Myra wanted to write to, in her 4 August memo, as her 'alleged cousin', making it clear that she didn't take this relationship on trust. There was no mention of such a cousin in the biographical notes about Myra. But Mrs Wing's suspicions appear to have extended no further than wanting to check whether Glenis was related to another life sentence prisoner whose family lived near Myra's mother in Greater Manchester. Once that had been ruled out, Myra was given the benefit of the doubt. She could correspond with Glenis.

At the end of August 1971, the first of a series of type-written letters from Glenis arrived at HMP Holloway. Myra replied to Glenis c/o her mother's address in Gorton. The cousins became great pen pals, exchanging at least 125 letters over the next two years.

But Glenis wasn't Myra's cousin. Glenis was a false name being used by Trisha Cairns who was writing to Myra, probably on Janet Harber's typewriter, without Janet's knowledge. The surname chosen for this surreptitious correspondence gave a clue to what was really going on. Trisha wrote to Myra as Glenis Moores, an homophonous surname that evoked memories of the Moors murders.

6

IAN AND MYRA

Before Trisha entered her life, Ian Brady was Myra's pen pal. The lovers started to write to each other from their respective prisons within days of their conviction. This was allowed, though their letters were read by staff who kept meticulous notes on everything Hindley and Brady said and did in custody, in the hope of finding clues to more victims.

An icy-cold man, Brady expressed himself in unusually warm terms in his first prison letter: 'Well, Myra, I hope you've now gotten over the initial shock of your sentence. I at least got what I expected, but you should never have been on any charge except harbouring [me] . . . The day you are released will be the happiest day of my life.' He wrote this on 12 May 1966, a few days after he was found guilty of three murders and Hindley of two, plus harbouring Brady knowing he had killed a third victim. 'I know that I will love you more as time passes. I know I can never love you less.'

The couple exchanged letters weekly from then on, for the next six years. Ian wrote to Myra every Friday for her to receive his love in Holloway on Saturday. They were as close as the most devoted married couple, doubly bonded by their crimes and secrets.

They met at work in January 1961 when eighteen-year-old Myra, her hair recently dyed blonde and piled high, her eyes heavily underlined, making her look older than her years, got a job as a shorthand-typist at Millwards Merchandise Ltd, a Gorton chemicals company that supplied the textile mills. The premises was a mile from where Myra now lived with her grandmother in Bannock Street (as Beasley Street had been renamed). Brady was a twenty-three year-old stock clerk at Millwards, a skinny, smartly dressed six foot tall Scot with a superior manner. Myra sometimes typed his letters. She developed an intense crush on the young man, who was different to most lads she knew. There was no knockabout fun with Ian. He was serious, and he seemed to take no notice of her. He later claimed he did not even know her proper surname at first. He thought she was called Indley (Mancunians tend to drop the H).

'Wonder if Ian is courting,' Myra wrote in her diary on her nineteenth birthday, and, in the months that followed, she wrote about him obsessively. 'Ian's taking sly looks at me . . . Not sure if he likes me . . . Gone off Ian a bit . . . I love Ian all over again . . . I hope Ian loves me and will marry me some day . . .' He continued to ignore her. 'I hate Ian,' Myra wrote at the end of 1961, by which time she had taken to mocking him as 'Misery'. They finally got together at the Christmas party. They went to the pub afterwards, and the pictures. After such a long wait, their first kiss was disappointing. Myra told the police that Ian didn't know how to kiss. Myra was a virgin, but she had dated, and had been briefly engaged at seventeen. Ian by contrast had little experience with the opposite sex.

The next night, Christmas Eve, they went to see another film, possibly *Judgement at Nuremberg*, which they saw together near the start of their relationship. Brady was fascinated with the Nazis. They also went to Midnight Mass, which was more Myra's speed. After church they went back to Myra's gran's house and made love on the sofa. 'Ian is so gentle he makes me want to cry,' she wrote afterwards. She later described a man who was far from gentle.

The inside truth about relationships is always hard to divine, and that is especially true in the case of Hindley and Brady, because both lied and changed their stories over time, but it soon became apparent to Myra that Ian was strange. Like most maniacs, he had a complicated and unhappy background. He was ashamed of the fact that he had been born out of marriage, to a poor Glasgow woman named Margaret Stewart, in 1938, making him a bastard in the language of his time. His mother passed him into the care of a couple called Sloan, who raised Ian as part of their family, making Sloan his second surname. Ian didn't adopt the name he made infamous until his birth mother married a Manchester market trader named Brady, in 1950, all of which was confusing and unsettling. Ian was convicted of housebreaking and theft in his youth, and got into more trouble, culminating in a borstal sentence at seventeen. He returned from borstal to live with his mother in Manchester, where he did various jobs and was unemployed for a time, as well as committing relatively minor crimes: mugging and stealing. He later claimed to have led a criminal gang in Manchester that carried out armed robberies, and he said that he committed impetuous acts of violence, including killing people, all before the Moors murders, but these claims were never substantiated. Brady was a fantasist, with personality disorders that degenerated into madness. He heard voices, had visions he described in terms of green and black light, and claimed to have met Death: 'I have seen Death . . . I had conversations with it.' He was later diagnosed as schizophrenic, and sectioned under the Mental Health Act.

Nobody ever thought that Myra was mad. Holloway governor Dorothy Wing considered Myra to be entirely sane and, moreover, a well-behaved woman blessed with intelligence, charm and resilience, though Mrs Wing's judgement was not always sound where Myra was concerned. (She also wrote, 'I think there is little likelihood of Myra attempting to escape.') Oddly, though, Myra remained staunchly loyal to her bad boy even after conviction. 'She is still obsessed with Brady,' wrote Mrs Wing, unable to comprehend this.

Myra's love for Brady is especially hard to understand in light of what she later said about the abuse she suffered from him, and the evidence of his mental delusions, which also would have made him difficult to be with on a daily basis. Sex was apparently rough and transgressive. Ian preferred anal sex, and he liked Myra to insert a candle in him. She claimed that he raped and beat her, gagged and strangled her until she almost passed out, and he bit her face. 'He did many other things to me, such as forcing my mouth open and urinating in it, or urinating all over my body,' she wrote. The couple took pornographic photographs of themselves. Myra later said that Ian drugged her beforehand, then used the pictures to blackmail her. She didn't say that at the time, though. On the contrary, she told her diary that Ian was so gentle he made her cry.

Neither of them had much formal education, but they were keen readers and autodidacts. Brady identified with Adolf Hitler's self-portrait in *Mein Kampf*; the murderer Raskolnikov in Dostoevsky's *Crime and Punishment*; the life and work of the Marquis de Sade, who connected cruelty with sexual excitement. He also read Nietzsche, whose writings were used by the Nazis to justify the idea of a master race. He talked of himself in existential terms as a man who operated by his own rules, and he persuaded Myra, in his softly insinuating Scottish voice, that laws were for little people, and religion was bunk. 'Within months he had convinced me that there was no God at all,' said Myra, who had enjoyed going to church up to then. Ian killed God and took His place. 'He became my god, my idol, my object of worship.'

Despite these eccentricities, Ian and Myra also behaved like any other young couple in love. They went to the pictures and sat together in the pub, wrapped up in themselves. They used baby talk, and gave each other pet names: he called her Kiddo; she called him Neddie, after Neddie Seagoon in the *Goon Show*. They had a laugh, and they were devoted to each other. Ian became a familiar sight in Gorton, riding down Bannock Street on his Tiger Cub motorbike to Myra's, dressed in black like the Devil, wearing a helmet and goggles. 'We never saw his face,' says Pat Garvey (*née* Cummins) who lived in the next street. The couple toured the countryside at weekends, finding isolated places to picnic. They often rode east out of Manchester, through the cotton mill town of Ashton-under-Lyne, where the moors rise up on the horizon beyond the chimney stacks.

Saddleworth Moor, fifteen miles from central Manchester, became their favourite destination. It is wild, open country. The bumpy terrain, with peat bogs and gullies, made walking difficult, but within a few yards of the A635 there was privacy and tranquility on the moors, with just the sound of the wind and the peep and chatter of birds in the long grass. From the top of Hollin Brown Knoll, the couple enjoyed a grand view down the valley to the reservoirs, with the grey blur of Manchester in the distance. Ian and Myra took photographs on these outings, little black-and-white pictures of themselves, which they stuck into an album, along with photos of themselves as children with their families and pet dogs.

These were the sort of outings any young lovers might enjoy, save for the fact that Ian started to talk about committing a murder: choosing a random victim because he, like Raskolnikov, didn't feel bound by laws. This would be a meticulously planned crime which could not be traced to them. But he needed Myra's help. He needed a vehicle. Myra was learning to drive, and although she hadn't passed her test yet she had the use of a van. Ian only had his motorbike. Myra would lure somebody off the street into the van, then deliver the victim to Brady on the moors. Their child victim would trust a woman. Brady's pretentious blather about Dostoevsky and Nietzsche was a cover for his true desires: he wanted to assault children, and he needed a female accomplice with transport to be his child catcher. In preparation for the crime, Ian practiced carrying Myra on his shoulder over the moors, telling her to make herself limp like a corpse. Then they did it for real.

Pauline Reade was a shy sixteen-year-old who lived with her parents on Wiles Street in Gorton, and had recently started working with her dad in a bakery. The Reades lived only two streets from Myra and her grandmother, and next door but one to a young man named David Smith who had started to date Myra's sister, Maureen. The Reades and the Hindleys knew each other, as everyone did locally.

On a warm Friday evening in July 1963, Pauline got ready to go to a dance in a workingmen's club near the train factory. Her parents were uneasy because there would be alcohol at the dance, while Pauline was shy of going on her own, but none of her friends could join her, including little Pat Cummins who often kept Pauline company. 'Pauline always had to be in early,' says Pat. 'They were very strict with her. She was a lovely girl, Pauline. Very quiet. Very timid.' Pauline dressed carefully for the dance, choosing a skirt, blouse and cardigan, with brand-new white shoes. Despite the warm weather she also wore a coat. Her mother lent her a medallion to complete her outfit. Out of childish curiosity, her little friend Pat followed her by foot with another girl as Pauline set off for the dance. 'I said to this [other] girl, "Let's see if she'll go . . . I don't think she'll go on her own." So we followed her.' Pauline walked to Gorton Lane, then down Froxmer Street, where Pat lost sight of her. 'Pauline went out of view and we stood there for a while and I thought, *Oh, she must have gone back home . . .* I was the last one to see her.'

Myra Hindley was in a black Ford van in Froxmer Street. Ian Brady was lurking nearby on his motorbike, dressed in black. When he saw Pauline, he flashed his headlight at Myra to signal that this girl would do. Myra caught Pauline's attention, and asked if she would do her a favour. She said she had dropped a glove on the moors, and asked if Pauline would come and help her look for it. She offered to give her some records in return. Pauline got into the van. '*I'd* have got in with her,' says her friend, Pat. 'We knew her [Myra]. We'd grown up with them.'

It was a longish drive through Stalybridge and past Mossley up to the moors. Once past the village of Greenfield, the A635 twists into a high barren landscape and then runs for several miles until another building comes into sight. To the right, the moors slope down to Greenfield and Dove Stone reservoirs. Myra rendezvoused with Ian in a lay-by opposite Hollin Brown Knoll on the left, introducing Ian to Pauline as her boyfriend. Pauline probably recognised the biker, who was often seen riding through Gorton. It is hard to believe that Pauline went willingly with Ian onto the moors, in her best clothes and new high-heel shoes, but that is what Myra ultimately claimed, after denying it all for decades. Pauline would have had to clamber over difficult terrain to get to the other side of Hollin Brown Knoll where, out of sight of traffic on the A635, Brady felt able to do what he did. He sexually assaulted Pauline. Then he slit her neck with a knife – two deep cuts.

Like Hindley, Brady denied knowledge of the murder for years. Then he said that Myra was with him at the scene, and she took a leading part in the crime. He also said that she stole the medallion from the dying girl, telling her, 'You won't need that where you're going'. Hindley said that Brady took Pauline onto the moors alone, while she waited in the van, and that his story about the medallion was a lie. But when Pauline's body was found, her medallion was missing.

Brady buried the body behind the knoll, using a spade he had brought for the job. It was easy to dig a shallow grave in the soft black peat. But if he tried to dig deeper, he hit bedrock. Afterwards, they put the spade and Brady's motor-bike into the van, and Myra drove back to Manchester. As they turned into Gorton, she saw the Reade family out on the street looking frantically for Pauline. She pointed them out to Ian. 'That's her mother and brother.' They went to Granny Maybury's where they cleaned the van, washed the spade and burned the clothes they had been wearing, and the wooden handle of the murder weapon.

The following day they went for another drive and Brady dropped the knife blade into a stream. He spent coins he had stolen from Pauline's pockets on cigarettes for himself and a Crunchie bar for Myra. The murderers then became worried that this money might link them to the body, and they could hang for stealing from a murder victim, so they went back to the moor and scattered substitute coins on Pauline's grave. With that done they went to the Odeon in Oldham to see *The Day of the Triffids*. Ian also gave Myra a record to commemorate the murder, the theme music to an army movie starring Sean Connery. Myra claimed that Ian said he would kill her if she told the police what they had done.

The terrible story of the murder of Pauline Reade was not fully known when Myra was in Holloway and it had not formed part of the Moors murder trial, because Pauline's body had not been found. She was still a missing person and, although Brady and Hindley were suspected of killing her, they claimed to know nothing about her disappearance. They were convicted of three other murders, where the police had recovered bodies. Brady and Hindley remained united through their arrest and trial. 'I loved him. I still love him,' Myra told the court, referring to Ian as her husband. But six years later, with no prospect of seeing Ian again, her love began to fade at the point that Trisha Cairns entered her life.

Then God got dragged in. Holloway prisoners had a card outside their cell door denoting their faith. Myra's card was white, meaning in her case that she had no religion, and when the Holloway priest, Father William Kahle, first tried to speak to Myra she turned him away. However, around the time that she met Trisha, Myra asked to see Father Kahle and she started to attend his mass in the chapel. '[She] was designated a Catholic and a red card [for Catholics] put on her door,' said Kahle. 'There is some good in Myra.' Personally, he was sceptical about how much she had changed, but Hindley's return to the church spread like the news of a miracle throughout the Catholic community.

Visiting prisoners in jail is known to the Catholic faithful as an act of 'corporal mercy', and Hindley became like catnip to nuns who queued up to become her friend. Aside from Trisha, herself a former novice nun, Sister Eileen now wrote to Myra from Glasgow, where she worked with deaf children, wanting to meet her in Holloway as soon as possible; and Sister Sophie, from a convent in London, also requested a prison visit.

Myra's return to the Catholic church greatly excited the penal reformer Lord Longford, a Catholic convert who was already visiting Hindley and Brady. Despite his dotty manner and his dishevelled appearance, looking like a Heath Robinson drawing of a mad scientist, Lord Longford was a useful friend. Wealthy and well-connected, the sixty-six-year-old earl had held high political office, as First Lord of the Admiralty and Leader of the House of Lords, among other duties. Brady and Hindley asked him initially if he could help arrange for them to see each other in prison. 'She was desperately anxious to be allowed to meet Ian Brady with whom she was still infatuated.' Longford couldn't arrange that, but he became friendly with Myra who confided in him. 'The truth of the matter is that after only five years of a life sentence I am obsessed with an inordinate desire to be free; in other words I have rampant gate fever,' she wrote to Longford in December 1970, adding that she lived with one foot outside Holloway's walls, 'metaphorically speaking'.

Longford was drawn to famous prisoners. He was pally with the gangster and convicted murderer Reg Kray, whom he found to be charming company; and he was impressed that Ian Brady discussed the novels of Charles Dickens with him when they met. Brady was a particular admirer of *A Christmas Carol*, which he read repeatedly. But Brady was a difficult man to know. 'It was obvious from the beginning that Brady was in some way mentally afflicted.' Myra was more agreeable company, and polite enough to tell Longford that she had read his books. He began to tell anyone who would listen that Myra had been grossly misrepresented by the popular press. 'I was astonished to find the peroxide gorgon of the tabloids was in fact a nice-looking, dark [haired], well-behaved young person.' The idea that the most wicked woman in Britain could be redeemed through faith was an irresistible challenge to Longford, as it was to Trisha Cairns, and to the nuns who visited her. Like them, Longford thought that he could see beyond Myra's crimes into the soul of somebody whom he liked to describe, with his wobbly R, as a 'good *weligious* woman'. Sceptics saw Hindley adopting 'prison religion' to wrap well-meaning but credulous people around her finger.

Myra was still in contact with Ian Brady, but not long after she became involved with Trisha she intimated that she wanted to stop writing to him. Trisha had replaced Ian in her heart, and the old association was hindering her attempts to gain more freedom in Holloway. She told Longford that she was preparing herself for the 'agonizing' decision to break it off with Ian. Around this time she sent Ian a bookmark she had woven in Holloway, embroidered with the Latin phrase 'carpe diem' (seize the day), a favourite of Brady's. This gift was accompanied by a letter making reference to her Catholic faith. Brady the atheist was contemptuous. 'Ian Brady returned the book marker to Myra with an unpleasant letter,' staff noted, 'she seemed upset by Brady's attitude.'

A few days later, Myra wrote to Longford to tell him that she had decided to end the relationship altogether. 'I wish to put him out of my life as totally as I do all the unhappy, destructive and Godless aspects of my past life with him, and

I must admit that I rarely think of him now,' she wrote in May 1972. She started to spin their story in a new way. 'At times I tend to blame him entirely for my involvement in things, which is unfair since I was not a mindless idiot without the ability to say no to the things I acquiesced to. Although, of course, had it not been for him I would never have been involved in any of the things that brought me to prison.' She was still insisting that she hadn't murdered anyone. Longford believed her. So did Trisha.

For months now, Myra had been asking to be downgraded from Category A status, so she could enjoy a freer, easier life in Holloway. The decision was not one that the governor could make alone, although Dorothy Wing was sympathetic. Breaking with Brady helped Myra's case considerably. When she signalled her desire to end the relationship, the Home Office allowed Mrs Wing to downgrade Hindley to Category B on a trial basis. Myra then sent Ian a letter formally ending it, asking Mrs Wing to forward her letter via the governor of HMP Albany, on the Isle of Wight, where Brady was being held, so that everybody in the Prison Service knew her decision. 'She also requested that any letters received from him should be returned without her knowing or seeing them,' Mrs Wing told the Home Office. As a reward, Myra's lowered security status was confirmed. She could now leave E Wing without a special escort. 'She moves freely around the prison without difficulty,' Mrs Wing noted with satisfaction. Myra had got her way – again.

The next challenge was to get out of Holloway altogether.

7

D WING

Shortly after she broke with Ian Brady, Myra, along with other long-term Holloway prisoners, was moved from E to D Wing in a reorganisation of the jail. Myra was assigned cell number '1' on the top floor, known as 'the fours'. Although it was the fourth floor of the prison block, this part of D Wing was split, so Myra's section was two storeys high, with an iron staircase leading from the flat to her landing under the roof. Her cell was the standard seven by thirteen feet, fitted with bunk beds, though she was alone. The lumpy mattress was stuffed with coir (coconut hair). The windowsill was six feet off the floor, so she had to stand on her bed to see through the bars. One tiny windowpane, no bigger than her hand, slid open for ventilation. The cell was furnished with a table and chair, and equipped with a chamber pot, bucket, metal meal tray and a locker for shoes and clothes, though women tended to hang clothes on the back of the cell door, hooking hangers through the spy hole. Myra made curtains, and she decorated the walls with pictures she snipped from magazines: kittens, landscapes and religious images, to make her cell look like a bed-sitting room. The dim ceiling light snapped off at 10:00PM. For many women this was best time, when they were safe from other inmates, and free to think alone in the dark, but Myra was restless at night and she asked for her light to be left on until dawn.

The rising bell rang at 6:30AM, after which cells were unlocked and Myra followed the other women with their chamber pots to slop out in the toilet recesses, a dangerous place out of sight of the staff where there were fights. Once unlocked, prisoners were allowed to move freely about D Wing which, although it had extra bars, locks and guards for the high security inmates, was run as an open wing.

After tidying their cells, the women queued up with their trays at 7:00AM for their breakfast, which generally consisted of cornflakes, tea, and a ration of two slices of bread, a pat of butter and a spoonful of sugar. They took the food back to their cells to eat.

At 8:00AM, Monday to Friday, the women left the wing for work. Prison work took many forms. Until it became one of the first parts of the old prison to be demolished, in the rebuilding, Holloway had a jam factory where the women made jam for every prison in the country. 'It was horrible. It wasn't washed and the stalks of the plums and everything went in the jam,' says former officer Veronica Bird. There were other work rooms where women were employed in such simple tasks as putting pencils in boxes, and ice cream scoops in sleeves. 'The prisoners used to lick the spoons before putting them in the bags,' reveals Bird. 'People would be horrified!'

Most prisoners were careless and slovenly at their prison work, especially those listless long-term inmates who had developed 'jail rot'. Myra by contrast was keen to work. She took pride in any task she was given and was rewarded for her conscientiousness with skilled work: weaving tapestry in a nice room with other well-behaved inmates. 'It was lovely.

You had a real place to work by yourself. It was quiet, and it had a window,' says former inmate Joan Kleinert, who worked with Myra on a large wall hanging in the tapestry room. 'I worked on the edging, but Myra worked on the intricate things: dragons, or swords, or shields.' The women chatted as they weaved. 'Myra was charismatic, very into the Catholic religion,' Joan recalls, 'a thoughtful person who read and appeared educated, [and] looked for ways to enhance her life within the confines of her physical existence.'

Joan was a twenty-eight-year-old American who had been caught smuggling a large amount of marijuana (250lb) into the UK, via the Glasgow docks. Having never been to prison before, she found life in Holloway an unpleasant experience. Apart from the smell and the din, the food was terrible, arriving by cart from the distant kitchen 'which of course meant that by the time food got to us it was usually cold. *Ugh!*' Equally yuk was the dishwater tea served twice a day. Then there was the vermin and lice. 'I remember a time sitting in church and seeing lice walking on the back of a woman's head in front of me.' Joan couldn't relate to most of the women. 'Most of the people there were very hard, they were the kind of people I wasn't used to being around.' Despite her crimes, Myra, who occupied the cell opposite Joan's, didn't seem to have that same 'criminal mentality', though Joan admits that she didn't have a clear idea at first of what Myra had been convicted of, having not been in England at the time of the murders.

'People wanted to tell me the story. Guards wanted to tell me,' she says. 'Why was I friends with this person, when I had kids?' Joan had two children, aged four and five. 'Don't you know who this is?' the screws asked her. 'Don't you know what Myra did?'

49

In fact, Myra paid little attention to Joan initially. 'I didn't have any goodies to give her.' That changed when Joan was given trusty status to make tea for the staff, which was the best prison job.

Each morning, the milkman delivered a crate of milk to the gatehouse on Parkhurst Road. 'I would go to the front gate, get the milk, and then bring it all the way up these many flights of stairs to this little kitchen and make tea,' explains Joan. The staff kitchen was at the top of the so-called Ivory Tower, the right-hand tower (viewed from Parkhurst Road) above the crenellated inner gate. There was a courtyard between the inner and outer gates, enclosed by a wall. The inner entrance was flanked by two giant stone dragons, emblems of the City of London, clutching keys and shackles. The prisoners nick-named the tower above this as the Ivory Tower, mockingly, because this was where the screws took their breaks, in a scruffy lounge furnished with a threadbare carpet and tired chairs. Joan made the tea in the adjacent kitchen, and carried it down on trays for the officers and civilian prison workers, including doctors, nurses and maintenance men. She also made coffee for the 11:00AM staff meeting in the boardroom. 'Then I would come down [again] and get the dishes, go back up and wash them. Then in the afternoon, do another set of teas. That was the period of time that I was told by Myra that she had this relationship with [Trisha] Cairns.'

Myra opened up to Joan after she saw that the American had 'goodies' to offer her, that is to say that as a trusty she could do a service for her and Trisha. Myra persuaded Joan to follow in the footsteps of Carole Callaghan and Violet Ali, and pass illicit love notes to Trisha. 'For a few months during that period of time, I delivered notes back and forth between the two of them,' says Joan, revealing this for the first time.

'The note would be scrunched up and put someplace behind a door in [the Ivory Tower]. I would pick it up and give it to Myra, and do the opposite thing.' Myra also spoke to Joan about her feelings for Trisha. 'She definitely saw this as a relationship, and a romantic one. She was very fond of [Trisha].' Joan noticed that Trisha often walked past the tapestry room to catch a glimpse of Myra at work. 'In many ways when I look back on it now, it was this incredible fantasy.'

Myra was a woman who had seen it all and, paradoxically, had led a narrow life. She had never travelled abroad, for instance. Her first trip to London was in a prison van to Holloway. By contrast, Joan had been all over the United States and Europe, and she had visited Mexico and Colombia, where her marijuana shipment originated. Myra listened with interest to Joan's travel stories, especially her adventures in Latin America, and she took note of the fact that Joan hoped to be deported back to the USA. This was useful information for the future.

Meanwhile, Joan still knew relatively little about Myra's crimes. She didn't know the grisly details of what had happened, for example, to John Kilbride.

The murder of John Kilbride, in 1963, took place four months after the murder of Pauline Reade, whose remains had not been found. In the meantime Myra had turned twenty-one and joined a shooting club in Cheadle, south of Manchester. Through contacts she made at Cheadle Rifle Club she purchased, illegally, two revolvers: a .38 Smith & Wesson, and a .45 Webley, with ammunition. She and Brady also bought a small calibre .22 rifle, which Brady practised and posed with on their country outings, wearing as his eccentric shooting outfit a long black coat, his motorcycle helmet (with side flaps) and goggles. He fantasised about shooting someone dead. Myra later said, by way of an example of the terror she lived under with Brady, that he sometimes aimed the rifle at her. 'He often used to sit cleaning the rifle and when I looked up he was pointing it at me . . . one day, I said, "Shoot me and put me out of my misery."'

If it were true that Myra was terrorised by Brady into taking part in the crimes, she had an opportunity to free herself from him around this time when she became friendly with a policeman. Myra had been given the van the couple used in the first murder, but she had failed to renew its tax disc. As a result she received a visit from a young constable named Norman Sutton, who offered to buy the van from her. Myra thought PC Sutton was handsome. She flirted with him, and they went on dates. She could have told PC Sutton what was going on, trusting him to protect her from Brady. Instead, she chose to tell Brady about Sutton, who thought her dalliance with the constable was a good way of getting inside information on the police search for Pauline Reade, which had made no progress. Myra then dropped PC Sutton.

The urge to commit another murder grew meanwhile, and the true motivation behind what became a series of killings becomes clearer in the case of John Kilbride. This time the victim was a small boy, and it was obviously a sex crime. Like the first murder, it was also carefully planned.

The couple decided to use a hire car this time. They first attempted to hire a car from Warren's Autos in Manchester on Saturday, 9 November 1963, but couldn't go through with it that weekend because Myra didn't have her full licence yet, having only just passed her test. This initial attempt to hire a vehicle was, however, evidence of murder aforethought. Myra returned to the garage with her full licence on Saturday, 23

November, and this time she successfully hired a Ford Anglia. It was the day after President Kennedy's assassination, the news of which was on everybody's lips. Ian gave Myra a record to mark what would be a special day for them: Gene Pitney's new release 'Twenty-Four Hours From Tulsa'. They put the .22 rifle and a shovel in the back of the hire car and Myra disguised herself with a black wig and headscarf. Then they set off for Ashton-under-Lyne, between Gorton and the moors.

It was like a night from a Sherlock Holmes story, with fog enveloping the market square. The stalls were lit up, many with early Christmas decorations, and the square was busy with shoppers, watched by the sleepy stone lion on top of the public library. It was 5:30 by the clock tower when they saw John Kilbride, a twelve-year-old boy with a prominent gap between his front middle upper teeth. He was wearing a hand-me-down check jacket with plastic football buttons, which his mother had sewn on, and blue jeans. John's family lived on an estate fifteen minutes walk away. That afternoon he and some friends had been to the pictures, after which the boys hung about the market running errands for the traders. Brady and Hindley gave different versions of which of them spoke to John first, but as before the child was offered a reward to help Myra find a glove. He got into the hire car next to Myra. Ian Brady got in the back.

They headed out to the moors where Pauline Reade had been murdered on a fine summer evening. By contrast this was a cold dark autumn evening. Once again, they drove through Greenfield and up onto the moors, 600 feet above the village, parking in the lay-by near Hollin Brown Knoll. Apart from the headlights of passing cars, there were no lights out here. Brady had brought a torch to illuminate the way as he took John onto the moor, walking down from the road on the opposite side to where Pauline was buried. Myra denied it all for years, but when she finally chose to speak she claimed that she watched them go. Then, on Ian's instruction, she drove down to the Clarence pub in Greenfield, giving Brady half an hour with the boy. Also at his instruction, she got the rifle out of the back of the car and put it on the passenger seat in case they ran into trouble.

It was easier to walk down from the road than climb Hollin Brown Knoll, and Brady and John Kilbride were soon out of sight. Like Hindley, Brady denied the crime initially, giving a partial confession decades later. In his account Myra came with them onto the moor. When he was sure that they couldn't be seen, Brady attacked the boy. He pulled his trousers and pants down, sexually assaulted and then strangled him. The murderer slapped his victim, shook his fist at the sky and taunted God: 'Take that, you bastard!' He dug a shallow grave in the peat, at a place named Sail Bark Moss, eighty-eight yards south of the A635.

Once again, Hindley and Brady covered their tracks carefully, destroying evidence, though when Myra returned the hire car it was very muddy, as if it had been driven off the road onto the moors. The Kilbride family reported John as a missing person. The police conducted an extensive search, with house-to-house enquiries, taking hundreds of statements, but they found no trace of the boy after he was last seen in Ashton market in the fog.

The following spring the murderers returned to the scene of the crime. Myra now had a puppy named Puppet, from her grandmother's dog, Lassie. She adored both dogs. The couple took many photographs of the dogs, and of themselves cuddling and petting the animals. Ian took a photograph of Myra with Puppet on John Kilbride's grave on the moor, as a memento of their second child murder, one of the three they were convicted of in 1966.

It was easier to rub along with Myra if you didn't know what happened to John Kilbride, or the other children; or if you could put that knowledge to the back of your mind, as some prison officers did in order to work with 'that woman' in Holloway; or if you believed Myra when she insisted that she was innocent. For women like Trisha Cairns and Joan Kleinert, it was possible to be friends with Myra. 'Not growing up in England, and not having this story as part of my formative years, made me, I think, on a different headset when I met Myra,' says Joan. They even had fun together in prison. 'Within this horrendous experience of incarceration there are these moments of lightness, and almost joy.'

Happy times were often thanks to Assistant Governor Joanna Kozubska, just twenty-five years old in 1972 when she was put in charge of D Wing. With the optimism and energy of youth, Miss Kozubska, known affectionately to the inmates as Miss K, encouraged the long-term prisoners to educate and entertain themselves, so they felt better. With her support, netball and volleyball teams were formed on D Wing. Myra played for both teams. When the D Wing netball team thrashed the girls from the Drug Unit, ten to four, Miss K rewarded her girls with cigarettes. There was also a D Wing choir, which Myra and Joan joined. Most significantly, with Miss Kozubska's support, Myra and Joan published a prison magazine, *Behind the Times*. This featured poems, jokes, puzzles and a light-hearted problem page in which Myra, as the columnist Betty Busybody, dispensed romantic advice to wing inmates, some of whom had formed crushes on Assistant Governor Kozubska. Betty (Myra) agreed that Miss K was 'rather dishy'. In addition to being the agony aunt and co-editor of *Behind the Times*, Myra typed the magazine (immaculately) and mimeographed it. She and Joan handed copies out on the wing, leaving a pile of magazines on a table for those women who would spit at Myra as soon as talk to her.

Miss Kozubska wrote a forward for *Behind the Times*, praising the editors, and she took a close interest in Myra personally. 'Everyone was aware of her presence – she was notorious. She was the top of the inmate hierarchy. New prisoners wanted to see her. Many women were vociferous in their condemnation and free with their threats as to what they would do to her if they had the opportunity,' Kozubska later wrote in her prison memoir, *Cries for Help*. 'I read her record soon after joining the wing. I had to. I had to sort out in my mind how I would relate to this most notorious of women. I was shocked and horrified as I read witness statements and other trial documents. Everything I read was beyond my understanding or any experience I had had so far. [But] I wasn't there to judge her – that had already been done.' Instead, she helped and supported Myra.

'She [Kozubska] was a very compassionate young woman who allowed things to happen that really encourage people [and] she had a very friendly relationship with Myra,' says Joan Kleinert, who was grateful to the assistant governor for the kindness she showed to them both. Being kind to Myra brought consequences, however.

One day, Myra and Joan gave Miss Kozubska money they had earned and saved in prison to go out to the shops and buy a chicken, which they then roasted in the wing kitchen. 'It was delicious!' says Joan, still delighted with their chicken dinner half a century later. Likewise, Myra never forgot their special meal. But other prisoners were jealous. 'Boy, did we get harassed,' says Joan, 'because of course it was something done nice for Myra.' It appeared to hostile inmates and staff as another example of Myra receiving favouritism in Holloway, which fuelled resentment and even hatred.

When a prisoner named Maxine Croft saw Assistant Governor Kozubska bringing a gift-wrapped book into the prison for Myra, on top of fetching her a chicken, she was outraged. 'Why would she have given her a book, all wrapped up?' she asks. 'This wing governor was infatuated with Myra Hindley . . . Joanna Kozubska sending wrapped-up presents, that angers me.' Intriguingly, this angry inmate would soon become mixed up in a conspiracy with Myra and Trisha Cairns to help Myra escape from Holloway.

8

A WALK IN THE PARK

On Monday morning, Dorothy Wing telephoned Joanna Kozubska, the assistant governor in charge of D Wing, with unusual instructions about Myra. 'She said, "I want you to bring her to my house tomorrow afternoon at two o'clock. I'm going to take Myra for a walk."'

The following afternoon, 12 September 1972, Miss Kozubska escorted Myra off the wing, through the security gate into the Centre, where she handed her keys to Chief Officer Isabelle Storrow, a senior woman in her fifties who hung her keys on the corresponding hook in the wall safe. Holloway staff were issued with the same set of keys every day, the lower the number on their personal bunch the more senior their rank. Kozubska had key bunch '6', showing her to be near the very top of the prison command structure. Handing her keys to Storrow meant that Kozubska was leaving the prison, and she appeared to be taking 'that woman' with her. The AG confirmed this startling fact to Storrow, who marked on the Roll Board that Hindley was being taken off the premises, creating astonishment among staff, many of whom already thought that Kozubska was too trusting. 'The problem for Myra was that very few people were ever going to believe she wanted to atone for what she'd done,' Kozubska wrote.

'I believed her insofar as I could only react and judge her by what I saw in front of me. My colleagues, who were older than I was, were much more objective and saw Myra as quite manipulative.'

While staff stared in surprise, Kozubska escorted Myra down the stairs and out through the gate house, past more astonished officers; past the outraged dragons, and across the courtyard to the outer gate house, which, unlike the rest of the prison, was staffed by men. It was built like the defensive barbican of a medieval castle, with an iron gate on the inside and an outer wooden gate. There was a wicket door in this great outer gate. Once she had stepped through this small door, Myra was back in the world.

A short, tree-lined avenue stretched ahead to Parkhurst Road. There were no more obstacles between Myra and the public walking past the prison on the pavement, oblivious to the fact that the most wicked woman in Britain was almost among them.

The governor's house was on the right hand corner of the avenue. It was a large red-brick building, built in the same antique style as the prison, with decorative crenellations, as if it was five hundred years old. Like the rest of Holloway, the house was shabby; the plasterwork around the light switches was black with fingerprints, and the whole place was in need of paint. Mrs Wing lived in the ground-floor flat, which smelt of dogs and cigarettes, and was stuffed with her collection of antiques. Other senior prison staff lived in flats above her. Mrs Wing was on leave that week, and she was waiting. 'The door opened almost before I knocked,' Joanna Kozubska recalled. Once Myra was safely inside, Kozubska returned to work.

Mrs Wing had decided to take her Cairn terrier, Piper, for a walk, and she had invited Myra to join them. Together with one of the few male members of staff, they got into the governor's car and drove out onto Parkhurst Road. This was only Myra's second glimpse of London beyond the prison walls in the six years since she had been brought south in a van from Cheshire, at which time she had peered greedily through the windows at a vast and bewildering city she only knew from what she had read and seen in films and on TV. Now she was being chauffeur-driven away from the prison, past countless Victorian villas, interspersed with modern flats where houses had been blown up in the war.

It took fifteen minutes to reach Hampstead Heath. The leaves were starting to change colour, but there was the lingering scent of summer where the groundsmen were giving the grass one last cut. 'Doesn't it smell beautiful!' sighed Myra as she and Mrs Wing set out on their walk, with Piper scampering in front of them while the prison officer lumbered behind.

Taking prisoners out of Holloway on short excursions was not unheard of. It was an established way of helping inmates who were approaching their release date to readjust to civilian life. One of the maxims of the Prison Service was that 'a person is sent to prison as a punishment, not for punishment'. Mrs Wing often quoted this, and she sometimes took her girls out of Holloway for an hour or two to help rehabilitate them in this spirit. In the past, she had taken a 'notorious murderess' to Cruft's ('knowing she was fond of spaniels'); other women were taken to the Tate Gallery, the Royal Tournament and Madame Tussaud's. Mrs Wing even took a prisoner to the British Museum to see the Tutankhamen exhibition, but she was put off by the long queue. Mrs Wing felt that she was within her rights to take any woman out of the prison, while the rebuilding work at Holloway meant that there was less room than usual to exercise in the jail. All the more reason to take Myra for a dog walk. Myra shared Mrs Wing's love for dogs. So did Trisha Cairns. 'I was on holiday and I thought the stroll would do Hindley a lot of good,' said the governor.

Mrs Wing steered Myra onto the paths that wind between the trees and the ponds of the heath, climbing to a high point where, when they turned around to admire the view, Myra could see London spread out below in a panorama, including St Paul's Cathedral in the east, and the Post Office Tower.

What a view!

If any parents walking past with their children had recognised Myra on the heath that afternoon they would have been astonished. In the language of the popular press, they probably would have been *horrified*. Because of what she did to children.

The third murder victim was another football-mad twelve-year-old boy. Eternally smiling in the black-and-white photograph that has become his enduring image, Keith Bennett had a pudding-bowl haircut, jug ears and spectacles, though he was without his glasses on the evening he went missing, because he had broken them at school. Keith was the eldest of three children by his mother Winnie's first marriage. She had remarried a man named Jimmy Johnson, who already had a child, and this blended family lived together in a terrace house in Eston Street, between Hindley's grandmother in Gorton and Brady's mother in Longsight, where the murderer still slept most nights. Winnie Johnson had arranged for her mother to look after her children on 16 June 1964, so she could play bingo. Just before eight o'clock on a summer evening she walked Keith to the busy Stockport Road, saw him across, then went on her way confident that he could walk safely from there to his grandma's house on his own.

Keith was wandering through the side streets when Myra cruised by in her new vehicle, a Morris Mini Traveller, a little van with solid side panels and rear 'barn doors'. Lanky Brady was curled up out of sight in the back, like a spider. Hindley, the driver and child catcher, was wearing her wig as a disguise as they searched for another victim. Their chosen theme song for tonight's obscenity was 'It's Over' by Roy Orbison. Ian had given Myra the record in advance. When he saw Keith, Ian indicated that this boy would suit him. Myra had already guessed, knowing his tastes. She pulled over to ask the boy if he would help her carry some boxes. Although Keith didn't know Myra, he got into her car. She then explained that the strange man cooped up in the back was her boyfriend. After they had driven a short distance, Brady invited Keith to come into the back with him.

Once again, they drove out of Manchester onto Saddleworth Moor but, this time, went half a mile further along the A635 to where a stream cuts under the road. It was dusk now. The empty moors rolled away from the road, a majestic, seemingly endless landscape in the slanting last light of day. Having denied any knowledge of the murder for years, Hindley finally admitted her part in abducting Keith Bennett. She said that he went willingly with Brady onto the moor, walking away from the road along the stream named Hoe Grain, and she followed them at a distance with binoculars as the lookout. This time, Brady, the keen photographer, had a camera slung around his neck, as he often did on their outings. She claimed to have lost sight of them near where Hoe Grain joins another stream, Shiny Brook, which meanders through a series of gullies. She waited for about forty minutes for Brady to return. She said that she wasn't present when Brady assaulted and killed Keith, strangling him with string. She said that Brady came back into view having already buried the body, telling her what he had done. When Brady gave his version of what happened, he said Hindley was with him during the murder: 'I couldn't keep her away – she enjoyed it!' he told Dr Alan Keightley in the 1990s. Myra said Brady was lying. The fact that she admitted to burning her shoes afterwards indicated to the police that she may have been closer than she said.

Brady photographed the body. He developed the picture at home and showed it to Myra as a grotesque memento of what they had done. The blurry picture showed Keith with his trousers down. Myra said that she told Ian to get rid of it.

The next day, the couple went back to work at Millwards as if nothing had happened, while the police searched for another missing child. The case baffled detectives. Despite three local children going missing in suspicious circumstances in eleven months, they had no clue what was going on.

Even if she was not on the spot when Keith Bennett was killed, Myra played a vital role in the crime, knowing what Brady would do to the boy. In fact, Brady couldn't have committed any of the murders without her. The children trusted Myra, even those children like Keith who didn't know her. 'It was probably because of me being a woman – they never showed any fear,' she admitted in middle age. At the time that Dorothy Wing took Myra for a walk on Hampstead Heath, in 1972, Myra claimed to know nothing at all about Keith Bennett's disappearance, a crime that she and Brady hadn't been charged with, because his body had not been found.

Two hours after they had left Holloway for their dog walk, Mrs Wing brought Myra back to the prison. Assistant Governor Kozubska collected her from the governor's flat and escorted her back to D Wing. The other prisoners watched Myra closely, knowing that she had been out. Myra behaved like a woman who'd had an intoxicating sniff of freedom, but didn't know if it would be her last, says her American friend Joan Kleinert. She seemed to be walking on air as she returned to the wing. 'How could she not have been excited?'

The backlash was immediate. 'I don't think it was something that was looked at very friendly-wise on the wing, either by the guards or by the inmates,' adds Joan. 'Some people didn't like it if she got something special . . . Why should she get things that other people didn't get? Whether that was a walk on Hampstead Heath with Governor Wing, or a chicken, or a book.'

It wasn't only the prisoners who were now angry. One prison officer was so disgusted about Myra's trip to Hampstead Heath that she tipped off the press.

9

ERROR OF JUDGEMENT

Dorothy Wing woke the next day to see Myra on the front page of the *Daily Express*:

MOORS KILLER SENSATION

Moors murderess Myra Hindley is being given her first taste of freedom since being sentenced to life imprisonment . . . The woman who along with Ian Brady was convicted at Chester of "calculated, cruel and cold-blooded" killing of children has been allowed out of Holloway jail for short spells as training for possible parole.

In its exclusive, the *Express* suggested that Hindley could apply for parole as soon as next year, and that she might be let out again on a shopping trip before that. 'This sounds like a good idea,' Lord Longford told the paper. 'She is no longer the person she used to be. She is very religious.' The families of Hindley's victims did not agree. 'How can the mother of any child feel safe after what happened to my John and the other children?' asked Mrs Sheila Kilbride, who had also been contacted by journalists for a reaction. 'What is six years in prison for what she did? I doubt if she has suffered as much as I have.'

Reporters hurried to HMP Holloway for a follow-up, and

they managed to get the governor talking on her doorstep. 'Hindley enjoyed the walk. She benefitted from it,' Mrs Wing told the journalists, forcing herself to smile as photographers took her picture. Still on leave, Mrs Wing looked hungover this morning as she tried to explain her reasons for taking Myra out of the prison. 'Can you imagine what it is like for a woman locked up in this concrete jungle? Everyone needs exercise and a breath of fresh air now and again. Hindley has spent six years behind bars and is not the person she used to be. You find the personality of most lifers changes after a few years in prison. Now that Hindley has been regraded, I thought it would be a good idea to take her for a walk. I have done it with some of my other girls – so why not with her?'

Mrs Wing found herself on the wrong end of a row, her words making the front page of both the *Daily Express* and *Daily Mirror* the following day, Thursday, 14 September 1972, when these national newspapers carried the authority that came with selling millions of copies each day. The *Express* splashed with the story for the second day running: 'WHY I DID IT – by Mrs Wing of Holloway'. London's *Evening Standard*, meanwhile, ran a mocking cartoon that afternoon showing the Kray twins in prison reading about Hindley's outing: 'I think it's disgusting, Ronnie,' Reg Kray tells his psychotic gangster brother. 'Who will they let out next?'

In parliament, the Earl of Mansfield asked how a woman 'so wicked and depraved' could visit a public park guarded by a woman near retirement age. 'Myra Hindley has on one occasion been allowed to leave the prison,' replied Viscount Colville of Culross, Minister of State for the Home Office, adding that a man accompanied Hindley and Mrs Wing (as if that made all the difference), and he knocked down the suggestion that this was one of a series of outings. He added that the governor was confident that Hindley would not try to escape. Liberal-minded peers defended Mrs Wing, and expressed hope that Hindley was not beyond rehabilitation, but few listened to or agreed with them.

Among the voices raised in bitter protest was that of Mrs Ann West of Manchester, who wrote to the Home Secretary, Robert Carr:

Dear Sir,

I am writing on behalf of my family and as the mother of Lesley Ann Downey who was murdered by Myra Hindley and Brady eight years ago. I see that Hindley has been let out of prison for walks in the park and is expected to be out on parole. This I just cannot understand because a few people think she is a changed woman . . . You must think I am very bitter and I am and there must be hundreds of people that feel the way I do about this. If it was me I'd feel safer where I was.

When Hindley got her sentence in 1966 the judge said life and he said he means just that, not six years . . .

Please help me as a mother who has suffered more than anyone knows to lose a little girl in such a cold bloodied murder.

Mrs A West

Mother of Lesley Ann Downey

Lesley Ann Downey was the fourth child to be killed by Brady and Hindley, and the murder that caused most outrage. The details retain the power to shock, and this time there was evidence that Myra was directly involved in the abuse as well as the abduction.

The crime took place at Christmas 1964, six months after Keith Bennett was murdered. Lesley Ann Downey was the youngest victim at ten years old. A shy, cherubic girl she was the second child of waitress, Ann West, who lived with her second husband and four children by her first marriage (to a soldier, Terry Downey) in a flat in the Ancoats district of Manchester. Around four o'clock on Boxing Day, Lesley Ann went with friends to the fair at Hulme Hall Lane, near her home, with instructions to be back by eight. Having seen advertisements for the fair, Brady and Hindley had also decided to go there to look for their next victim. Once again, Ian gave Myra a record to mark their anticipated crime. 'Girl Don't Come' was a new song, sung by Sandie Shaw, about being stood up for a date.

Having spent her pocket money, Lesley Ann was last seen by her friends standing near the dodgems at about half past five that afternoon, by which time the fair with its garish attractions was a blaze of electric light, and ringing to the sound of pop music. Brady and Hindley sidled into the scene, Myra disguised with her wig and a head scarf. They watched the girl to make sure she was alone. Then they walked towards her with some boxes, which they contrived to drop in front of her as a trick. Nice little girl that she was, Lesley Ann helped them pick the boxes up and carried them to their van. They then persuaded her to help them take their shopping home, and drove off with her in the van.

They were not going directly to the moors this time. Three months earlier Myra and her grandmother, Nellie Maybury, had been given a new council house, prior to Bannock Street and several other old Gorton streets being demolished for redevelopment. Their new house was eight miles away on a new estate at Hattersley. Number 16 Wardle Brook Avenue was a small, two-bedroom end of terrace, built on an embankment. Myra and her grandma moved in along with Ian Brady and three pets: Mrs Maybury's dog, Lassie; Myra's dog, Puppet; and a budgie named Joey. Earlier that Boxing Day, Myra had taken her grandma to visit her son from her first marriage, Myra's

Uncle James Burns, meaning that 16 Wardle Brook Avenue was empty when Myra and Ian returned from the fair with Lesley Ann. They had to park the Morris on the street below the house and either scramble up the steep embankment or, more likely, walk along the raised path past their neighbours to the front door. Either way they risked being seen bringing a victim to their home. They were taking more risks now.

Lesley Ann was taken upstairs to Myra's bedroom, where Ian had set up photographic equipment to take indecent pictures of her. Lesley Ann screamed when she realised something was very wrong, pleading with Brady and Hindley to let her go.

'Shut up,' said Hindley, as she tried to restrain her.

'Please God, help me. Ah. Please. Oh.'

'Come on,' whispered Hindley, who later said that she was worried the neighbours might hear the child's cries. 'Shut up.'

'Oh . . . Help – Oh . . . I cannot while you have got hold of my neck . . . Oh [screams]. Help [followed by gurgling sound].'

One of the murderers left the room and came back with a handkerchief, which Myra tried to make the child take in her mouth, coaxing her but also ordering and ultimately threatening her. 'You are all right. Hush, hush. Put it in your mouth and keep it in,' said Hindley, as the child continued to struggle and cry. 'If you don't . . .' She kept crying. 'Shut up or I'll forget myself and hit you one. Keep it in.' Hindley later claimed that all the victims went quietly to their deaths like lambs, but it is more likely that they all struggled and screamed like Lesley Ann Downey when they realised they were in dire trouble.

'Can I just tell you summat? I must tell you summat. Please take your hands off me a minute, please,' the child pleaded. 'Please, Mummy, please . . . I can't breathe. Oh . . . I can't

– Dad – will you take your hands off me? . . . Please God . . . What are you going to do with me?'

Brady: 'I want to take some photographs, that's all.' He was setting up a camera light. The tripod legs made a snapping sound.

'Don't undress me, will you?' The child was stripped. 'It hurts me. I want to see Mummy, honest to God . . . I have got to go because I am going out with my mamma. Leave me, please. Help me, will you?'

'Put it in your mouth and you'll be all right,' said Brady, frustrated that they hadn't gagged her.

'I'm not going to do owt.'

'Put it in,' repeated Brady. 'If you don't keep your hand down, I'll slit your neck.'

They asked her some questions, including her name. She answered and said: 'I have to go home before eight o'clock . . . I'll get killed if I don't. Honest to God.'

'Yes,' said Brady.

Lesley Ann continued to cry and protest.

'Now listen, shurrup crying,' Hindley told her. 'Pull that hand away and don't dally, and just keep your mouth shut, please . . .'

'I want to go home.'

Finally, they wrapped a scarf around the child's head and forced her to lie on the bed. Brady took his pictures.

Ian Brady liked to portray himself as a Macavity-like master criminal who was too clever for the police to catch, but that was the opposite of the truth. What took place in Myra's bedroom is known about, including exactly what was said, because Brady tape-recorded everything for his pleasure. The tape was recovered by the police, and when it was played in court it was devastating evidence against Brady and Hindley.

For many people it was Hindley, though, as a woman, who seemed to behave with particular and unnatural cruelty. The police also recovered the photographs Brady took and developed the night of the murder, which was additional crushing evidence of their guilt.

Myra couldn't deny all this. She accepted from the start that she was the woman on the tape, but in court she and Brady claimed that teenage tearaway David Smith, who had recently married Maureen Hindley, becoming Myra's brother-in-law, brought Lesley Ann to the house, having arranged to pay her to pose for indecent photographs. The defendants said that the child left the house with Smith. Myra later changed her story, saying that she was in the bathroom when Brady raped and killed the girl. But Brady seemed to let slip an admission in court that indicated that once again Myra may have been closer than she said. While insisting that Smith was part of what happened, Brady said that when it was over, 'We all got dressed and went downstairs', suggesting that he and Myra stripped off when they were with the child. Cross-examined on this point, Brady said that he misspoke. He meant that the child got dressed and went downstairs. The judge reminded the jury of Brady's original remark in his summing up, suggesting that it might cast a 'flood of light on the nature of the activities that were going on'.

The murderers took the child's dead body from the house that night, either sliding the corpse down the embankment, or carrying it the long way past their neighbours to the road, where they loaded the body into the back of the Morris and set out for the moors.

It had started to snow, and the A635 was slippery. Myra wasn't confident driving in icy conditions. Although she denied in court that they were moving a body, she admitted that she and Ian took the Morris out that night and there was the ring of truth to her evidence when she said, 'I was very tense and Ian was a back-seat driver and complaining'. It is easy to imagine the couple arguing in the car as they climbed to the moors, the road getting icier with every mile. Ian wanted to go on. Myra decided to turn back. Like characters in a black farce, they were stuck with a body they couldn't hide, and Myra had to go to her uncle's house to say that she couldn't drive granny home that night because the roads were too bad. There was a row about that. Back at Wardle Brook Avenue, Ian and Myra stashed the corpse in her bedroom, sleeping downstairs in the lounge.

The next day, they loaded the body back into the Morris and drove to Saddleworth Moor, parking near Hollin Brown Knoll. Brady dug another shallow grave in a boggy place close to where he had buried Pauline Reade, while Myra waited with the van. Anybody could have come past and seen her in broad daylight, with a body in the back of her vehicle, including the police who were out searching for Lesley Ann.

A policeman did stop. He asked Myra if she had broken down. As with her friendship with PC Sutton, here was an opportunity to tell the police what was going on, if she had only been helping Brady because she was in fear of her life. Brady was out of sight on the moor digging the grave. He couldn't hurt her. Instead of coming clean with the officer, and bringing the murders to an end, Myra lied to the police as she later reminded Brady, in the presence of her brother-in-law, David Smith. 'She said, "Do you remember that time we were burying a body on the moors and a policeman came up? . . . I was in the [car] with a body in the back. It was partitioned off with a plastic sheet. Ian was digging a hole when a policeman came and asked me what the trouble was. I told him I was drying my sparking plugs and he drove off."'

When the officer had gone, Brady retrieved the corpse from the van, hoisted it over his shoulder, as he had practiced with Myra, and carried it to the grave. Meanwhile, Lesley Ann's family were searching for their daughter.

No mother could forgive Myra for what she did to Lesley Ann Downey, and Ann West became Myra's implacable enemy. In the press coverage of her 1972 outing to Hampstead Heath, Mrs West made her feelings clear. 'If Myra Hindley leaves prison during my lifetime, I'll hunt her down and kill her,' the bereaved mother told the *Daily Mirror*. The Home Office wrote to Mrs West assuring her that this would not happen again. 'The Home Secretary has no intention of releasing Myra Hindley in the near future and is very conscious of the extremely strong feelings which this abhorrent case still arouses, not only in yourself and other close relatives of the victims, but among the public in general.' Mrs Wing was publicly reprimanded for making an 'error of judgement'.

Within Holloway, there was a belief that the walk on the heath had been authorised at a high level to test public opinion, and that Dorothy Wing had been acting on instructions. 'I think [Mrs Wing] ended up being a fall guy . . . it was an exercise to see how the public would act if Myra Hindley was out, and course it backfired on them – big time. So somebody had to be blamed,' says Kath Moores, who even as a junior member of the prison staff was certain that the governor could not have made the decision on her own to take Myra out. Assistant Governor Joanna Kozubska agreed. 'Dorothy Wing alone "carried the can" for the Myra Hindley walk in the park episode,' she wrote. 'I believe it is highly likely that she had consulted her superiors in the prison department about this disastrous event and they chose to distance themselves from a huge error of judgement.'

Unseen hands seemed to be pulling strings where Myra was concerned.

It was Christmas, a difficult time of year for prisoners in Holloway but not a Christmas that Lesley Ann Downey or her family could enjoy. Joanna Kozubska tried to bring some festive cheer to D Wing. The women had a Christmas tree, and games of bingo. Myra sang in the carol concert. On Christmas morning all the women received a gift, and they ate a turkey lunch. They also watched Christmas TV, like people across the country. It was the year that André Previn tried to conduct Eric Morecambe playing the piano in the *Morecambe and Wise Christmas Show.* 'I am playing all the right notes, but not necessarily in the right order.' Everybody laughed at that. But even at Christmas the women bickered, fought and stole from each other in Holloway. At least one inmate returned to her cell on Boxing Day to discover that another prisoner had pinched her cigarettes.

While the prison resounded to games, carols, laughter, and some tears, Dorothy Wing cleared her desk. Taking Myra to Hampstead Heath, and the row it caused, had ended her career. She was retiring under a cloud. Despite her part in the governor's downfall, Myra came to see Dorothy Wing in her office to interview her for *Behind the Times,* before she left, and Mrs Wing promised to come back to visit Myra, who had almost become a friend.

Mrs Wing's successor was a South African physician named Dr Megan Bull, a married woman of forty with children. In her handover, Mrs Wing gave Dr Bull an account of Holloway's most famous inmate, describing the progress Myra had made. 'As a prisoner she presents herself as a well-disciplined, very controlled person, anxious never to transgress prison rules.

Under this façade she is a rather insecure young woman [who] is slow to trust anyone and, despite her intelligence, and apparent strength of character, she has a great need for approval.' Mrs Wing believed that breaking with Brady had been a relief to Myra, while in another positive development she was reconciled with Maureen, the sisters having fallen out when Maureen gave evidence against Myra at her trial. She also referred to Myra's good relationship with Assistant Governor Kozubska. She appeared to let her guard down with Miss K, was 'able to weep quite normally' in her office, and 'discuss her feelings of guilt that her family has had to suffer on her account'. This did not mean that Myra had faced up to her crimes. 'In my opinion when Myra talks about the enormity of her crime[s] this relates to the pornographic photographs and her part in this offence in relation to the young child Lesley [Ann Downey]. To my knowledge she has never given any indication of admitting guilt to murdering the victims.'

Mrs Wing didn't believe that Myra expected to be released soon. 'She realises and always has done that she is likely to serve a very long sentence and has no illusions about parole in the foreseeable future . . . She envisages about twenty years in custody at the least.' In her heart, Myra did not accept that. She had gate fever, and her own ideas about getting out of Holloway, ideas that involved the prison officer Trisha Cairns, who had twice now been accused of smuggling notes under Mrs Wing's nose, as well as trying to give a prison key to Myra. Mrs Wing didn't mention Trisha in her handover to the new governor, but Myra and Trisha were Dr Bull's problem now.

10

LITTLE MAX

The furious reaction to her trip to Hampstead Heath sent Myra into a depression. She went to see Assistant Governor Joanna Kozubska, and wept in her office, receiving sympathy in return from a young woman who appeared to understand her almost as well as Trisha did. 'I supported her as best I could,' said Kozubska. Myra turned up the charm. 'You have this special "knack" of seeming to share implicitly people's sorrows and sadnesses,' she wrote in a note of thanks to Miss K, just one of the many little notes which Myra sent around Holloway. Hindley was a prolific and prolix correspondent, who may have written nearly as many letters as all six Mitford sisters combined (one of whom, the fascist Diana Mitford, was interned in Holloway during the Second World War) and she could be almost as charming. Kozubska was won over. 'The furore was staggering. No one had foreseen the immense reaction or the orchestrated press campaign against Myra, the governor and the Home Office,' she wrote of the negative reaction to Myra's outing, as if the press was to blame. 'After that we all knew Myra would never be released.'

Myra had other ideas. The first day of January 1973 is recorded as day one of her plan to escape from Holloway.

★

The new year had a strange beginning. On 1 January, Myra helped organise a meeting of prisoners to discuss running D Wing as 'a community'. The initial proposals were modest: the women agreed to clean up after themselves when they used the wing kitchen, to sweep the 'flat' and TV room, and clean the baths and slopping out recesses. Hindley reported this in *Behind the Times*. 'Perhaps due to the fact that so much is done and decided for one in the prison system, we have tended to rely too much on the staff for routines which, with a little thinking about, could have been organised by ourselves,' she wrote. 'For even these small improvements to last, each woman must be aware of her personal responsibilities in a united community.' Less sympathetic prison officers feared that the inmates were taking over D Wing.

While Myra was organising the prisoners, she was deepening her illicit relationship with Trisha Cairns, and finding new ways for them to meet and communicate. Trisha passed her principal officer exam in 1973, with the second highest mark of all the officers sitting the test. She was now senior enough to take charge of the key safe in the Centre when the need arose. Meanwhile, Myra had more freedom in the prison, having been downgraded from Category A status. Taking advantage of the situation, the women started to meet secretly in the prison chapel, where love blossomed.

One day, Trisha opened her heart about her feelings to a colleague. 'Cairns told me she loved Hindley more than anything else in the world, they seemed to have the perfect understanding in every way. This was not only on a physical level, but also on a spiritual level, and that she thought this was to be her destiny,' said Miss Taylor, a young prison officer from the south-west.[1] Once she started talking to Taylor, Trisha couldn't stop herself. She explained how she and Myra met, and she spoke about the Violet Ali affair. 'She said that although the relationship was in existence, the actual allegations were not true.' So saying, Trisha admitted that she had misled the Visiting Committee eighteen months earlier. 'Pat [Cairns] told me she was meeting Myra Hindley in the chapel occasionally. She also said that she spoke to her in an adjoining office through a gap in the wall where pipes ran through.' Trisha was working in the Discipline Office. There was a hole in the wall through which she could whisper to Myra in the tapestry room. There was more. 'Pat [Cairns] showed me knitted articles in the form of animals which Myra made for her. [Cairns] also showed me books Myra had sent her.' Trisha admitted that she wrote to Myra from outside under a false name. Surprisingly, Taylor did not rush to share this information with the new governor, Megan Bull.

Coming from a medical background, Dr Bull had relatively little experience of running a prison and was out of her depth. 'I think in a way she should have been given more training to be governor, because it is not an easy job,' says Judy Gibbons, who was the third most senior member of the governing staff at the time, after the deputy governor and Dr Bull, having previously worked at Bullwood Hall. 'I think she had some difficulties.' Gibbons had more experience of dealing with complicated women like Myra, and she didn't take what she was told on face value. 'This is the thing with working in prisons. You are working very closely with very difficult people, who can be extremely manipulative, and you have to know when you are being manipulated . . . I knew [Myra]

---

1 Name changed.

very well, and for a long time. As far as I was concerned I felt that she was highly manipulative. I *always* felt that, [meaning] that people [like her] dispose themselves in such a way that they become acceptable to whoever they are speaking to.'

Myra spoke to Dr Bull regularly, and made as many requests to her as she had to her predecessor, Mrs Wing. The new governor agreed to most of what Myra asked, sometimes with dubious logic. Dr Bull sanctioned Myra's request to correspond with her American friend, Joan Kleinert, who had just been deported back to the USA, on the snob basis that Joan was of the same social class as Myra. 'Although many people wish to write to and visit Myra, apart from her own family, they are people of good will above her social standing,' Dr Bull noted, no doubt thinking of Lord Longford and similar moneyed supporters who had befriended Hindley, 'and it might be helpful for her to have a more natural pen friend.' In fact, Myra had a secret motive for staying in touch with Joan. A plan was forming with an American connection.

Meanwhile, Myra and Trisha still needed a new go-between. They chose Maxine Croft, known in prison as Little Max due to her diminutive size. Maxine had recently been transferred to Holloway from HMP Styal in Cheshire, where she had climbed over the wall. 'The governor there hated me.' Maxine was put in isolation for her escape attempt, in the punishment block which was aptly named Bleak House. 'But I still wouldn't give in.' So she was sent to Holloway, where she arrived in time to celebrate her twenty-first birthday, in July 1972. 'Mrs Wing was still the governor at the time and they threw me a big party.' The governor gave Maxine cigarettes and embraced her. 'Mrs Wing gave me a hug and said, "I'm never going to send you back to Styal."' It was a mark of how much trouble

Little Max could cause, however, that she was locked up in D Wing with Myra and the most serious offenders.

Like many women in Holloway, Maxine had a difficult childhood. She was born in London in 1951 to Irene Croft and a hotel waiter, Michael Abrahams, who didn't stay together. Irene had been raised by an adoptive mother, Grace Croft, on a council estate in Harold Hill, Essex. Grace had also adopted a boy named Dennis, six years older than Maxine. When Maxine was still small, Irene handed her over to Grace to raise as another adoptive child, alongside Dennis, who having been Maxine's uncle now became her brother, shortly after which Irene went to live in Canada. It was a confusing start in life, and Maxine became a troublesome child. Clever but mischievous there was 'a little devilment in her', says Dennis. 'She mixed with the wrong people from school . . . I don't know how she got into so much trouble . . . She doesn't care what anybody thinks of her, not really. She is a little bit of an oddball.'

When Maxine was fifteen, Dennis told Grace that his little sister had stolen some money. As a result she was marched to the police station, for which she blamed her brother. Maxine was convicted at a juvenile court of obtaining money by false pretence, and released on probation after Grace spoke up for her. '[Grace] got up and pleaded, "Please don't send her away, I'll look after her,"' says Dennis, who felt that Maxine didn't appreciate how much Grace had done for them both. Six months later, Maxine was convicted of possessing an offensive weapon (a knife), together with other offences, and sent to an approved school where she was unhappy. After Maxine absconded, she was sent for borstal training at Bullwood Hall. This was another traumatic experience, starting with the drive to the borstal with other girls. 'I remember one girl was frantically trying to open her wrists up with a piece of plastic. One girl stood there and wet herself.'

Life in Bullwood Hall was made bearable by the kindness of the young prison officer Trisha Cairns, and her colleague Janet Harber, who the inmates nicknamed Flipper after a children's TV show about a dolphin. 'At Bullwood, the officers weren't that much older than us. We were sixteen. They must have been in their twenties, and most of them were lesbians,' says Maxine, who remembers Trisha at this time as 'one of the nicest people you could ever meet, [and] one of the funniest'. Trisha liked Maxine, too. Shortly after her release from Bullwood, Maxine claims that Trisha sent her a letter with a photograph of herself asking to meet in a pub in Southend. Grace burned the letter, so there was no date. But their paths would cross again.

Maxine's next conviction was for sacrilege, which made her laugh as most things did when she was young. She was with two men who stole a safe. 'And they said I carried it across the churchyard.' Little Max argued that, at seven stone, she was too weedy to lift a safe and, absurdly, it turned out to be empty. Together with thirteen cases of taking and driving away cars, she was given a prison sentence, varied on appeal to probation. She was becoming well-known to the police in Essex. 'Romford police had a handbook on me.' Then she travelled around the continent passing forged £5 notes. Dennis says that his sister brought a carrier bag full of dodgy money home. 'I said, "Just get that out of the house."' Arrested for the forged fivers, Maxine was initially held on remand in Holloway where she kicked up rough. 'I said, "I'm not eating that food!" So we rounded everybody up and I organised a riot.' One of the prison officers sent to quell this food riot was her old friend Trisha Cairns. Maxine hit her. In Christian spirit, Trisha turned the other cheek. 'She wouldn't press charges.' But Trisha didn't speak to Max for a while.

Maxine was convicted at the Old Bailey in 1970 of passing forged five-pound notes and given a suspended sentence. Convicted of the same offence five months later, plus assault on a woman police officer, the judge sent her down for three years. Maxine was still only twenty. Grace and Dennis found Maxine unrepentant. 'She had just come out of court and [sort of said], "I can do this standing on me head." Cavalier . . . She didn't have a care in the world. Didn't take life seriously.' The next time he visited his sister, Dennis noticed that Maxine had a small mark tattooed on her face. 'That's how one prisoner could recognise another on the street.'

Maxine settled into life at Holloway. 'It didn't bother me at all . . . I was always laughing. I thought everything was funny.' Maxine could be funny herself. She told a good story, and she was witty. 'We had that traitor in who was done for spying. We had a game of netball. She passed it to the wrong person. I went, "You traitor!" I lost a week's wages over that.' The welfare officer, Valerie Haig-Brown, took a benevolent interest in Little Max, concluding that having spent so much of her youth in care homes and prison she was, at twenty-one, institutionalised. 'She lacks confidence and has grave doubts about her ability to be able to cope with life in the community.'

Then something odd happened. One day, while she was leaning on her broom in the prison, 'kicking time', Maxine says that she was approached by an officer – 'I can't remember what her name was' – with a proposition. 'She collared me and said, "I want a word."'

'Yeah?'

'You are going to be given a green band.'

At the time, there were red- and green-band Holloway trusties, the green-bands having less freedom. It was still a coveted privilege. Maxine laughed. 'Because obviously somebody like me was never going to be given a green band, you are never going to be made a trusty: you've escaped from prison, you have lost all of your remission; I had so many VCs . . . I organised riots . . . If you are going to pick a trusty, you are not going to pick somebody like me.'

The officer was serious. 'But the string attached is I want you to get as much information and evidence [as possible] that Pat Cairns is having an affair with Myra Hindley.'

'Well, it's common knowledge, isn' it?' said Maxine. Only there was a problem. 'I don't have anything to do with Hindley.'

'You are going to have to, because you could get early parole for doing this.'

'Oh, no, I'm not really into baby killers. I can't be mixing with them.' Like many prisoners, Maxine didn't want to be seen associating with nonces. 'The people I was friends with were the usual hoisters, prostitutes – you didn't mix with baby killers.'

'What are my friends going to say?'

'You either do it, or you don't get parole. And you could get a longer sentence.'

Maxine felt that she was being forced into agreeing with the officer, who seemed to be acting on instructions from people higher up. 'There were no ifs and buts about it. Who she was working for, I don't know.' The officer painted a rosy picture of the life of a trusty. 'You get to run around the prison, and you get to work upstairs in the kitchen . . .You're the ideal candidate because you know Pat [Cairns] so well.'

'I remember Pat from Bullwood, but I don't know Hindley.'

'You better start making friends with her. But don't push it. She'll make friends with you. The minute you get your green band, she'll get in touch with you.'

Holloway records confirm that Maxine Croft – riotous troublemaker and escapee – was made a green-band trusty on 20 January 1973, allowing her to move about Holloway freely. Could it be true, as she claims, that she was hand-picked by staff to befriend Myra and spy on her and Cairns? Indeed, she claims that this was just the start of what she was asked to do. One former prison governor who came to know Myra believes that Maxine's story is credible, alleging that there was corruption within the service where Myra was concerned. 'I've long believed that money changed hands in Prison Service headquarters to make her life as miserable as possible,' says Chris Duffin, a governor of HMP Cookham Wood in the 1990s. In light of her experiences with Myra then, she doesn't rule out Maxine Croft's story: 'It sounds very possible.'

Like Joan Kleinert before her, Little Max started to collect the milk from the gate and make the staff teas in the Ivory Tower, carrying trays up and down the stairs, and washing up the dishes in the little kitchen at the top of the tower, which had a gas stove, sink and table. A cloth was put over the tea things to stop rodents eating the sugar. The metal cutlery was counted daily to make sure the trusties didn't pinch anything that prisoners could use as a weapon downstairs, where inmates were only allowed plastic knives and forks.

Myra was sent upstairs to help Maxine, who was intimi-dated at first by the notorious child-killer. 'She was like very tall, very kind of big-boned, but quite slim, and it was like quite daunting if you was tiny [talking to her]. Quite a square face, square jaw.' But as she got to know Myra, she noticed that the Moors murderer avoided confrontation, even when she was provoked. 'She would never retaliate, very subdued.'

One day, when Maxine and Myra were in the Ivory Tower, Trisha Cairns joined them. Myra asked Maxine to keep watch while she and Trisha went into the lounge. Assistant Governor Kozubska then came up, and Myra left with the AG, who Maxine thought treated Myra like a pet. 'The next day I went to work after the dinner hour. Miss Cairns was in the sitting room and asked me would I pass messages,' said Maxine, who agreed at this stage to be their go-between.

That evening before lock-up, Myra spoke to Maxine, telling her that she carried a photograph of Trisha in a pouch next to her skin. Maxine later remembered Myra using another hiding place. 'She had pictures sewn in her knickers.' Myra said that she and Trisha wrote to each other, with Trisha using the name Glenis, but that her flatmate Janet was suspicious. 'Myra then became very friendly with me and told me that Miss Cairns sent all her clothes in, and bought everything she needed. She had also given Myra the divisions of the officers [work shifts] so that Myra could tell her duties.'

After this conversation, which Myra may have regretted as indiscreet, Trisha had a quiet word with Maxine. She told her that if an inmate made an allegation against a prison officer, like herself, they wouldn't be believed, because 'an officer is above an inmate, [which] gave me some kind of warning.'

Maxine felt that she had no option other than to do what she was asked. 'At first, I was only asked to deliver personal messages. After some time I was asked to deliver letters, fruit and other things to Myra.' These items were left on a shelf in the Ivory Tower kitchen, or in an old clock in a sideboard in the adjacent lounge. The clock no longer worked. Its mechanism had been removed.

Then Trisha went on holiday, and she returned to Holloway with a gift of handkerchiefs for Myra. She couldn't deliver the gift personally. So she gave the hankies to Maxine, who stuffed them down her trousers. As she walked through D Wing to give them to Myra the hankies slipped further down her trouser legs and fell out onto the floor. 'Myra was watching me from the landing where her cell was, and shouted to me to pick them up.' To their fright, a screw saw the hankies first. She took them into her office. An unhappy Myra ordered Maxine to go and get them back. Being Myra's gofer was making Maxine stressed, and then the trouble started.

11

MYRA SPENCER

Myra's mind was now fixed on getting out of Holloway, and she obsessed about what she would do, and how she would keep herself safe, on the outside. The furore over her trip to Hampstead Heath had made it clear that her crimes had not been forgotten, seven years since her conviction. She would have to take steps to avoid being recognised. That involved changing her name, as criminals sometimes do to disassociate themselves from their past.

As early as 1968, two years into her sentence, Myra adopted Clare Stewart as a pseudonym, Stewart being the surname of Ian Brady's birth mother. Then, towards the end of Dorothy Wing's time as governor, Myra changed her name again, with the assistance of the Cheshire solicitors who had represented her and Brady at the time of their arrest. This was done legally, with Mrs Wing's support, for her life after parole, for most life prisoners are allowed out on parole eventually, though Myra was nowhere near the stage when parole was likely in her case.

Curiously, Mrs Wing didn't tell the police about Myra's second name change. 'The only document relating [to this] which we hold is that which gives permission to change her name and instructs us to notify the police. There is no record that this was done,' a Holloway officer later informed the Home Office. Nonetheless, by February 1973, Myra's solicitors, Chronnell & Fitzpatrick, had changed her surname by deed poll to Spencer. This was not a name she used in Holloway. It was kept secret for when she left prison.

She then asked her solicitors to do another service for her. On 5 February, they sent an application on behalf of Miss Myra Spencer, of 1 Parkhurst Road, London N7, to the driving licence office with a copy of her deed poll name change and a one pound postal order. Back came a driving licence in her new name, which was a useful form of identification for somebody with a devious mind. Like the assassin in Frederick Forsyth's recent bestseller, *The Day of the Jackal*, which was released as a film in 1973, Myra was building a new identity for herself with a sinister purpose.

It is also true that Myra took pride in being a motorist, as she did in all her accomplishments: her shorthand-typing, her German 'O' level, being a Holloway ping-pong champion. Not many people in Gorton in the 1960s owned a car, and few women were motorists. Being a driver with transport made Myra a cut above then, and having an up-to-date, valid driving licence in Holloway gave her a sense of achievement and hope for the future.

Her ability to drive had also been a vital element in the first four Moors murders as it was in the last murder, committed in 1965, by which time Myra was driving a blue Austin Mini Countryman, a small estate car similar to her Morris but with a half-timbered back. It was the perfect vehicle for a busy working woman on a budget whose interests included weekend drives with her boyfriend, country picnics, photography, and murder.

★

Edward Evans was the oldest of the five murder victims, but not yet a fully-grown adult. Edward was a small, seventeen-year-old apprentice engineer, five foot six and slim and spotty as a boy. He lived at home with his parents and siblings in Ardwick, which was just down the road from Gorton in Manchester. Around 6.15PM on Wednesday, 6 October 1965, Edward went out for the evening, telling his mother that he was going to watch Manchester United play. Around the same time, Hindley and Brady set out in the Mini Countryman to look for their next victim, Brady having given Hindley another record to mark the occasion. This time it was Joan Baez singing 'It's All Over Now, Baby Blue'.

They went to the Central Station in Manchester around 10:30 that evening. Brady had already stashed two suitcases in the left luggage office at the station, containing incriminating evidence he didn't want at home in case something went wrong and the police searched the house. Myra waited outside on a double yellow line while Ian went into the station to buy wine (they said), or to look for a likely victim, or both. A policeman told Myra that she wasn't allowed to park there. She replied that she was waiting for her boyfriend, and they wouldn't be long. The murderers were so bold now that casual contact with the police, even when they were engaged in crime, didn't faze them. Brady emerged from the station moments later with Edward Evans, whom he had met inside and apparently already knew; introducing him as Eddie to Myra who, he said, was his sister. Evans seemingly agreed to go home with them for a drink.

It was a thirty-minute drive to Hattersley, and, by the time they got home, Granny Maybury was upstairs in bed. Brady and Evans went through to the lounge, which had been stuffed full with granny's knick-knacks and old furniture from Gorton, including her ancient sofa and easy chair. Two types of wall-paper had been hung, with novelty stone effect paper behind the fireplace, making the front room look busier still. There was a clock on the mantlepiece, a china horse and a pair of candlesticks. An old-fashioned mirror hung on a chain above the fireplace. Although the house was brand-new, they had made it look like a cramped and scruffy Beasley Street parlour.

Myra went upstairs to change into casual clothes, later described as her 'killing clothes'. Although it was almost midnight, she then left the house and walked around the corner to Underwood Court, a new block of flats on the same estate where her sister, Maureen, and her husband, David Smith, were living. The Smiths had suffered the loss of their first child to bronchitis the previous April, and Maureen was pregnant again. Brady had started to groom David Smith, known locally as an 'head case', as a new follower and possible accomplice in crime. Ian lent David books about the Nazis and the Marquis de Sade, and discussed committing a robbery with him. He told him that it was OK to murder because 'people are maggots'. David tended to agree but he wasn't sure whether to believe Ian when he boasted, when they were drinking together, that he had already killed people, and buried their bodies on the moors.

The Smiths were in bed when Myra rang the buzzer, asking to come upstairs to have a word with Maureen about the weekend. When the sisters had spoken, Myra asked David to walk her home. Although it was very late, and Myra only lived five minutes away, he agreed. She said that Ian had some miniature bottles of wine to give him, which was some incentive.

Oddly, Myra asked David to wait outside the house until Ian flicked the landing light to signal that it was OK for him to come in. After the signal, Ian opened the front door and showed David through to the kitchen where the wine was, then went next door to the lounge apparently to get some more, which is when it happened.

'I heard a hell of a scream . . . really high-pitched . . . the screams carried on, one after another, really loud,' recalled David Smith. 'Then I heard Myra shout, "Dave, help him" very loud.' David dashed into the lounge to see Brady beating Edward Evans about the head with a hatchet, hitting him left and right, 'it sounded horrible'. Brady was swinging the hatchet with such frenzy that he chipped the fireplace with one back swing, also accidentally grazing David and Myra. He was out of control. Vomit rose in Smith's throat. Edward was dying, making a gurgling sound, 'like when you brush your teeth and gargle with water'. Brady put a cushion cover over his head, and fastened an electrical flex around his neck. He yanked it tight. 'All the time Ian was doing this, he was strangling the lad, Ian was swearing, he was saying, "You dirty bastard" . . . Then Ian looked up at Myra and said something like, "It's done, it's the messiest yet . . ."'

There was blood everywhere, blood on the floor and up the wallpaper. Blood and brains, said the attorney general when it came to court, for Brady had bashed the boy's head in. The dogs were barking. Granny Maybury shouted down to ask what the racket was. Myra replied by saying that she had dropped Ian's tape recorder on her foot.

Edward Evans was clothed save for the fact that his fly was down and he didn't have his shoes on. It is possible that there had been sexual contact with Brady before he turned on the boy. Brady had calmed down now, and Myra didn't appear shocked or upset by what had just happened. Brady began trussing the body up, and told the others to help him lift it onto a blanket and a sheet of polythene which Myra had fetched. 'We placed the lad in the middle, and then Ian came out with a joke,' said David Smith. 'He said, "Eddie's a dead weight", and both Ian and Myra thought it was bloody hilarious.' They carried the corpse up to Myra's bedroom, then came down to clean the lounge, drinking alcohol as they washed and scrubbed the floor, walls and door. Ian even cleaned the top of the door in case blood had splattered up there. Myra filled buckets with water, emptying them when the water turned red. When they were finished, she made tea for them all. Then she sat in grandma's chair, with her feet up on the fireplace, chatting to Ian.

Smith recalled the conversation: '[Ian] said, "I held the axe with my two hands and brought it down on his head."'

Myra said, 'His eyes registered astonishment when you hit him.'

Brady had hurt his ankle during the attack. Because his ankle was tender, he decided not to move the body to the moors that night. David promised to come back the next day, with his dead child's pram, and help them wheel the body down to the car in that. The murderers let him go around 3:30 in the morning, apparently satisfied that he had passed their test – the murder clearly having been stage-managed for him to witness – and that he was now one of them. By helping in the clean-up, David literally had blood on his hands. But they could not read his mind. Smith was sickened by what he had seen, and he was now terrified of Brady. He ran home to Underwood Court, washed himself frantically and scrubbed blood from his nails, then he went to bed.

He could not sleep. He woke Maureen and told her what had happened. He was white with shock. Ian was a murderer and her sister was Ian's accomplice. 'Then she got up, she was crying and upset, and we sat down and tried to decide what to do . . .' They waited until dawn. Taking a screwdriver and a knife for protection – 'I expected Ian and Myra to be outside . . .' – the terrified couple crept downstairs and dialled 999 from a phone box.

The police soon arrived. Having been warned by Smith that Brady and Hindley owned firearms, Superintendent Bob Talbot borrowed the white coat of a bread-delivery man and approached the rear of Number 16 in this disguise. Myra opened the back door. She was dressed for work. Talbot asked to speak to her husband. She said that she wasn't married, and that there was no man in the house. Talbot identified himself and pushed past her into the lounge, followed by a detective sergeant. Brady was sitting up on the sofa, writing a sick note for Myra to give to their boss, explaining that he couldn't come to work that day because he had hurt his foot. Talbot told Brady that the police had received a report of violence and they intended to search the house.

'There is nothing wrong here,' said Myra.

The officers went upstairs, anyway, and found her bedroom door locked. Although the house was new, Myra had had a lock fitted to her door, which was odd. So was her explanation to the police that she kept guns in the bedroom, and the key to the lock was at work. The officers said that they weren't leaving until they had looked inside. 'She then became silent and looked at Brady for some time,' said Talbot.

'Well, you had better tell him,' Myra said.

Brady stood up and told the police: 'There was a row last night. It's in the back bedroom.' He told Myra, 'Give them the keys.' The police found Edward Evans's body wrapped in a blanket, one foot protruding. The hatchet was in a plastic bag. They also recovered two loaded pistols.

★

Life as Myra had known it ended that day: job, home, boyfriend, killing – it was over for her. The police seized her dog, Puppet, which died in their care. She screamed at the police officer who gave her the news: 'You fucking murderer!' The police also took her car away. It proved to be a rich source of evidence. Brady's 'to do' list for the murder was still in the vehicle, including a shorthand note to himself to clean the murder weapon and wipe all fingerprints. Brady headed his murder list, 'Destroy all Lists'.

In her Holloway dreams, Myra imagined herself picking up the pieces of her life where everything stopped in 1965. Her new driving licence, in a new name, represented the life that she hoped to resume. It helped keep her going. Maybe the licence would have another use, too.

She hadn't yet given up all hope that she might get parole at some stage, but when? Myra asked Lord Longford to clarify the parole process for a lifer. The trial judge had not speci-fied how many years she should serve, and she didn't know when she could even apply for parole. Longford went straight to the top. In July 1973, he wrote to Lord Hunt, Chairman of the Parole Board, whom he knew well enough to address as John. He was seeing Myra next week in Holloway, after lunch with the governor, and wondered if they could have a private word first about when Myra might apply for parole, though he conceded that it was early for her to think about this. He signed off as Frank (Frank Pakenham being his given name). Despite the old-boy network, John couldn't offer Frank any help. No politician wanted to think about letting Myra Hindley out, however notional or distant the parole date. Judging by the outraged reaction to her recent walk in the park, such a decision could force a Home Secretary out of office. When Longford told her, Myra began to realise that public opinion and the weight this carried with the press and, therefore, politicians, was going to be the main obstacle in any legitimate attempt she made to regain her freedom. In a letter to Longford, she lamented 'politically inspired cautiousness' around her case.

She tried to distract herself with a project, and applied to study with the Open University (OU). Higher education was an unusual aspiration in Holloway, where many women were barely literate. Myra wanted to learn, which chimed with the principles of rehabilitation. Yet her Open University application was referred to the Home Office as another potential public-relations headache. This proved to be the final straw: Myra's new gofer, Maxine Croft, says that Hindley went 'absolutely ballistic' when she was told that her OU application was being questioned. 'The fact that a decision about a comparatively mundane thing as a degree for someone who had spent eight years in prison . . . had to be handled with such fear-lined kid gloves increased my fears and depression,' Myra wrote. 'If the authorities (at the Home Office) were afraid of criticism about a mere degree, how much more afraid would they be about criticism regarding a release?'

It was time to take the law into her own hands. She shared her decision with Trisha Cairns. 'I told Trisha that I felt there was really no alternative to an otherwise almost unendurable situation – the *whole* situation – than for me to escape from prison, and I asked her to help.'

12

ESCAPE PLANS

'The first duty of the prison official must be to see that the prisoners are kept safely in custody,' an old Holloway governor wrote, 'and if they are not censure is to be expected.' For a prison officer to help a woman escape would be a total professional failure, and a betrayal of her colleagues. It would also be a criminal offence, punishable with a jail sentence, as a notice at the prison gate reminded the staff when they came to work each day at HMP Holloway. But this is what Myra was now asking Trisha Cairns to do and, amazingly, she agreed.

'We were first drawn together by the fact that we are of the same age, come from the same part of Manchester, and share a deep love of the same Catholic faith. We often discussed the faith, and she told me that due to my influence she made her confession to the prison chaplain, and has regularly attended mass and communion since then,' Trisha later explained the basis of her relationship with Myra. 'I became convinced that she had finally freed herself from the yoke of Ian Brady's influence, sincerely amended her ways, and desires only to do good in the future.'

Even if they bonded over Catholicism, and even if that was not put on by Myra to impress a gullible guard, Myra soon steered conversations around to her desire to get out of

Holloway, and Trisha was easily co-opted. 'We often spoke of the day when she would get parole, and I promised to do all in my power to help her.' As time passed, and parole seemed to be an impossible dream, Trisha became concerned about Myra's well-being. 'During recent months, I was distressed to observe that prison was becoming too much for her. I think that even her [prison] doctors were aware of her distress. Also, being such a political hot potato it seemed that no government would wish the criticism of letting her free. The slightest incident would spark a violent outcry from the press, so what would be their reaction when she came to be considered for parole? . . . It seemed to be a hopeless situation, and that she would never be free.'

By Trisha's account, an escape plan evolved during conversations with their latest go-between. 'Maxine Croft is a friend of Myra Hindley's. I used to see Maxine every day because she used to make tea for the civilian staff in the kitchen where I used to take my meal breaks.' This was the scruffy staff kitchen-cum-lounge at the top of the Ivory Tower. 'On numerous occasions we had spoken of the days when Myra would be free, but at the end of September '73, we began to consider getting her out of Holloway.'

Maxine tells a different story. She had already become nervous about helping Myra and Trisha, and wanted to stop carrying their messages, but they wouldn't let her stop. 'By this time there was a lot of pressure, and if I refused at any time to carry things across then the attitude of both Myra Hindley and Miss Cairns was I would be fitted up.'

One day, Hindley, Cairns and Croft were talking together in the Ivory Tower. Myra was complaining about the Home Office reaction to her attempt to study with the Open University, when she sighed, 'They're never going to let me out.'

'The only way you are going to get out is over the wall,' joked Maxine. The solemn faces of the other two women told her that this is what they were thinking.

'We've decided,' said Trisha, 'we're going to do an escape.'

'How?' asked Maxine.

Ever since Holloway had opened in the mid-1800s, prisoners had tried to escape. Early escapees were men, for Holloway was originally a mixed prison that held mostly men, with some women and boys. One of its most famous male inmates had been Oscar Wilde, with Holloway becoming a prison for women exclusively in 1902; and of course, women were just as keen to escape. Some of them succeeded. More than one woman escaped from Holloway in the bold style of Mr Toad, the irrepressible character in *The Wind in the Willows* who is incarcerated in a grim old prison very like Holloway for stealing a motor car. With the help of the jailer's daughter, Toad dresses up as the prison washerwoman and strolls to freedom via 'the wicket-gate in the great outer door'. One Holloway inmate pulled off this trick for real while wearing the prison matron's clothes; and in 1954, two more women walked out of Holloway dressed as workmen.

The self-proclaimed Queen of the Underworld, Zoe Progl, also known as Blonde Mickey, exaggerated when she claimed to be 'the first woman ever to climb over the twenty-five foot wall that surrounds the grim London prison for women'. She wasn't the first, and the perimeter wall was eighteen feet high. But Progl was the best-known recent example of a woman getting over the wall successfully. Her 1960 escape remained fresh in the minds of Holloway inmates and staff, and served as an example to Myra and Trisha of the challenge they faced.

Born in east London in 1928, Zoe Progl was by her admission 'an inveterate criminal', a professional burglar who had served several custodial sentences in Holloway and elsewhere. In 1960, she found herself back in Holloway doing two and a half years for theft. Like Violet Ali, Zoe became a red-band trusty and she used this privilege to place sneaky phone calls from a staff telephone to her boyfriend, Barry, arranging for Barry to meet her at a section of the wall adjoining a side road. Coke was used to stoke the prison furnace. A load of coke had been left piled up against the prison wall, on the inside, and this was the spot that Zoe chose to make her escape on Sunday, 24 July 1960.

'As I scrambled up the pile of coke, I slipped back three times and the gaps in my outsize [prison] shoes filled each time with small pieces of coke. Finally, I managed to grab the low wall, and haul myself to the top,' she later explained. This was only the inner wall, which was about seven feet high. There was then a gap, known as the 'sterile area', beyond which towered the perimeter wall. Simultaneously, Barry put a ladder up outside. 'Suddenly, Barry's head appeared and a rope ladder with metal rungs was dropped.' Zoe grabbed the rope ladder and climbed towards Barry. Then she made the mistake of looking down. 'The sheer drop below terrified me.' She reached the top of the outer wall, and followed Barry down to where he had a car waiting. Meanwhile, friends of theirs were scuffling with prison staff who had sounded the alarm. Every prison officer had an Acme whistle chained to their key ring and one long blast signalled an escape attempt. Progl was bundled into the getaway car as whistles shrilled. 'As we roared off round the back streets, the others pushed me to the floor of the car, out of sight,' she wrote in her memoir, *Woman of the Underworld*.

Zoe spent a fortnight with her daughter in a caravan in Devon. She then returned to London, where, after forty days on the run, she was caught. The women cheered her return to Holloway, where she was locked in a cell with 'E' for 'Escapee' on the door.

There were less-inspiring stories of women who tried to climb the wall. Several would-be escapees were found crumpled up on the pavement outside the prison, writhing in agony, having broken their bones falling from the top.

Was there another, safer way? 'Various plans were discussed between us,' admitted Trisha. There were rumours of a back door in the wall. Zoe Progl claimed to have found it, only to discover that it opened onto a second door with a lock that could not be picked. Trisha tried to find out if this back door existed. Meanwhile, Myra thought she might be able to get into the chapel loft, but there was no way down from the roof without being seen.

Over eighty prison officers worked in Holloway, plus civilian staff, making the prison busy during the day, with many eyes on the inmates. It was much quieter at night after the prisoners had been locked in, the lights dimmed, and most of the staff had gone home. As they left work, the guards handed their keys to Chief Officer Storrow, who locked them in the safe in the Centre. Before she went home, Storrow gave the safe key to the Sleeping Officer who was the only person in the secure part of the prison overnight with cell keys. 'You were locked in with the key, actually in the condemned cell . . . so if anybody had to be taken out of the prison at night – we had women who could give birth, or whatever – you were the one who had to wake up to unlock the prison,' explains former officer Monica Carden. 'You slept with the [key] under your pillow.' Other officers were on patrol in the prison at night, but not many.

Nighttime was Myra's best hope of escaping, but she would have to get out of her cell first. The fact that Myra was on D Wing meant that she was held in the most secure, most heavily guarded part of the prison. As she was on the top floor, she couldn't tunnel out. Some parts of the Victorian prison were so decrepit by 1973 that the rusting bars could be bent by hand. Maxine did it once for a laugh. 'I said, *It's wide enough, I think I can get through*, and I got as far as my waist and got stuck . . . they had to call the fire brigade.' But new bars had been fitted on D Wing for the lifers.

If she could find some way to get her door open, Myra's next challenge would be getting off D Wing. That meant making her way down the stairs to the flat, past the duty officer who watched the wing all night, through the locked gate into the Centre, then down a spiral staircase, and out through another locked door which was also watched overnight. She would have to overpower the guard. It was then downstairs to the gatehouses. Even if she got through the inner gate, she would never penetrate the second gatehouse that faced the street. To avoid the gatehouses, Myra might slip out into the prison yard, but doors to the yard were double locked at night with the so-called master key, which was in the safe. If she managed to overcome that problem, Myra would face the wall. Like Zoe Progl before her, she would have to climb the inner wall and then the eighteen-foot outer wall, and get down without injuring herself. Progl had had the advantage of the coke pile, which gave her a leg up, and she had Barry to help her. Maxine had noticed a builder's skip in the yard, which Myra could climb onto, but Trisha would probably have to help her with a ladder on the other side.

It seemed all but impossible, but Myra was willing to try, and she had an advantage over Zoe Progl and practically every other prisoner who had ever tried to escape from Holloway: her girlfriend had prison keys.

Trisha had to hand her keys in every night at the end of her shift, like every officer, and her keys were locked in the safe when she wasn't using them. She couldn't let Myra out personally. But they might copy the keys Trisha had access to during the day, giving Myra forged keys to let herself out at night. This became the plan.

This was where Maxine Croft came in useful again. 'Myra was like, "We can get keys, and you can make [copies] because you are really good at forging stuff" . . . That's how it started,' recalls Maxine, whose conviction for passing fake fivers had given her an unwarranted reputation as a forger. She now found herself central to an escape conspiracy with the most infamous criminal in England.

'[Trisha] asked me if I knew of anyone to make keys. I replied that I knew people, but wasn't interested in the escape and I didn't think that they would be, either. She, Miss Cairns, replied, "Well, you're in it now, you have family outside and you have no protection in here."' Half a century later, Maxine says there was another element, a secret she didn't share at the time. The prison officer who first approached her to make friends with Hindley, and spy on her and Cairns, told her to go along with the escape plan in order to get Myra in so much trouble she would never be let out. 'You can't prove I'm telling the truth. I could be being a Walter Mitty. The Home Office are never going to turn around and say, *Yeah, we set the whole thing up*, [but] the whole thing was to keep her in, to stop her getting parole,' claims Maxine. 'I was told it was a set-up.'

Maxine found herself caught between her handler and Myra and, despite Myra's non-confrontational manner, Maxine sensed that she could be dangerous if crossed. 'You had to really be in that room, and get to know her, to understand in depth what she was really like,' says Maxine, who felt increasingly nervous around the Moors murderer, 'and I'm a tough person.'

Trisha saw Myra differently: as a deeply religious woman with whom she wanted to spend her life. The plan to break Myra out was a plan for them to be together. Once she had helped Myra down from the wall, they would drive to Heathrow Airport and catch a night flight to Brazil. 'I suggested going at about 9PM.' By the time of the rising bell in Holloway in the morning, they would be halfway to paradise. 'Myra and I would have all night to reach our destination, before she was missed.' The travel tales Joan Kleinert shared with Myra, while they worked together in the tapestry room, may have partly inspired the idea of running away to Latin America, while Brazil was one of the few countries in the world that would not automatically extradite them back to the UK. Trisha also thought that they could do God's work in a Catholic country. 'I suggested my taking Myra to São Paulo, where we could do missionary work.' A Moors murderer and a former nun hiding out as missionaries in a country that harboured escaped Nazis and the train robber Ronnie Biggs, the idea made Maxine laugh. 'I think she had an illusion that they were going to live happily ever after.'

The women were serious, though, and escape was now urgent. Holloway was alive with gossip about Myra and Trisha, who had rashly revealed her feelings to at least one other prison officer. At the same time, Trisha's flatmate, Janet Harber, was becoming jealous of Trisha and Myra, which was especially dangerous because Janet worked in Holloway. '[Myra] said she was worried in case Janet went to the Chief [Officer],' said Maxine. 'She said that Miss Harber was becoming a nuisance and had twice threatened to go to the chief.' As a precaution, Trisha stopped sending Glenis Moores letters to Myra. The last of fifty-one such letters, probably typed on Janet's typewriter, some including money, arrived at the prison on 18 September 1973. The pressure was on to get Myra over the wall before Janet or someone else turned them in.

13

PHOTOGRAPHING MYRA

Myra ordered Maxine to do exactly what Trisha Cairns told her as they planned the escape. 'I would be given instructions on what to do and at no point to show any anxiety. She said that Miss Cairns would talk to me, and to wait and see her. Myra Hindley seemed quite confident that the escape would come off.'

Trisha soon briefed Maxine about the first job. '[She] told me she would supply me with an instamatic camera and flash bulbs to take photographs of Myra Hindley. I refused at first, being as it was too dangerous, but she said that there was too much involved now, and that she would leave the camera and I was to carry it to the wing.'

To leave the country, Myra needed a passport, and to obtain a passport she needed proof of identity and a photograph. Her new Myra Spencer driving licence was one proof of identity, but the conspirators could not risk using an old photograph of Myra when she was blonde. That was the face of the Moors murderer. Since her incarceration the only new photographs of Myra to have been taken were the prison identification pictures that staff took at intervals. These came in a strip of three black-and-white images: a body shot, a head and shoulders, and a profile photo; dated and marked with the prisoner's name and number (Hindley was 964055). The woman depicted in these images was quite different to her 1965 mug shot, and indeed to Myra in her early Holloway photos, when she wore the prison uniform of lisle stockings, grey skirt and floral blouse. No longer blonde, and now fashionably dressed, Myra also diverged significantly from her public image when she smiled. A smiling, trendy brunette Myra Spencer would not have attracted attention strolling through Heathrow, bound for Brazil. Unable to obtain her recent prison pictures, however, the conspirators had to take new photographs of their own.

Trisha bought a camera especially. The Kodak Pocket Instamatic was small, cheap and supposedly easy to use. It was not much larger than a packet of cigarettes, and used miniature film. For taking pictures indoors, the Pocket Instamatic came with 'flashcubes', a cube of four bulbs that snapped into the top of the camera and rotated with each flash frame, so the photographer could take four flash images before changing the cube. As each flash went off, the spent bulbs went cloudy. 'Little Camera, Big Sharp Pictures,' promised Kodak. 'No settings.' It was new technology in 1973.

Trisha left this little camera in the clock in the staff room for Maxine, who tucked the camera into her bra, and pushed the flashbulbs down into her knee socks. Worried that the camera might fall out, like the hankies had, she walked very carefully down the stairs from the Ivory Tower, through the Centre onto D Wing, past the screws, and climbed the stairs to the fours, where she took a roll of pictures of Myra in her cell.

The next day, Maxine replaced the camera in their hiding place in the tower. 'Miss Cairns picked it up from the clock and said she would take [the film] to a shop and get them developed. She then said to me that things were going well.'

A few days later, an agitated Trisha rushed into the staff lounge, where Little Max was clearing up. The pictures

hadn't come out. None of them. *You must have done it wrong!*
Maxine was sure that she hadn't. She suggested to Trisha that
they might have been found out. 'I asked her if the shop-
keeper might have recognised the photographs as being Myra
Hindley.' Trisha said she would have to go back to the shop.

It was a ten-minute walk from HMP Holloway to the
Nag's Head corner of Parkhurst Road, Seven Sisters Road
and Holloway Road. This busy junction, named after the pub
on the corner, was lined with shops. Cairns crossed over to
Bishop's camera shop and showed the assistant her camera,
and the blank prints she had got back, asking nervously what
had gone wrong.

The camera had a lens cover, which you had to slide back
before taking pictures. This was explained in the instructions.
Apparently, neither Trisha nor Maxine had read the instructions, and Little Max had left the lens cover on. Greatly
relieved, Trisha took the camera back to Holloway where
she asked Maxine to try again. Maxine didn't want to risk a
second attempt. She said that their initial failure was 'a bad
omen', signifying that they ought to drop the idea.

Trisha laughed. 'Wait a while,' she said.

A week later, Myra told Maxine that there was something
for her to collect in the clock again. Dreading what she would
find, Maxine climbed the Ivory Tower at lunchtime and looked
in the sideboard. 'There was a paper bag containing the camera,
two sets of flash bulbs and instructions on how to use the camera
properly.' Feeling apprehensive, she smuggled the camera back
to D Wing in her bra, then steeled herself to return for the
flash cubes. Every time she made the journey between the
Ivory Tower and D Wing, she risked getting caught, just like
Violet Ali and Gail Payne were caught smuggling contraband
for Hindley and Cairns. 'I might easily have been searched.'

Myra dressed up for her second photoshoot with Maxine. She chose a favourite patterned blouse with a brown singlet, matching skirt and dark tights. She had washed and combed her hair, which had grown down to her shoulders, and she had applied heavy make-up to disguise her prison-grey complexion. She put so much product on her face that she looked like she had just come back from Spain with a deep tan. She posed for Maxine sitting on her bed, having closed the curtains to hide the cell bars. Maxine took twenty shots of Myra, winding the film forward for each frame, and making sure this time that the lens cover was open.

The flash cubes created an alarmingly bright light in Myra's dingy cell as they went off – *pof, pof, pof* – which risked drawing attention. When all four flashes had gone cloudy, Maxine took the spent cube out and fitted a new one. Twenty pictures required five cubes. A guard could come in at any time, but Myra didn't appear nervous. Displaying the same composure under pressure she had shown during the murders, she instructed Maxine to stand three feet away from her, and make sure the pictures were good. She then allowed herself to enjoy the photo session, as she had posed like a coquette for that keen photographer Ian Brady. In one picture, she sat with her legs crossed and her chin on her hand. In another, she had both legs up. In a third, she cuddled a Snoopy toy. These were not conventional passport photos, but they could be cropped and printed in monochrome to satisfy the Passport Office. Apart from the escape plot, they were pictures for Trisha. 'She wanted them as keepsakes,' says Maxine. Later, there would be talk of taking other pictures more suitable for use in a passport.

Back went the camera to the clock. Maxine smashed and binned the spent cubes. Once more, Trisha collected the camera from the lounge, sneaked it out of the prison and down the road to Bishop's shop to have the film developed. This time, she gave a false name. Changing her name to hide her identity was becoming a habit for Patricia Cairns, also known as Pat or Trisha, Sister Therese and Glenis Moores; and that wasn't the end of her many aliases.

The former nun had to wait a few days to collect her prints, praying that they had come out. *Hallelujah!* They had! Trisha was so excited that she dashed into the Quality Fish Bar next door to Bishop's to look through the prints without delay. The new pictures were curved slightly by the developing machine, and so fresh that they stuck together. Myra looked lovely in the photos. She seemed to gaze into Trisha's eyes. Trisha had to share her excitement with someone, and she risked taking the snaps back into Holloway to show to Maxine.

Doesn't Myra look sweet?

Look at her with Snoopy!

As the women flipped through the prints, Trisha told Little Max that she might be asked to take more photographs.

Colleagues noticed Trisha was in a tizzy. 'I was very aware that Cairns was behaving in an excitable way,' says Judy Gibbons, the third most senior member of the governing staff. She had started to hear whispers that the officer was up to something, and decided to have a word. 'What's the matter with you?' she asked Trisha.

'Oh, no, nothing. I'm just happy.'

Gibbons raised an eyebrow. 'I thought, *All right, you're happy*.' She kept her counsel for now, not sure what was going on, but it seemed to involve Maxine Croft. She made a note to speak to her, too.

'In the meantime, Myra Hindley told me things had been prepared for her escape,' said Maxine. 'She told me there was a lot of outside help.'

A few days later, the US Mail delivered a package to Joan Kleinert in Santa Rosa, California, a town north of San Francisco, where she was now living, having been extradited from the UK at the start of the year. 'It had some photographs in it [of Myra] with some sort of note from Pat [Cairns], saying, "I'm going to get Myra out . . ." some allusion to an escape plan, and, "We'll come by and pick up this package", or, "We'll write and let you know where to send the package."'

Trisha had sent copies of Myra's prison-cell photographs to Joan for safekeeping, and possibly with a mind to ask her to do something with them. Around this time, Trisha persuaded Janet Harber's Uncle William in Kent to accept a package that she said might come from America. She evidently didn't want this item delivered to her home. Trisha and Myra may have hoped that Joan could use her contacts to forge a passport for Myra in California. 'Maybe, but I was never asked to do that.'

The motive remains unclear, but as the escape plan developed, Myra and Trisha used several women they knew from Holloway – ex-cons and staff – women whom they felt might be sympathetic to Myra, and women about whom they knew compromising information. Joan had of course been in prison, information which might be used to coerce a weak person. 'It's amazing no one connected me in any way,' says Joan, revealing this part of the story only now. But she didn't co-operate. 'I wasn't part of the escape plan. All I got was this thing saying something is going to happen.' That spooked her. 'I remember being slightly uptight. *You're going to come to my house*? I'd had enough of being in jail.' She sent the photographs back to Trisha, refusing to help, and frustrating the escape plan.

14

KEYS TO THE CASTLE

Despite the setback with Joan Kleinert, the conspirators moved ahead with the escape plan, turning next to the vital matter of the keys. When Trisha looked at her prison keys, on a large ring with a metal tag stamped with the number '58', showing that she ranked fairly low in the staff hierarchy, she held three keys. The first was a big old iron key that opened every cell door, including the door to Myra's cell. In keeping with the prison, this universal key looked like something from the middle ages. Its antique design was crudely replicated on a massive scale in stone, clutched by the dragons that guarded the gate. Also on the key ring were two modern keys, with holes in the ends. These opened office doors and internal gates, including the gate at the end of D Wing. Trisha was issued with this set of keys every day, and she handed them back before she went home. While in her possession, the bunch was chained to her belt. Otherwise, it was in the safe.

The conspirators had decided to get Myra out of Holloway by copying keys, but prison keys were worn by use, and as forensically distinct as fingerprints, so making copies of the fifty-eight bunch would put Trisha at risk. Also, these three keys would only get Myra off D Wing. To get out of the building, she needed a fourth key, the so-called master key, which was used to double lock external doors at night. The master key was not handed out as part of a standard bunch, but kept in the safe. The master key would still not allow Myra to let herself out of the prison. For that she would also need a fifth, gate-house key, and Cairns never had access to that key, which was why Myra couldn't attempt to leave through the gate. She would have to scale the wall, as Zoe Progl had, and somebody would probably have to be on the other side with a rope ladder. But Trisha could help Myra get from her cell into the yard after lock-up, to make her escape attempt at night, if they copied four prison keys, and if she was clever she would copy another officer's keys rather than her own bunch.

Copying keys was one of the black prison arts, like smuggling notes or making a shiv to stab an enemy. If they got a close look at a key, some prisoners were able to memorise its shape and carve a duplicate key in wood, or from a plastic toothbrush. 'That is why prison officers are never allowed to have their keys in view. That's why they have the key pouch,' explains Veronica Bird, who like all Holloway guards wore her keys on a chain, in a leather pouch, which she kept in the pocket of her skirt. Keys were only visible for the few seconds it took to use them. Myra needn't worry about that. In her case, unique as she was in many ways, a prison officer was willing to collude in copying keys for her, though making impressions of the keys would fall to Maxine Croft, who had acquired an unmerited reputation as a forger.

Trisha told Little Max that she would smuggle materials into the prison to make key impressions, from which duplicates could be cast. 'I asked her if she could do the impressions herself,' said Maxine, who did not wish to be drawn further into the escalating conspiracy. No, said Trisha, Maxine could do it upstairs in the Ivory Tower.

One prison trick was to press a key into a bar of soap to make an impression that could be used as the basis of a mould. Trisha and Maxine tried this technique first. They had some rough brown prison soap, and three bars of scented pink Camay, which Cairns brought into work especially, and which seemed more appropriate. Making keys to what was sometimes called Holloway Castle (not to be confused with the pub of that name opposite the prison gate) was also a romantic matter for Trisha and Myra, and Camay was advertised with pictures of beautiful women under the slogan, 'you'll be a little lovelier each day with fabulous pink Camay'. Trisha and Maxine softened the soap with water before pressing the flat of the keys into the surface. The results were disappointing. 'Soap never really works that well,' says Maxine. Still, Trisha took the impressions home.

For their second attempt, they tried to make plaster casts of the keys. Trisha said that this was Maxine's idea, 'so that we could be sure of getting good copies. I brought in a bag of plaster of Paris'. On her way up the Ivory Tower, Trisha almost bumped into another prison officer coming down, and had to hide the bag. 'It was like a French farce,' said Maxine. '[Cairns] ran down and threw me the plaster as we passed. We were throwing it to each other for several minutes so the other officer didn't see.' When the coast was clear they mixed the plaster up in a metal tea pot, but couldn't get the mixture right and had to throw the whole lot away.

'A few days later Maxine asked me to bring in some modelling powder,' said Trisha, who bought a packet of art plaster, a brand 'recommended by parents and teachers' for model-making. Again, Trisha arranged to meet Little Max in the Ivory Tower.

Trisha was delayed by being sent on escort duty that morning, which typically meant escorting a prisoner to court.

After she got back to Holloway, she was given the dinner patrol, which further detained her. While the prisoners and staff ate their lunch, Trisha was briefly in charge of the Centre, which gave her rare access to the key safe. This was a large steel-banded iron cupboard set into the wall under the clock. It was a golden opportunity. Trisha nipped upstairs to alert Maxine, then hurried back down to open the safe and remove the master key. 'As the escape plan was to be put into effect during the night, a copy of the master key was needed,' she later admitted.

She hurried back upstairs with the precious key. Trisha was still wearing her trench coat from being outside on escort duty. Before they started work, she took her coat off and hung it on the back of a chair in the kitchen. Trisha and Maxine then mixed up the modelling powder with water on a plate using a plastic spoon. They poured the mixture into a PG Tips tea packet to contain it. Their hearts were pounding. Making a mould took time, and anybody might walk in and catch them. Trisha couldn't get the hang of the work. 'I failed in my attempt to make a plaster cast, so I kept watch outside the kitchen while Maxine made up the mixture and took impressions.'

They heard footsteps. Someone was climbing the tower stairs. They peeked to see. It was Carol White, a prisoner friend of Maxine's, with a similar background. White had first been convicted of stealing and burglary when she was fourteen. Approved school led to borstal and prison. Aged twenty-nine, her previous convictions now ran to four pages. When Maxine realised it was Carol, coming upstairs to chat about her divorce, she told Trisha who pushed her out of the room, telling her to keep White talking while she went into the lounge to finish the moulds.

Carol White entered the kitchen. 'As I walked into the kitchen, on the first chair I noticed a white trench mac, which I knew belonged to Miss Cairns,' said White. 'Maxine whispered that there was someone in the dining room. I took no more notice of this. We went on talking about my divorce.'

While the prisoners chatted in the kitchen, Trisha tried to finish an impression next door. She gave up after a few minutes and hid her aborted attempt in the old clock. Then she went into the kitchen, smiled at White as if nothing untoward was happening, washed her hands, collected her trench coat and left, probably taking the master key, which she had to return to the safe before it was missed by her colleagues. 'There was no conversation with the officer [Cairns],' White said later, 'because I don't like her.'

The conspirators reconvened downstairs outside the discipline office, where Trisha worked. She told Maxine off: 'You've messed things up, having your friend up there.'

It wasn't my fault!

'You will have to do the keys this afternoon.'

Poor Little Max trudged back upstairs, cleaned the mess they'd made, did her tea duties, and the washing up, then got things ready for yet another copying attempt. When Trisha joined her, they mixed up a second batch of powder with water. 'I poured the plaster into three cardboard boxes which Miss Cairns had made up. She then took the keys off the ring, and I made three impressions. She told me she had already made one soap impression herself.'

This session ended with a warning, by Maxine's account. 'You're in it now,' Trisha told her. 'If you say anything to your friends, or anybody, I'll have you nicked.'

The unhappy drudge went downstairs to eat her meagre supper before being banged up for the night. But Little Max had something to give Trisha first, a woman whom she had liked since their Bullwood Hall days, though the prison officer wasn't so kind to her now. Maxine passed her gift over in a PG Tips packet. Trisha was surprised to receive the most valuable impression of all. Maxine had managed to copy the master key, by carving it in prison soap, with Trisha's penknife, when she wasn't looking. With this impression the conspirators had everything they needed to begin making four new keys.

The strain was starting to show on Maxine, who was observed downstairs looking glum by Assistant Governor Judy Gibbons. 'There is something going on around here,' Gibbons told Maxine. 'For goodness sake, tell me. I won't implicate you. At least if you tell me I can start to do some work on it.' But Maxine wouldn't explain. 'Why can't you tell me about it, Maxine? We are on our own.'

Finally, Maxine said, 'It's the staff here that drive me mad.'

In her way, Little Max was telling the assistant governor the truth. Officer Cairns was driving her crackers with her love for Myra Hindley, and their escape plan. Judy Gibbons already had her suspicions about Cairns, and her friendship with Hindley. Unable to get any sense out of Maxine, she went to see the governor. 'I did say to her, "Megan, you have to watch Pat Cairns and Myra Hindley. They're up to something, and I don't know what . . . You'd better keep an eye open."' Around the same time members of staff noticed bits of soap stuck to one of the keys in the prison safe.

15

SAYING HER PRAYERS

When she stepped into the witness box in 1966, to give evidence in the murder trial, Myra was offered the Bible. 'Do you wish to take the oath in the normal form, or do you want to affirm?' the judge asked her.

'I want to affirm,' she replied, meaning that she would solemnly swear to tell the truth, but not by God.

'That is because you have no religious beliefs?'

'Yes.'

Ian Brady also chose to affirm. Brady and Hindley were a godless couple, and proud of it, but Myra changed her tune in prison.

She wasn't the first woman to come into Holloway caring nothing for religion only to become a devout Christian in custody. While Trisha Cairns and Lord Longford hailed a Damascene conversion, others saw cynical 'prison religion': an inmate paying lip-service to faith because she thought it might give her advantages: more time off the wing, and the trust and support of people in power who equated faith with goodness and rehabilitation. It was remarkable how many women in Holloway professed to be Roman Catholic, about thirty-five per cent, treble the proportion in the general population. Cairns and Hindley made a feature of their faith, as the basis of their relationship, and proof of their integrity, but that didn't impress everyone. 'I'm a Catholic as well. She [Cairns] knew that. She didn't try to pull much wool over my eyes,' says Judy Gibbons, who left Holloway at this time having warned the governor to watch Cairns and Hindley. 'If I can be candid, it was a bit more manipulation.'

When the Victorians built Holloway they put religion at the heart of the prison. The chaplain's house flanked the governor's residence at the entrance, indicating that the vicar was equally important, and the prison chapel was at the literal and metaphorical centre of Holloway castle, located above the entrance hall and administration offices, and accessed via a gothic arched door on the third floor. Its roof rose above the battlements, with crosses at the gable ends. The chapel was a big, bright space, with the largest barred windows in the prison, allowing the light of God to flood across the polished pews and gleaming brass candlesticks. Fresh flowers also gave the chapel a sweeter smell than the noisome wings. This was the nicest part of Holloway, and the hub of prison life.

The chapel was a place to come to pray, of course, whatever your faith. There were Anglican, RC and Methodist chaplains, with visits from a rabbi and an imam, and a little side chapel for Catholics. 'That was where we saw [Hindley] on Sunday morning,' says former prison officer Kath Moores, also a Roman Catholic. 'She was going to church and found religion again, but to me it was all a ploy.' The chapel was also a place of entertainment, where the women came to sing and hear music; and somewhere to go to simply 'break up the boredom, or to see your girlfriend, or other friends, or to pass goodies,' says former staff member Veronica Bird. Women traded all manner of items in Holloway, from cigarettes to their wedding rings. Chapel was a place to pass this contraband.

Myra came to chapel more than most women. Apart from attending services, she sang in the choir, and she was allowed to play the chapel's grand piano. Myra was musical to some extent. She played acoustic guitar and she sang in the folk style of Joan Baez. What sort of pianist she was is a moot subject. Staff don't remember hearing her play, and it isn't clear if she ever even learned. Yet she persuaded the assistant governor that she was a pianist who needed to practice. 'These people will convince you of anything,' chuckles Judy Gibbons. Myra went for piano practice in the chapel on Monday, Tuesday and Wednesday lunchtime, and Thursday and Friday after tea; it was almost enough practice time to raise her to concert standard. A junior officer escorted her to the chapel, and came back to collect her when she was finished.

One lunchtime in October 1973, while the escape plan was being assembled, Myra asked the dinner-patrol officer, Barbara Bates, if she would take her to the chapel for her piano practice, which Bates did at 12:20PM. Before she left, Bates checked all the chapel doors were locked, save for the door to the Centre.

She returned an hour later. 'I could not see Myra Hindley . . . On going further into the church, I noticed that the door between the altar and the side chapel, which opens into the church, was being slowly closed by someone whom I could not see.' This door had previously been locked. Myra emerged suddenly, as if caught by surprise. 'I asked her what she had been doing, and she said she had been saying her prayers.'

Bates took Myra back to D Wing, and then returned to the chapel to investigate further. 'I went through the door I had seen closing.' Bates descended the back stairs, which brought her to the discipline office where Trisha Cairns worked, adjacent to Myra's tapestry room. Looking through the window,

Bates saw the back of a woman who looked like Cairns. She went past again to be sure. This time she looked the woman in the eye and verified that it was Cairns. 'I looked at her and she looked at me. She gave me the impression that she knew I was checking on her.'

Bates didn't report Trisha Cairns as having had an illicit assignation with Hindley in the chapel, thinking that she didn't have enough evidence. She did tell a colleague, though. She spoke to Miss Taylor, telling her about walking into the chapel in time to see someone apparently closing the connecting door behind them, then finding a prison officer downstairs who appeared 'very flustered'. She also said that she had seen Hindley chewing gum, a treat she suspected had been supplied by this officer. Bates didn't name Cairns, but Taylor guessed who she meant. She already knew. Taylor was the officer whom Trisha confided in about her love for Myra earlier in the year. Trisha told Taylor on that occasion that she and Myra were meeting in the chapel. It now appeared that Cairns was unlocking doors in order to be alone with Hindley. Yet there is no record in prison files that Bates, or Taylor, told the governor this at this time. 'The officers stuck together,' comments Veronica Bird. Grassing on a colleague in Holloway, where many officers shared digs, as well as working together, was as much of a sin as grassing was among the prisoners. 'If you are a grass, life can be very difficult.'

After work, Trisha took the Tube home to Gloucester Road, then walked the short distance through Earl's Court to her hostel. This was a Victorian mansion block at 18 Collingham Gardens, one of two hostels used by Holloway staff: a good address in the salubrious borough of Kensington and Chelsea. Letting herself into the hostel, Trisha checked the post in the hall, and looked to see whether there had been any telephone messages for her. The communal telephone was the bane of her colleague Angela Glynn, who occupied the downstairs flat. Angela had to answer the phone when it rang, shouting upstairs to whoever was wanted. When the phone rang for Trisha, Angela had to climb five flights of stairs to alert her, because the flat Trisha shared with Janet Harber was right at the top of the building in the eves.

Trisha and Janet had been together for five years, but the relationship was going wrong. Janet had suspected something from when Trisha and Myra met, in 1970, at the time of the ping-pong tournament on E Wing, with the Carpenters on the record player. Janet looked in Trisha's bedside locker at home (where they had separate bedrooms) and discovered a letter in Hindley's inimitable handwriting. 'I showed Pat [Cairns] the letter and she agreed it was from Myra Hindley, but said it was an old one she had received a long time ago.'

Considering that they had only just met, that didn't make sense, but Janet was a simple soul, later characterised as 'not a particularly bright individual', and she loved Trisha. So she let it go. Trisha had subsequently become infatuated with Myra, which shut Janet out. Janet wasn't being told things, but she worked out that Maxine Croft was involved, and she suspected that twenty-two-year-old Miss Taylor was being dragged in. 'During October 1973, I asked Pat Cairns if she was using [Taylor] to pass messages to and from Myra Hindley,' Janet later said. 'Cairns agreed this was so.' Janet was furious. 'I told Cairns I though it was wrong to use [Taylor] for this because she was so young.' She threatened to report Trisha, who warned Myra that they had a problem.

Janet noticed that Myra wasn't speaking to her at work. 'When I saw Hindley in prison we always said good morning and good afternoon to each other, but from the middle of October when I saw Hindley, although I knew she had seen me, she pretended she hadn't.' It was humiliating to be snubbed by a prisoner. Janet also noticed that Trisha was making notes about Myra, seemingly lists of things that Hindley wanted. When Janet confronted Trisha about this, they had a row.

What are you doing in my room? Can't I have any privacy?

Trisha told Janet not to come into her bedroom again. Slammed doors. Tears. 'From that time, she refused me access to her bedroom by locking it.' It is likely that Trisha had the key impressions hidden in her bedroom, the impressions that she and Maxine had made in secret. She couldn't allow Janet to find them. Locking her door against her friend was the final insult. Janet felt that she couldn't live with Trisha any more, and she couldn't work with her. 'I was so upset by Miss Cairns's attitude, and the fact that I could no longer discuss work problems with her, that, on 24 October 1973, I put in my resignation from the Prison Service.'

When Janet handed in her notice, the conspirators feared that she would tell the governor everything she knew, and what she suspected. They had to act first. Myra's escape from Holloway was now urgent.

'She [Cairns] was frightened of being caught in her flat with the keys,' explained Maxine. They had to get the impressions away at once. 'I asked her, couldn't she leave them with any of her friends and she replied, *No, they will have to go to yours.*' Ideally, the impressions would be sent to somebody who could make new keys from the impressions. Trisha was out of her depth here. But Maxine thought she might know someone who could help. Trisha urged her to contact her friend at once. 'She hadn't a clue really,' says Maxine. 'She believed everything I told her.'

16

USING PEOPLE

Before her time in prison, Maxine drank in the Three Rabbits in Ilford, east London, with Lenny Thompson, a local man in his thirties who was later acquitted of involvement in a gangland murder case. Maxine and Lenny knew some colourful people, such as the armed robber Roy 'Pretty Boy' Shaw, a nightclub owner known as Ronnie the Pig, and a scrap dealer named George Stephens, whose salvage yard was just around the corner from the Three Rabbits.

George was like a character out of the TV cop show, *The Sweeney*. In his forties, with red hair and sideburns, he customarily wore a chunky fawn cardigan with leather buttons, drove flash cars, enjoyed a cigarette and a drink, and gave the impression that he could take care of things. If he couldn't, he would know someone who could. Maxine says that George was 'just a friend', though she thinks that he would have liked to have known her better. Married with children, George was certainly a ladies man. 'He used to have all the women after him. All the time, really. He was a very social man,' says his daughter.

Born in east London in 1932, George competed in bicycle races for the Stratford Hammers cycle speedway team as a youth. He was convicted of stealing at nineteen, three years after which he married his girlfriend, Joyce, with whom he had three children: Kevin, Ian and Julie. By 1973, the Stephenses were living in a council maisonette near George's yard, where he broke up old cars for parts. There are sometimes links between scrap dealers and criminals, and George had shady contacts. 'My dad wasn't a nasty villain type of person. He was just on the dodgy side,' says Ian.

There was a mismatch between George's work and his life-style. 'He always had wads in his wallet,' says Julie, laughing. She has fond memories of her father, but knew that he was a bit of a lad. George was forever changing his cars, and he once turned up at the flats in a Rolls-Royce. He brought a present home for Joyce every Friday, and not just flowers and chocolates. On one occasion, he came home with a diamond tiara and necklace; another time it was a valuable painting, which he hid in a cupboard.

George and Joyce liked to go out on the town. George was a Freemason, and they attended black-tie dinner-dances at the Masonic lodge in Upminster. George also enjoyed lock-ins at a pub on the Isle of Dogs in London where there were drunken sing-songs into the early hours of the morning. George was fun, 'the best dad in the world' says Ian, until he ran off with a woman from the pub. There were two sides to George Stephens, sometimes known as George the Liar.

In a gap in the houses on Wanstead Park Road, a long resi-dential road connecting Redbridge and Ilford, was a potholed alley that led into a warren of car spray shops, repair garages and scrap yards. George's scrap yard was at the end of this alley, behind a corrugated iron gate guarded by a chained up Alsatian dog. He used an old caravan as an office. George sat here in his caravan most days surrounded by smashed cars, a wood burner going in the winter. When his kids came to visit, Julie played in the puddles, and Ian shot rats with an air gun. Nobody touched the dog.

This was the dodgy geezer Maxine Croft suggested Trisha Cairns send the Holloway key impressions to, when Trisha felt under pressure to get them out of her flat. 'Maxine said she knew somebody called George who could help.' But his phone number was in her address book, which was at home in Harold Hill with her elderly foster mother, Grace. Trisha told Maxine to get hold of it. 'She told me to ask my brother [Dennis] to collect the address book.'

Dennis and Maxine were quarrelsome siblings, and Dennis wasn't keen to get roped into one of Maxine's schemes. He'd had a scrape with the police, when he was convicted at nineteen of taking a car for a joy ride with some mates. Dennis had lived a law-abiding life since then. He worked in the fruit 'n' veg trade, and lived with his wife, Jackie, above a friend's greengrocer's shop in Dagenham. Every other Sunday, Dennis, Jackie and Grace visited Maxine in Holloway, which was a bitter-sweet experience. Dennis remembers the inmates yelling at them from their cell windows when they arrived at the prison, then being led through the complex to a gloomy room where inmates and family members were reunited over a cigarette and a cup of tea, while the screws watched to make sure no contraband was passed. 'Maxine sat on one side, we sat on the other . . . Weren't allowed to touch or give her anything.' Gifts had to be handed in at the gate. 'Maxine may have asked for something – soap.' Sometimes arguments broke out in the room, as happened one afternoon when Veronica Bird was supervising the visits. 'This young prisoner had a fight with her boyfriend because he was drunk and late, and so I was trying to separate them.' The lovers started throwing chairs, at which point the governor Mrs Wing piled in and there was a jolly good fight.

Maxine didn't seem to have a care in the world as she sat across the table from her family in the visits room in October 1973. 'She was always cheerful and pleased to see you, always in good spirits,' recalls Dennis. When Grace needed the loo, Jackie went with her, leaving Dennis and Maxine to talk on their own. Leaning forward, Maxine told her brother quietly that she wanted him to retrieve her blue address book from home. 'She didn't tell me why . . . later she would let me know an address to send it to.'

Trisha didn't want the address book sent to her hostel. That would be too risky, with her flatmate Janet on the brink of handing them in. She would use another woman, Susan,[1] who had recently served a short sentence in Holloway for minor offences including theft, 'something I regret very, very much'. Susan's family had disowned her, and she was frightened of anybody knowing about her time inside. She was, as a result, easily manipulated. Trisha was kind to Susan in Holloway, and like many of the women Trisha came into contact with, Susan was made a trusty. 'I was a green-band and she [Trisha] looked after me.'

Susan was a hairdresser by trade. After she was released from Holloway she moved to a flat in central London, and got a job in a salon in a big West End hotel. Trisha came to the hotel regularly to get her hair done. 'I used to do her girlfriend's hair as well. They used to come in together.' Trisha kept her hair short. 'I would say she was the more manly one of the two.' It was now time for Susan to do Trisha a favour, in return for the kindness she had shown her in prison. 'She said she was expecting some mail, which she didn't want to go to the hostel, she asked if I would receive it for her at my address.'

---

1 Name changed.

At the same time, Maxine requested a parole day out of Holloway in preparation for her release – Monday, 29 October would suit her. The conspirators began to work towards this date.

Myra knew that her best chance of escape was to let herself out of her cell, with a copied key, after 8:45PM, when the day staff had gone home. A duty officer patrolled D Wing at half-hourly intervals through the night, but she spent most of her time sitting in the office below Myra's landing, or snoozing in the chair outside the office. Unfortunately, Myra's cell was directly opposite this office, putting Myra's door on plain view. To solve this problem Myra requested permission to move cells.

Although the cells on D Wing had bunk beds, most women had a cell to themselves, because the prison wasn't full, but friends could share if they wished. Two convicted thieves lived together in one cell as a couple, for example. Myra had something else in mind when, on 14 October, she moved her things around the fours landing to cell thirteen where her friend Anna lived. Crucially, '13' was above the duty office, so the night watch officer could not see the door from her chair. Also, Maxine Croft had the cell next door, which was doubly convenient.

Myra's new cellmate was the terrorist Anna Mendleson, who later changed the spelling of her surname to Mendelssohn, like the composer; and another woman in her twenties from Manchester. In 1972, Anna, Hilary Creek and two male accomplices, all members of the Angry Brigade, were given ten years for conspiring to plant bombs. The Angry Brigade saw themselves as part of an international working-class movement whose enemy was the Establishment. During a short bombing campaign, starting in 1970, they planted explosives at high profile locations, including the residence of the Home

Secretary. The Angries didn't kill anybody, but people were terrified and one person was injured. The Metropolitan Police became so concerned that the Bomb Squad was formed in response to the threat. The authorities viewed the group in a similar light as the Provisional IRA, which started to bomb London in 1973, hitting the Old Bailey and Scotland Yard that March, causing the death of one person and injuring 174. In recent weeks, the IRA had exploded two more bombs, at London's King's Cross Station, injuring five people; and nearby Euston Station later the same day injuring eight more. These outrages sent the IRA to the top of the list of terror threats in a capital city suddenly gripped by the fear of further attacks, which had unforeseen consequences for the Holloway conspirators.

The fact that Myra was able to move cells easily is a mark of how well-disposed Dr Bull was towards her, the new governor proving to be almost as accommodating as her predecessor. There is also no doubt that Lord Longford's support helped win Myra favourable treatment in Holloway. Longford was quick to leap to Myra's defence if she had any complaints. He was chiefly concerned at this time about securing permission for Myra to begin her Open University course, which remained contentious. Longford telephoned the Home Office on 17 October, expressing his frustration that Myra still did not know for sure if she could begin her studies. 'Lord Longford, who seemed very angry, said that Myra had told him that she had been accepted, and he had told the *Daily Mirror* so,' a ministerial aide noted. 'If she had not been accepted he would get in touch with the Vice Chancellor of the Open University and bring pressure to bear, by publicity or otherwise, to have her treated as a special case.' The Home Office dreaded Longford's frequent calls and letters regarding Hindley, while

Myra Hindley poses in a fitted dress and dark glasses in one of the snapshots Ian Brady took of her, and which the couple kept in an album.

Ian Brady poses with his .22 rifle, wearing his motorcycle helmet and goggles. He dressed like this the night Pauline Reade was murdered.

Myra Hindley was a keen motorist and a dog lover. Here she is in her car with a pet, in a photograph taken by Brady.

Hindley and Brady took pictures of each other on top of Hollin Brown Knoll, Saddleworth Moor, near to where victims were killed and buried. Hindley's car can be seen below her on the A635.

Hindley poses for Brady in the living room of her Hattersley council house, 16 Wardle Brook Avenue, standing where Edward Evans was murdered.

Pauline Reade, aged sixteen, became the first Moors murder victim in July 1963.

John Kilbride was twelve when Hindley and Brady lured him away from Ashton-under-Lyne market in November 1963 as their second victim.

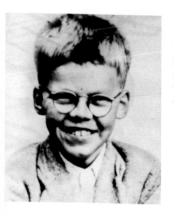

The third murder victim, Keith Bennett, disappeared in June 1964, also aged twelve. His body, buried on the moors, has never been found.

Lesley Ann Downey was ten when she was killed on Boxing Day, 1964.

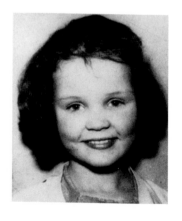

The fifth and last murder victim, Edward Evans, was seventeen in 1965 when Brady battered him to death at Hindley's council house. The police found the body in her bedroom.

Lesley Ann Downey's mother, Ann West, is seen in 1965 at the Manchester fairground where her daughter went missing, not yet certain that Lesley was dead.

Prison officers walk to work under the stone dragons that guarded the inner gate at HMP Holloway. E Wing, where Hindley was held when she met Trisha Cairns, is the block to the left.

The outer gate of HMP Holloway, with the Ivory Tower rising behind it on the right. A corner of the Governor's House can be seen in the foreground on the left.

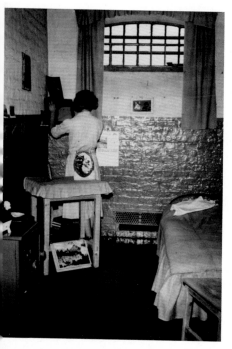

Myra Hindley occupied cells like this at Holloway. She had to stand on the bed to peek out of the window to see Trisha Cairns walking to work across the courtyard below.

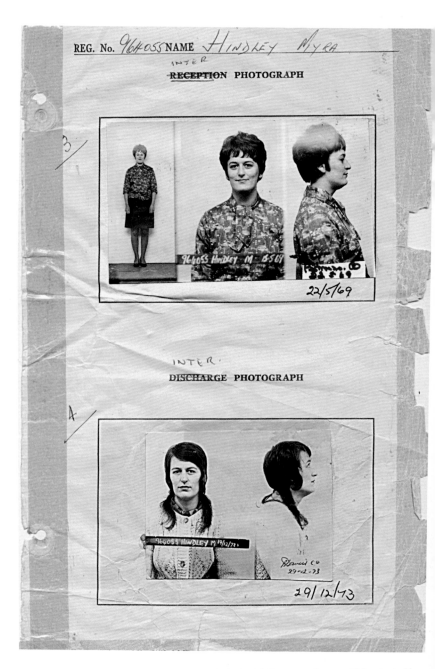

Myra Hindley was photographed regularly by Holloway prison staff for their files. On this page she is shown in three pictures at the top, in 1969; with a different hair cut below, in 1973, at the time of the escape plot.

Violet Ali was one of several prisoners who acted as a go-between for Hindley and prison officer Cairns.

Governor Dorothy Wing in the Centre at HMP Holloway. Prison wings radiate behind.

This is one of the illicit photographs Maxine Croft took of Hindley in her prison cell in Holloway in 1973.

Hindley was held on the upper level of this part of D Wing at the time of her planned escape.

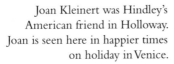

Joan Kleinert was Hindley's American friend in Holloway. Joan is seen here in happier times on holiday in Venice.

Veronica Bird was one of Hindley's jailers. In this recent picture, she holds her old prison key chain while wearing the key pouch and whistle attached to her belt, as her colleague Trisha Cairns would have done.

the fuss he made was a mere sideshow for Myra, if not useful cover for her escape attempt. Maxine Croft says that Myra mocked the earl behind his back, saying, 'He's useless, he's not going to get me out.'

Maxine's parole date was pencilled in for the following week, which was the ideal opportunity for her to pass the key impressions to the scrap dealer George Stephens, but they still hadn't spoken to George, because Maxine's brother hadn't sent her address book to Susan the hairdresser. A frustrated Trisha cornered Little Max in Holloway and complained that her brother hadn't done what he had been asked, and reminded of in this letter, written on prison notepaper:

> *Monday*
>   *Dear Dennis,*
>   *When you visit Maxine on Sunday she is going to ask you to get hold of her address book from her mother's (I think it is a blue one) and post it to this address:*
>   *Miss [Susan's name and address in London].*
>   *In case you don't remember the address from the visit I am writing it down here.*
>   *It is most important that you do this, so please make an effort.*
>   *Max sends you all her love.*
>   *A friend*

This letter reads as if it was written before Dennis visited Maxine in Holloway, suggesting that Maxine would have already given him Susan's name and address, or at least that he had been alerted. By Dennis's account, however, he didn't receive the letter until a few days after his Sunday visit. In any event Dennis hadn't sent the book. 'Cairns got a bit annoyed and didn't believe I had asked him,' said Maxine. Trisha said she would send him a telegram to chivvy him along.

The letter Dennis had received obviously related to something underhand. Dennis says that he no longer remembers the details, but he insists that he had no idea that his sister was planning to help Myra escape. 'I wouldn't have done anything if it was Myra Hindley . . . I have done a few silly things in my life, but do I want to be banged up inside? No, I don't.' But he wasn't allowed to ignore his sister's request. A telegram soon arrived at Dennis's flat: 'PLEASE POST THE ADDRESS BOOK URGENT'. This time the sender called herself Marie, which was Trisha's latest alias.

A further complication arose over Maxine's friendship with another prison officer, Lyn Summers, a vivacious woman of twenty-three from Bristol. 'As well as being very kind, she was bloody funny,' remembers her sister, Jane. 'She was a strong character in a quiet way – everybody loved her.' Lyn started work at Holloway in 1971, and moved into the other prison hostel in Hampstead. Jane came to visit her sister in London and recalls Lyn talking about Hindley, saying that she had a 'magnetic personality and was very wilful and able to manipulate quite easily.'

Although Lyn had a private side, she made friends in Holloway. 'She was well-liked by the women and she was fun. I think you have to have something to laugh about when you are in prison,' says fellow officer Kath Moores, who became Lyn's best friend. 'Some people go around with their chins down to their knees, but Lyn was not like that. She was always finding some way to laugh about something or other. In that environment you have to.' Lyn and Kath got on so well that they rented a flat together in Finsbury

Park, close enough to Holloway to walk to work. They were both friendly with Trisha Cairns, who had helped train them. 'I thought she was a good officer,' says Kath. 'She seemed straight down the line.' Unbeknownst to Kath, Lyn also made friends with Maxine Croft.

Little Max describes Lyn Summers as an emotional woman who wasn't cut out to be a prison officer. 'There was very few that were really into the job, but she wasn't one of them. I liked her. I liked her a lot.' Lyn liked Maxine, too. She made it plain that she would miss her badly after she was paroled. 'Her story was, *Oh, you girls, you go out and you'll get married*. Of course we would. That was par for the course. It's not in your nature [to live as a lesbian]. When you go in so young, it is more like a buddy system. You need a buddy . . . you can't be on your own.' Lyn told colleagues a different story: she said that Maxine developed such a crush on her that she had to leave Holloway.

Lyn did leave Holloway, in August 1973, but probably for another reason. She had recently been arrested for the theft of six cassette tapes, with another case taken into consideration. This may have been shoplifting, there is little more detail in the files. Despite being very petty offences, they led to a criminal conviction. Maxine seemed to know that Lyn had got into trouble, but Lyn didn't tell her flatmate Kath Moores. 'You are telling me a lot of things now I haven't heard. It's eye-opening,' says Kath. 'I'm flabbergasted.' Women with convictions were not allowed to serve as prison officers. Lyn may have been sacked from Holloway, or resigned before she was fired, which shows her in a different light. 'I thought Lyn was straight down the middle, and she wasn't,' says Kath. 'If I had known, I would have nicked her.'

Lyn became tearful when the time came to leave Holloway. 'She got really upset, she was crying,' says Maxine. She found a new job as a print room assistant, and continued to live with Kath in Finsbury Park, but she didn't explain her sudden career change to her flatmate. 'She was my friend. I thought if there was anything happening she might have confided in me, but she obviously didn't.'

Although she no longer worked in Holloway, Lyn still met friends in the prison officers' social club at Holloway, where there was a lively bar. 'On one of these visits, in October, Pat Cairns told me that Maxine Croft was having a day out and wanted to see me,' said Lyn. 'She said Maxine would like to meet me at Speaker's Corner.' A date with Lyn in Hyde Park was, perhaps, an incentive for Maxine to do what was required of her on her parole day. Former prison officer Lyn was being used by Myra Hindley, along with Trisha, Maxine, her brother Dennis, Janet Harber and Susan the hairdresser.

Maxine's request for a day out of Holloway was granted on Friday, 26 October. She would go shopping with her parole officer the following Monday. Trisha was off work that Friday, but she turned up at the prison unexpectedly to talk to Maxine. 'She said I will see you Monday,' said Maxine. 'I asked her where we should meet and she told me to be at Speaker's Corner by a quarter to twelve. She said to get rid of your probation officer as soon as possible.' Maxine thought that might be difficult.

'Just get rid of her,' said Trisha, sounding less and less like the nun she had once been.

Around five o'clock on Saturday afternoon, Trisha telephoned Susan, who told her that Maxine's address book had arrived at her flat by post. Dennis Croft had caved into pressure and sent it. Trisha told Susan to bring the book to her salon on Monday. Trisha would collect it before meeting Little Max in Hyde Park.

17

IS IT A BOMB?

Trisha was due to report to Holloway at six o'clock on Monday morning, 29 October, to escort a prisoner to Winchester Crown Court. It was still dark out when she telephoned the prison to say she couldn't come to work, because she wasn't feeling well. She was going to stay in bed. Having lied to her colleagues, the former nun got ready for a very different kind of day. After she dressed she left her flat with the Holloway key impressions in a box, wrapped in paper, a heavy parcel slightly larger than a brick.

It was a short walk from Trisha's hostel to Gloucester Road underground station, and it was five Tube stops from there to Piccadilly Circus. She arrived in the West End around 9:30AM, and went into the hotel where Susan, the former Holloway inmate, worked. Susan gave Trisha Maxine's address book, which she had received in the post. Monday mornings were quiet in the salon, so Susan had time for a cup of coffee and a chat with Trisha. 'I noticed she was carrying a brown paper package.'

'What have you got there?' she asked.

'It's nothing.'

'It looks like a bomb!'

Since the IRA had bombed the Old Bailey and Scotland Yard in March, with more explosions in recent weeks, everybody in London was looking out for suspicious packages, fearing another blast. 'I remember my mother ringing me up and asking me if I was OK,' says Susan, 'because there were bombs going off.' In this febrile atmosphere Trisha's parcel looked suspect. Trisha laughed nervously, and assured Susan that she wasn't carrying a bomb.

Meanwhile, in north London, Maxine Croft was being escorted by prison officer Sylvia Hurford through HMP Holloway to the gate. Little Max had dressed in a blouse and trousers for her parole day, and she was carrying a fur coat because it was chilly. She was met in the gatehouse by a young probation officer named Maggie Powell. Officer Hurford gave Maggie an envelope containing £5, which was Maxine's spending money for 'a day out for shopping and rehabilitation' in preparation for her release, having served most of her sentence. Maxine and Maggie then left the prison, crossed Parkhurst Road and walked around the corner to Maggie's office in Penn Road, where they completed some paperwork. Then they got into Maggie's car and drove into the West End.

As grim as Holloway was the prison was a secure, well-ordered place where women were shielded from some of the problems they faced in the outside world, often involving men who abused or exploited them. That was Myra's story, or at least how she was starting to explain how she got into trouble. While women were relatively safe in prison, it was easy to become institutionalised. Everyday tasks like work, shopping and paying bills can seem daunting to a long-term inmate for whom every day is planned and everything is provided. Crowds and traffic overwhelm a woman who has been locked up for years, and the world changes fast. Decimal currency had been introduced during Maxine's time inside, with the public making the transition from pounds, shillings and pence to new money with its 'p' coins. Maxine still thought in old money. If she was to make it on her own after release she had to understand and be comfortable with everyday life, which was the purpose of giving her a day's escorted parole with Maggie the probation officer.

Maggie drove towards Marble Arch, parking in nearby Upper Berkeley Street. She and Maxine then walked into Oxford Street, which was busy with people and traffic. They visited two or three shops, including one department store. Maxine found a pair of trousers she liked, and bought them out of the £5 provided. But she was distracted.

Around half-past eleven, Maxine asked Maggie if she could go off on her own for a while. Maggie agreed and she gave Maxine the telephone number of her office, and thirty pence to make calls from a public pay phone in an emergency. They agreed to meet in a restaurant near Oxford Circus by four o'clock, at the latest, at which time Maggie would have to escort Maxine back to prison. 'I told her I would be in the Old Kentucky restaurant from about three o'clock onwards.' Assuring Maggie that she would see her there, and she wouldn't be late, Maxine headed towards Hyde Park. Her rendezvous with Trisha Cairns was at Speaker's Corner, in the north-east corner of the park, opposite Marble Arch.

There was a sense of autumn in the park, where the trees were turning brown and fallen leaves covered the grass. Trisha nervously checked her watch. Where was Maxine? The package was feeling heavier the longer she carried it. Could Maxine be relied upon to shake off her probation officer and make her way through the crowds to the park as arranged, without getting lost, or being distracted? Then she saw her, with her shopping bag and fur coat. Trisha waited a few moments, to make sure that Maxine wasn't with her probation officer. Trisha knew that she shouldn't be meeting Maxine outside prison. Every time a police car came screaming around Marble Arch she almost jumped.

When she was sure that Maxine was alone, Trisha whistled to her. 'At twenty to twelve I heard a whistle and behind me was Miss Cairns . . . carrying a package which was wrapped up in brown paper.'

'That parcel looks a bit iffy,' said Maxine, walking over.

Trisha said she hoped that nobody thought it was a bomb.

Although it was early, Trisha suggested that they have a drink. They walked through the Marble Arch underpass to the Cumberland Hotel where Trisha ordered vodka and lime for two. This was Maxine's first drink in a bar in years. She soon asked for another one. Today was going to be a vodka day.

Alcohol loosened Trisha's tongue and she talked more freely than before about the escape. 'She seemed quite confident that everything was going OK,' said Maxine. The photographs Maxine had taken of Myra would not work as passport photos, however. Trisha was going to arrange another photo session. 'She said she would be taking passport photographs of Myra Hindley in the church later in the week, with wigs on.' Trisha seemed oblivious to the fact that Myra had worn a wig to disguise herself when she abducted children to be raped and murdered. For a former nun she also seemed remarkably relaxed about their use of the prison chapel, which was supposed to be God's house.

As they drank their vodka and limes, Trisha asked Maxine if she thought that a visa was required for South America. They discussed prison security, the night patrols, and which part of the perimeter wall would be easiest to climb. They talked about the rumoured back door in the wall. Trisha mentioned the costs she was incurring in planning the escape, including today's expenses. She had £1,335 in the Halifax building society, which had taken six years to save out of her wages, and she was drawing on this money to free Myra. 'She was explaining to me how expensive all this was to her.' It was an altogether extraordinary conversation for a prison officer to have with a jailbird in a bar.

Fortified with booze, it was time to call the Essex salvage man George Stephens, using the phone number in Maxine's book. They went to a phone booth and fed the machine with coins. Cairns crowded close while Maxine dialled George's number. The fact that George happened to be by his phone, and answered at once, suggests that he had been expecting this call, though he later denied he had advance knowledge of what was going on. 'I was very surprised and asked [Maxine] how she could make a phone call from prison. She said she was out for the day.'

Maxine was super friendly, asking George if he could do her a favour and look after a package for her. 'He asked what was in the package, I told him it was something personal, and it wasn't to be opened, and that someone would be picking it up from him if I couldn't pick it up myself.'

Stephens: 'She said she couldn't get down to me in the time she had, and went on to say if she left [the package] at Paddington Railway Station, in the left luggage office, and sent me the receipt, would I hold onto it for her? She said she was due out in a few weeks. I asked her what the personal effects were.'

'It is nothing to worry about, but it is stuff I cannot take back in with me.'

Stephens: 'I thought she had been doing a bit of Christmas shopping.' That was hardly likely, considering that it wasn't yet Halloween. He gave Maxine the address of his scrap yard. Maxine thanked him and hung up.

The call had gone well. The women left the bar in good spirits and took a taxi to Paddington.

Criminals tend to use the same methods again and again, and the idea of using a left luggage office as part of the plan may have originated with Myra, repeating her *modus operandi* with Brady. When detectives searched Myra's house, in 1965, they found a luggage ticket tucked into the spine of the prayer book she had been given by relatives to celebrate her first communion. That ticket led them to the Central Station where they recovered suitcases containing the audio tape of Lesley Ann Downey, and nine indecent photographs of the dead girl.

In London, the conspirators wove their way through the crowds at Paddington to the left luggage office. All they had to do now was give the parcel to the porter, and post the ticket to George. That part of the plan would be done, and Trisha would be relieved of a cumbersome package which everyone thought looked like a bomb. But there was an unexpected hitch. 'When Maxine and I arrived at Paddington, we discovered that because of the bomb scares luggage wasn't being accepted.'

Trisha telephoned Euston Station, in north London. The clerk there said that they were open, despite the fact that Euston had suffered a bomb blast the previous month. So Trisha decided to take the package there instead. She told Maxine that she should write a note to George explaining the change of plan. They walked out of the station and across the road to a shop in Sussex Gardens, where Trisha bought notepaper and envelopes. Then they got a taxi back to Marble Arch, and went into the Quality Inn restaurant for lunch, choosing a table downstairs. It was a liquid lunch with more vodka. Before Maxine got too drunk, Trisha told her to write the note. It read:

> Dear George,
>   Sorry Darling but I couldn't leave it at Paddington. So I left it at Euston. I'm sending you the receipt, I wish I had more time to [talk] and been able to come [illegible] and have a Drink with you but I am sending you a VO [Visiting Order] to Come and see me. I'll write to you tonight, it's not long Darling until Xmas then you will be My Number ONE, I have to close. So please see what you can do with the package.
>   I'll write soon
>   All my love to you,
>   Maxine XXXX

This note makes it clear that, contrary to what he said, George knew that the package contained key impressions ('please see what you can do with the package'), either because they told him earlier that day on the phone, or he was briefed in a previous communication which nobody admitted to.

Having written the note, Maxine addressed an envelope to: 'Mr George, 47a Wanstead Park Road, Ilford, Essex'. Then she realised the time. She was due to meet Lyn Summers. It was already after two and there was a queue in the restaurant to pay. Maxine told Trisha to push her way in, 'because I wanted to go'. When Trisha had settled the bill, they hurried back along Oxford Street towards Marble Arch where they parted company. Trisha said she was going to Euston. Maxine went into the park for her date.

Lyn Summers had driven into town in her Austin van to meet Maxine as arranged at Speaker's Corner, the same place Trisha had met Maxine that morning. Little Max showed up later than expected, around a quarter to three, and the worse for wear. 'I noticed Maxine had been drinking, and she told me she had been drinking with her probation officer,' said Lyn. 'I asked Maxine where she wanted to go, and she eventually said for a ride, and we went to Hampstead Heath. She said she had to be back at the prison by 5:30PM.' Maxine was in a drinking mood, so Lyn bought a bottle of vodka.

Although Lyn was no longer working at Holloway, it would still be unusual for a former prison officer like her to socialise with a prisoner. Most people who have worked in prisons are wary of criminals knowing about their personal lives, for fear that they may be intimidated, or used in criminal schemes. The fact that Lyn didn't tell her best friend and prison officer flatmate that she was meeting Little Max shows how irregular this assignation was. 'She never mentioned anything at all about that. Not a peep,' says Kath Moores, who is shocked to learn about it now. 'That fact that she knew [Maxine] had a crush on her, and then she met her outside, is so dangerous. Why would she have done something so daft?' Lyn had crossed the line prison officers have to tread with inmates. 'You don't do those kind of things.'

By the time the women got to Hampstead, there was less than an hour's daylight left, and as the sun sank it got cold. It was also muddy on the heath. The girls trudged about for an hour or so, in the footsteps of Myra Hindley and Dorothy Wing on their dog walk the previous year. Unlike Myra and Mrs Wing, however, Lyn and Max also sat under a tree and swigged vodka from the bottle.

The girls were close, though who liked who best is unclear. 'I liked her a lot,' says Maxine, though she denies that they were in a relationship. 'A lot of people said there was a lesbian affair [between us]. There wasn't. And Lynda knew, I think Lynda knew what was going on.'

The conversation became emotional. Lyn was worried about Maxine, but she also had her own problems. She was due to appear at Barking Magistrates Court the following day to answer the theft charge that had almost certainly ended her prison career, a secret she had kept from everybody else. Meanwhile, Maxine was in an excitable state because she had to go back to Holloway, which was a depressing prospect, and because of what was going on there with Myra and Trisha. Also, she was drunk.

When the street lights came on, just before five o'clock, the women walked back to Lyn's van. It was then that Maxine admitted that she had not been with her probation officer all day, as she said, but had slipped off to see Trisha Cairns. Lyn was surprised and angry. 'When I heard she had not been with her probation officer all day I started shouting at her.'

'I'm frightened,' wailed Maxine. Then she let the cat out of the bag. 'Pat [Cairns] is going to break Myra out.' If this came as news to Lyn, it was a bombshell: prison officer Trisha Cairns was going to break the Moors murderer Myra Hindley out of HMP Holloway. She didn't alert the prison or the police, though, which surprises her sister. 'I know Lyn wouldn't have colluded in anything like that. But not immediately going to the authorities . . .' muses Jane. 'She would have been in a real dilemma about what to do about that.'

'You're a bloody fool, Maxine,' said Lyn. 'What are you supposed to be doing?'

'I am supposed to be getting the passports for them . . . I have already taken the prints.' But she said that she wasn't going to help with the passports now. She wasn't going to get into any more trouble.

'If you get caught, you are going to get years.'

'Don't worry about it, don't worry about it,' slurred Maxine.

Lyn drove to a phone box. She told Maxine to ring her probation office and say she was on her way back. Then she put her in a taxi.

There was a nervous watchfulness at all the big London train stations, but especially at Euston where the IRA had struck so recently. The concourse was still being repaired six weeks after an IRA bomb had gone off in a snack bar, ripping the station apart.

Having walked into the damaged building, Trisha looked about for the luggage office. She soon found it, and was pleased to see that it was open. Then she saw to her dismay that British Rail staff were searching the bags that members of the public were checking in. She couldn't risk the staff finding the key impressions in her parcel. So she turned around and walked straight back out of the station. The IRA was complicating matters enormously. Everywhere she went, Trisha was made aware that her parcel looked like a bomb, attracting attention to herself when she needed to be discreet. Almost at her wit's end, Trisha decided to post the parcel direct to George Stephens. She scribbled a note on the back of Maxine's original message:

> *George,*
> *They were searching everything at Euston. Had to send it by post.*
> *Hope you understand.*
> *Max's friend,*
> *Marie*

Once again, this shows that Stephens knew what was being planned was illicit, even if he didn't know every detail. It then occurred to Trisha that George might wonder why Maxine hadn't written this note herself. So she added:

*Max didn't have the time left to pop up to Euston. So I went
to do it for her.*
Thanks

Trisha taped the envelope to the parcel and took it into a
nearby post office, writing 'Letter enclosed. First Class' on the
front. She just caught the last post. Almost twelve hours after
she rang in sick, this was the end of her mission for the day.
Being a criminal was exhausting.

At the same time, Maxine finally rolled up at her probation
office in Penn Road, asking the staff for money to pay the
taxi driver. A few minutes later Maggie Powell arrived back at
the office, having waited all afternoon for Maxine in Oxford
Street. She saw that Maxine had got herself into a terrible
mess. 'She was in an emotional state bordering on hysteria, she
may well have been drinking. I attempted to calm her down.'
It took almost an hour. Just before six o'clock, Maggie took
Maxine back to Holloway, where they had to bang on the
gate. 'I ended up knocking on the door, can you believe it,'
says Maxine, 'and they all came running, *Where have you been?
We've been worried!* I was as drunk as a skunk. *We thought you'd
done a runner.* They took me back to my cell.' Maxine was back
home on D Wing, where Myra Hindley was waiting for her.

18

UNCLE PHIL

At lunchtime the next day, George Stephens drove down Wanstead Park Road and turned into the alley leading to his scrap yard. Ted, who worked in the yard breaking up cars, told George that he had collected the post from the corner shop as usual and a package had arrived. This was a surprise. George was expecting to receive a left luggage receipt in the post, not a package.

He went into his caravan and saw the brown paper parcel on his desk. There was an envelope taped to the front, addressed skittishly to 'Mr George'. He picked the parcel up, felt its weight, then lit one of the countless cigarettes that would one day kill him, and thought very carefully about what to do.

A couple of hours later a smart-looking gent in his fifties, dressed in a suit and tie, with highly polished shoes, pulled into the yard in a well-used Austin Cambridge. His name was Phil Thomas. George came out to greet him, and they went into the caravan to talk in private.

Phil Thomas came from a mining family in Pontypridd. He told his children that when he was a boy he sledded down coal slag heaps on a pit shovel, and although he had lived most of his life in England he retained his Welsh accent. Phil turned twenty the year that World War Two broke out, and he served in the Intelligence Corps. 'My uncle said Dad was in MI5 during the war,' says his son. 'All I know is that he was in military intelligence.'

After the army, Phil Thomas joined the Metropolitan Police, starting his career in Plaistow, east London, where he met Mary. They married in 1948, and had two children: Joanna, known as Jo; and Phillip, known like his dad as Phil. 'He was a good copper,' says his son. 'He got several commendations and awards, for initiative and intelligence on a difficult murder investigation.' Moving around east London, Thomas was promoted through the ranks, and he came to Dagenham in Essex in 1972 as a detective chief inspector. Approaching his fifty-fifth birthday in 1973, DCI Thomas was in the final months of his police career when the biggest case of his life dropped into his lap.

According to official records, including his own statement, DCI Thomas just happened to drive into George Stephens's scrap yard that Tuesday, in order to get his Austin fixed. But George wasn't a mechanic, and he didn't run a repair garage. 'He wouldn't be getting his car fixed – definitely not,' says George's daughter, Julie.

Phil and George were good friends, though, close enough for George's children to call DCI Thomas 'Uncle Phil'. The men first met in east London years earlier when Phil was a junior detective and George was a local wide boy. Both came from poor backgrounds, and George made Phil laugh. As Phil and George became friends, their families grew close, so much so that they had caravans on the same site at Herne Bay in Kent, where they holidayed at the same time. 'I spent all the summer holidays at the caravan, six weeks at a time, and Phil's caravan was right next to ours,' says George's son,

Ian. 'I used to play with his daughter, Joanna; and me brother [Kevin] was friends with his son, Phillip.' George and Phil also socialised together in London. They enjoyed lock-ins at the City Arms on the Isle of Dogs, and shared many adventures. 'I remember me dad telling a story that he was coming back down the A12 one night, he and Phil were racing in their cars, and me dad got pulled up [and] said, "I'm with Phil Thomas." And the copper said, "OK, off you go, sir."'

The men were both Freemasons. 'They used to have these police dos, and my mum and dad would go,' recalls Julie, who owns photographs of the couples at Masonic functions. In one picture, good time George is hugging Mary, making everybody laugh.

According to their contemporaneous accounts, when DCI Thomas went into George's caravan that day, at the scrap yard, and saw the parcel on his desk, he asked his friend out of innocent curiosity what it was.

'I think it's a bomb,' said George, the joker. He later explained more fully: 'I went on to tell [Phil] that I was a little bit worried about the parcel because I wasn't expecting one.' George claimed to have no idea at this stage who might have sent the package to him, and he hadn't opened the envelope. 'It struck me as odd because [of it] not being addressed in the ordinary way.'

Phil Thomas told him that the only way to find out what was in the parcel was to open it. 'I'll open it for you.' He sniffed the parcel first, 'to see if there was a smell of explosive'. On the contrary. 'It smelt of soap.' So Thomas opened it, 'and looked utterly surprised,' according to George.

The package contained three blocks of plaster, three bars of pink soap, and a block of brown soap in a tea packet, all bearing impressions. Together with these impressions were three corresponding notes, written in a rounded hand different to the handwriting of whoever addressed the letter, but the same as the person who added the words 'First Class' to the package when it was posted in the Euston area of London the previous afternoon. The notes obviously referred to copying keys. The first note went with a plaster cast and a bar of pink Camay, and gave George the following instructions:

2 impressions of same key ⅛" [inch]
1 copy needed

These instructions were repeated on the reverse of the note for the second key, while the instructions for the third key read:

2 impressions of same key ¼" [inch] thick
1 copy needed

The fourth note referred to a 'master key'. This impression had been carved into brown soap. The note read:

Impressions not very accurate! Master key! Part of key which goes into lock is on the side of the key stem, not in the centre.
Stem ⅛" [inch], key part ⅛" [inch]

'My first thought was that they were impressions of safe keys,' said Phil Thomas.

Then George told his friend, Phil, the chief inspector, that he knew a woman named Maxine Croft, an inmate at HMP Holloway, and she had telephoned him the previous day, on a day out of prison. It was at this stage that the men decided to open the envelope, and together they read Maxine's covering letter.

Afterwards, Phil told George that he was going to take the parcel away for closer inspection. 'He told me it was something I shouldn't have.'

The following day, DCI Phil Thomas called PC Trevor Scoble into his office at Dagenham Police Station. An affable, garrulous constable, Trevor Scoble tended to take five minutes to say what most people said in one minute. 'That's the joke that's made about me.' DCI Thomas told PC Scoble that he had a special job on, and Scoble was to keep absolutely quiet about it. 'I was sworn to secrecy.' Maxine Croft's name was then mentioned. Scoble knew Maxine from his beat. 'She was a local wide girl . . . blondish-haired, thinnish, chatty, typical Essex/East End girl.' He thought he had been selected because he knew her. DCI Thomas gave PC Scoble the impressions parcel, and told him to drive to the Home Office in London at once. He was to hand the parcel to a senior officer there.

Around five o'clock that afternoon, PC Scoble arrived at Eccleston Square, Pimlico, where he asked for Detective Chief Inspector John Hoggarth in Central Services (police on secondment to the Home Office). 'He was working on government stuff, Special Branchy-type stuff.' Part of DCI Hoggarth's job was to do with the security of Her Majesty's prisons, which, with the current terror threat, and bombers and suspected bombers in custody, was especially sensitive. The little that can be gleaned about Hoggarth personally indicates that he wasn't a run of the mill copper. If elegant handwriting is a mark of character, he was an intelligent, cultured and well-educated policeman, though appropriately for an undercover detective he remains otherwise mysterious. Trevor Scoble can't even describe what Hoggarth looked like. 'I've got no memories of his face.' Trevor has no doubt, though, that as DCI Thomas's messenger, he was playing a minor role a significant intelligence operation. 'I'm very minor in most things, except talking.' Despite his modesty Trevor was not a fool, and he didn't buy the story about DCI Thomas stumbling upon the key impressions in George Stephens's scrap yard. 'I've always thought that seemed too slick.' More was happening in this case than met the eye.

19

NOT THE IRA

The information that Detective Chief Inspector Thomas gave to DCI John Hoggarth at the Home Office, together with the key impressions and notes delivered by PC Scoble, led Hoggarth to Holloway, where he met with the governor and her senior staff the next day, Thursday, 1 November. 'My principal concern at that time was to establish whether, or to what extent, the security of Holloway prison had been breached,' Hoggarth said. He asked the staff about Maxine Croft, whose name George Stephens had given to Thomas, asking what she was in for, and what sort of person she was. It was decided that an officer whom Maxine knew and trusted should speak to her first.

This job was given to Maxine's welfare officer, Valerie Haig-Brown, who saw some good in Maxine, 'an intelligent young woman who, due to her disturbed background, has never been encouraged to find her true potential'. She thought that Maxine had shown encouraging signs of maturity in recent months. She coped well when told, in February, that her request for parole had been denied. It had since been decided to free her on 12 December. This news had only just come through. Haig-Brown was dismayed to be told that Maxine may have got herself in trouble in the meantime, which would almost certainly jeopardise her parole.

The kindly welfare officer seemed upset to Maxine when she took her aside in the prison that day. 'What have you done?' she asked her tearfully. She wanted to know what had happened on Monday, when Maxine went out of Holloway, and whether she had met anyone she shouldn't have met. Maxine said, no, but she had spent some time alone in Hyde Park. Haig-Brown didn't believe her. But Maxine wouldn't say more.

When Haig-Brown had gone, Maxine hurried to D Wing to tell Myra Hindley that their plot had been found out. Myra's thoughts flew at once to Trisha. 'She panicked and said, "You can't say anything about Patricia, because they won't believe you."' Maxine reminded her that Trisha had enclosed handwritten instructions with the key impressions. The police surely had these, if they had the package, and it wouldn't be long before they discovered that Trisha hadn't spent Monday at home. Myra reacted by destroying letters and photographs she had received from Trisha, and she told Maxine to warn Trisha that they were all in danger.

They couldn't reach Trisha at once. She was at Croydon Crown Court on escort duty. 'She [Myra] said that Miss Cairns would get herself out of it,' said Maxine. Myra added angrily that Maxine was 'just like Ian Brady'. Maxine was nothing like Brady, but it is an indication of how furious Myra was that she hurled the worst insult she could think of at Little Max in the heat of the moment.

Prison officer Miss Taylor was also out of Holloway on escort duty. When Taylor returned to the prison, around two o'clock, Maxine was standing outside the discipline office pouring the staff teas. She came over to her at once. Taylor recalled that Maxine asked her, 'to tell Pat [Cairns] to get rid of everything as she was having a police visit. I did not pass this information on to Pat'. As Taylor made her way to D Wing, however, Myra followed her upstairs. 'She then asked me to pass a written message to Janet Harber, who is Pat Cairns's flatmate.' Having retracted her recent resignation, Janet was still working in the prison. 'Myra said the message was really urgent.' Taylor took the note – which she said she didn't read – to Janet in the assessment unit.

'This is for Patricia,' she told Janet, 'it's urgent.'

Janet thought that the note was personal, from Taylor to Trisha, so she didn't read it either. If she had, she would have seen that it was from her nemesis, Myra Hindley.

Maxine then saw Taylor again and reminded her to warn Trisha to 'get rid of everything, because the police knew about her and Euston'.

'What's it about?' asked Taylor.

'The key impressions.'

This was the first that Taylor had heard about key impressions. The prison officer now found herself in a very awkward situation. She was being asked to be a messenger in a crisis involving copied keys and Myra Hindley, with the police sniffing around.

It was Myra who spoke to Taylor next. 'Myra again saw me and asked if I would phone Pat [Cairns] in the evening and tell her, in case Janet hadn't passed the note or message on.'

At the end of a frantic afternoon of secret messages and whispered conversations, prison officer Valerie Haig-Brown spoke to Maxine again. 'I told her that the key impressions had been intercepted in transit, and it was known she was involved.'

'I thought they might be discovered,' said Little Max.

Haig-Brown begged Maxine to tell her the whole truth, but Maxine refused, so she sent her to the governor. Maxine wouldn't tell Dr Bull either. So the governor sent her to the prison hospital to be segregated. They would speak again on Friday. '[I] was told the police were coming the following morning.'

Meanwhile, Janet met Trisha returning from Croydon. Janet gave her Myra's note, which warned her that the police had found the impressions, which they had traced to Maxine. This was a disaster. Trisha tried to see Myra in the chapel, but the lock on the door had already been changed. Myra whispered through the closed door, telling Trisha to get rid of the evidence of their escape plan.

All was not well at home in Earl's Court. Angela Glynn, the prison officer who occupied the downstairs flat in the staff hostel, was forever answering the phone for Trisha, and more than once, she said, the caller was Miss Taylor, the young jailer who had been roped in as another prison messenger. Angela was fed up with this. A woman in her forties, between marriages, she was one of those officers who were prejudiced against gay colleagues, and she disliked Trisha. 'I think that was part of [why] she didn't like her,' says her daughter, Dee, who often visited her mother at the hostel, adding frankly that Mum was a nosey, stroppy woman. Angela also disliked Myra Hindley. She said that Hindley was a horrible, manipulative person with 'dead eyes' whose faith was bogus. The fact that Trisha was friends with Hindley compounded her dislike for her colleague.

Dee was at Mum's flat around this time, waiting for her mother to return from work, when the hall phone rang yet again.

'Can I speak to Pat Cairns?'

'Yes, I'll go and get her. Who's calling?'

By Dee's memory, the caller said that her name was Maxine, or 'something beginning with M'. When Mum came home from work she asked Dee if there had been any calls. Dee said, yes, there had been a call for Cairns. Her mother looked at her colleague, Yvonne, who also lived in the hostel, as if this was significant. 'She went "Oh Really!" I said yes. She looked at Yvonne and said *Hmmm*.'

One night when Angela had to go to bed early to report for duty at 5:15 the next morning, she answered two calls from Miss Taylor asking for Trisha (though Taylor later told the police that she didn't call Trisha the night Myra Hindley asked her to). The first time the women spoke for forty-five minutes. The second call, at 10:20 that night, got Angela out of bed. 'I asked Miss [Taylor] if her call to Miss Cairns was urgent, and explained my situation to her, and that it was too late to shout up the stairs as this would awaken the other residents . . . She said it was not urgent, and therefore I did not call Miss Cairns.'

The next day, Angela had cross words with Trisha Cairns who 'was extremely rude and abrupt to me and told me that I had no right to refuse to fetch her in response to Miss [Taylor's] telephone call.' Angela resented her colleague's attitude, and decided to report her. This was the fraught and dangerous situation at home as Trisha faced the biggest problem of her life at Holloway.

The first thing Trisha did when she arrived at the prison on Friday was to visit Maxine on the hospital wing, where she had spent the night, bringing her cigarettes. They spoke about the events of Monday, and Maxine asked if Trisha had left the package at Euston Station as they agreed.

'No, I posted it.'

This was a significant change to the plan, and not one that George Stephens could have known about. Dropping the package at a train station meant that George could collect it discreetly. By posting the package to his work, Trisha put George in danger. The postman, the people in the corner shop on Wanstead Park Road who accepted post for the works, and Ted in the yard who collected the post, were all now witnesses to the fact that the key impressions had come to George's work place.

Maxine told Trisha that she was due to go back to see the governor, and the police would be present. 'You'll have to carry this one on your own,' Trisha warned her, according to Maxine.

'I can't.'

Trisha asked Maxine to follow her. They walked to the top of the wing where she dropped a letter for Maxine to pick up without anyone seeing. 'Read that,' she said, by Maxine's account, adding that she would be back. The letter contained instructions about what Maxine should tell the police. 'The story was, "Say that the AG [Assistant Governor], who has left the prison now, left her keys in the boardroom one day and made a regular habit of it. I took it in my head to make impressions of these keys, hoping that I would be able to sell them once out of prison."' Maxine was also instructed to tear this note up.

Trisha soon returned. 'I told her the story was silly,' said Maxine. 'AGs just don't happen to leave their keys lying about.' Not only was it an unbelievable alibi, it meant that Maxine would have to admit to a criminal offence. Maxine said Trisha then applied further pressure. 'Miss Cairns replied, "If you say anything to the police I'll do you for allegations, and remember that you have no protection in here."'

The former nun also said, 'I'll pray for you.'

Pray for yourself, thought Maxine. 'She [Trisha] wasn't a bad person . . . But Myra had a way of drawing them in, and she fell hook, line and sinker for her. Don't ask me why, but she did. And she was still with Flipper [Janet Harber] at the time, who was a decent person, so God knows why.'

It was time for Maxine to go back to see the governor. DCI Hoggarth was with Dr Bull, and he made an immediate favourable impression on Little Max. 'He was a good guy . . . special branch guy . . . he knew everything about me.' She asked if they could speak in private, so Hoggarth asked Dr Bull if she would leave them alone, which she agreed to reluctantly. Hoggarth didn't make notes, wanting to keep their interview as informal as possible, but Deputy Governor Leissner was present as his witness.

Maxine started by giving DCI Hoggarth the runaround. 'She at first denied all knowledge of the key impressions, but then she said she was responsible for making them.' When the chief inspector asked her how she had obtained prison keys, Maxine tried to palm him off with the story Cairns had given her: that a former assistant governor had left her keys lying around, and she had copied them to sell. Hoggarth didn't believe that.

Maxine now insists that she had been briefed by the unnamed prison officer who initially told her to make friends with Myra Hindley to ask for her case to be heard outside the prison, rather than by a Visiting Committee, because Violet Ali wasn't believed when she made allegations against Hindley and Cairns before a VC.

She also says that DCI Hoggarth seemed primarily concerned that the key impressions might be intended to free women linked to terror groups. Two members of the Angry Brigade were in Holloway, one sharing a cell with Myra. In addition, Marian and Dolours Price had been in Holloway recently in connection with the IRA bombing of the Old Bailey and

Scotland Yard. The Price sisters were currently on trial at Winchester. If convicted, it was likely that they would be returned to Holloway. Hoggarth seemed to fear that somebody might be plotting to get terrorists out of Holloway with forged keys. Only Maxine didn't seem the type to have terrorist connections.

The chief inspector sat on the governor's desk and spoke to her gently, as she recalls: 'He said, "Listen, Maxine, this is not your game."'

'What are you talking about?'

'The keys . . . the IRA . . . you are into a lot of things, but you are not into that.'

'I'll tell you everything on one condition.'

'What's that?'

'You'll get me an outside court.'

'Done.'

'It's not for the the IRA. It's for Myra Hindley.'

20

McGUINNESS, LIKE THE DRINK

By two o'clock that Friday afternoon, Detective Chief Superintendent Frank McGuinness was starting to think about the weekend. His wife, Christina, was a good cook and they usually had fish for supper at home on Friday, with wine and one of Christina's homemade desserts, maybe lemon meringue pie. Afterwards, McGuinness would watch the evening news and smoke his pipe. After years of smoking cigarettes he was moving to a pipe for his health. He was also trying to cut back on drinking. Like many detectives, McGuinness drank whisky (Grant's Standfast, mixed half and half with water) and he sometimes drank too much. He had started to develop the swollen nose of a boozer. Otherwise, he was a fresh-faced man of forty-seven, with fine silver hair. After dinner he and Christina might listen to some music. 'He liked the Bruch violin concerto. He was quite cultured,' says his daughter, Catherine.

DCS McGuinness was based at King's Cross Police Station, near the train station. This was area headquarters for N Division, with two prisons in its patch: HMP Holloway on Parkhurst Road; and the men's prison, HMP Pentonville, nearby on Caledonian Road. If something happened in either prison that required the attendance of the police, officers came from one of the stations in N Division, and McGuinness was one of the most senior officers.

The white phone on McGuinness's desk rang, interrupting his thoughts. It was the Home Office detective DCI Hoggarth calling to introduce himself to the chief superintendent, who was senior to him in rank. A big job was on. High security. Top secret.

If you could come to Holloway right away, sir, it would be appreciated.

McGuinness's plans for the evening were scrapped. Christina understood when he called quickly to say that he wouldn't be home for supper. He didn't have to explain himself. 'He did work very, very long hours. He was very dedicated. I think he loved every minute of it,' says his daughter. 'Family was important, but quite honestly we hardly ever saw him.'

Frank McGuinnness's family were Irish Catholics, though McGuinness had been born in England, in 1926. He was privately educated and, like DCI Phil Thomas, he served in the army Intelligence Corps before joining the Metropolitan Police, and was selected to learn Japanese in the army as an officer of high intelligence. As well as being clever and cultured, McGuinness was known at work as Gentleman Frank: a fair and honourable policeman with a calm manner. He didn't throw his weight around, though junior officers knew to always address him as sir. 'There was no way I would have called him anything else. He was like God to me in terms of rank,' says Paul Barr, one of his junior detectives.

When he had got off the phone from speaking to DCI Hoggarth, McGuinness called Detective Sergeant Ron Peace at Caledonian Road, another station within N Division. Ron was the old man of Caledonian Road. Close to retirement, he was the liaison officer for Holloway and Pentonville prisons.

He knew both prisons inside out, and he kept a framed photograph on his desk of Ronald Marwood, who was hanged in Pentonville in 1959 for killing a police officer, as a trophy of his part in the case. 'His claim to fame was that he took [one of the last men] hanged in England for killing a cop,' recalls colleague John Dixon, who was also stationed at Caledonian Road, as was Paul Barr. 'When new guys would come on board, Ron would show them that picture.' Ron liked a drink and he smoked cigars. 'I used to go home every night stinking of [tobacco], especially working with Ron because of all those bloody Hamlet cigars,' says Barr.

Chief Superintendent McGuinness, DCI Hoggarth and DS Peace all met at HMP Holloway later that Friday afternoon. Hoggarth explained to his colleagues that impressions of prison keys had been intercepted by the police in Essex, and the impressions had been traced to a Holloway inmate named Maxine Croft, who he had spoken to briefly. After lying to him initially, Croft had admitted her involvement in copying keys, and she had made the sensational claim that this was part of a plot to spring Myra Hindley. That famous name secured everyone's attention. Croft had also implicated a serving prison officer, Trisha Cairns, who had to be spoken to. Hoggarth was handing the case over to McGuinness to investigate further.

At four o'clock, McGuinness had an initial interview with Maxine Croft while Ron Peace took notes, puffing on a Hamlet. The chief superintendent showed Maxine the key impressions which had been posted to George Stephens. She admitted making some of them, and said that the rest must have been made by Cairns, who supplied the original keys, 'so that somebody could escape from the prison'.

'What is the name of the person you intended to escape from the prison?'

'Myra Hindley,' she said, confirming the name she had given to Hoggarth.

'Why did you wish Myra Hindley to escape from the prison?'

'It was not my wish,' said Maxine. It was Cairns's idea. She said that Myra didn't even know about it, probably not wanting to grass on a fellow inmate to the police. When McGuinness asked her how the impressions got to Essex, Maxine became coy. 'I really don't feel like answering any more questions,' she said.

The chief superintendent then spoke to Trisha Cairns, who denied meeting Maxine in Hyde Park on Monday, as she denied virtually everything Maxine had told the police. 'Have you ever spoken to Maxine Croft about Myra Hindley?' McGuinness asked her.

'No.'

The detective asked Trisha for her prison keys, and she handed him bunch fifty-eight. 'Have you ever handed these keys to Maxine Croft?'

'Certainly not.'

Shown the impressions and the note that had been posted to George Stephens, Trisha denied having seen them before. Informed that Maxine had told the police that she made the impressions at her instigation, to help Myra Hindley escape, Trisha said: 'Certainly there is no truth in the accusation.'

'Have you any strong feelings about Myra Hindley?'

'No. I have been accused of it in 1971. An inmate made an allegation,' she said, referring to the Violet Ali affair. 'An inquiry was made and [the allegation] was found to be groundless.'

Trisha was then allowed to go. The police made a show of leaving Holloway, too, but this was not the end of their work for the day.

DCS McGuinness went back to King's Cross, and summoned Paul Barr to his office. Barr was a twenty-two-year-old Temporary Detective Constable (TDC), which meant that he was a very junior officer on probation, trying to earn his place alongside the older detectives in the Criminal Investigation Department at Caledonian Road. 'I didn't want to be a uniform bobby. I knew I wanted to be in CID.' He and fellow TDC, John Dixon, close to him in age, spent a lot of their time out and about in north London gathering intelligence. They wore plain-clothes, and let their hair grow long, to blend into the background, like the detectives in *The Sweeney*. One day when Dixon was at the Old Bailey, *Sweeney* actors John Thaw and Dennis Waterman sat next to him in court, doing research for their roles as fictional detectives Jack Regan and George Carter. Their lives were not dissimilar. 'You had to prove yourself, that you could get out on the streets and be a "thief taker",' says Barr. 'We were encouraged to be in the pubs to see who was drinking with who. Jot down car numbers. So you knew the villains.'

McGuinness took an interest in his young temporary detectives, and he brought Barr onto the Holloway investigation as his exhibits officer, which would be useful experience for him. Barr would assist the chief superintendent on his enquiries and collect and label items of evidence. McGuinness warned him at the outset not to talk about the case. 'Frank McGuinness made it quite plain from day one that the inquiry was to be kept between us. There was to be no conversations with anybody else. No contact with the press . . . *Nothing from this office can get out.*'

Having put the fear of God into his junior officer, McGuinness and Barr reconvened with DCI Hoggarth, and together they all went back to HMP Holloway, which had been locked down for the evening. The prisoners were in their cells, and most of the staff had gone home, including Cairns, which meant that the police could continue their investigation unobserved.

The old prison seemed even gloomier and more like a castle after dark, with the autumn wind whistling through the cracked windows and battlements. The governor met the police, and took them to see Maxine Croft, who agreed to show the officers where she and Trisha had made the key impressions. Together, they climbed the dark stairwell of the Ivory Tower. Looking around, TDC Barr was struck by the cramped medieval look of the prison, with its arched doors and poky rooms. The place was very scruffy and rather dirty. In the staff kitchen, Maxine showed the police the cheap metal teapot that she and Trisha had mixed plaster in, and the plastic spoon they used. She also showed them a hidden packet of modelling powder, left over from the copying attempts; likewise pieces of soap; and the broken clock in the lounge where she and Trisha hid things. TDC Barr removed the items, putting them in bags which he signed and dated. As he catalogued potential exhibits, he watched Maxine from the corner of his eye, a woman near to him in age, and decided that she was an impressionable young woman who might have been manipulated.

After Maxine had shown them everything, the police drove to Earl's Court to pay a surprise late night visit on Trisha Cairns.

Since she had got home from work that Friday afternoon, having had one interview with the police, Trisha had been disposing of evidence at her hostel flat, including: Myra's letters; tourist information about Brazil obtained from the Brazilian consulate; and luggage she had bought for their flight to South America. She was still doing this at ten o'clock that night when she heard an unexpected, commanding knock at the front door.

Trisha was startled to find three detectives standing on her doorstep, and not pleased to see them there. 'She was indignant that we were there . . . that we had the audacity to be there,' recalls Paul Barr. 'It was incredulity that we were there, and we could possibly suspect her of having done anything!' There was a bit of an argument. '*Have you got a warrant?* That sort of thing,' says Barr. '*Who do you think you are?* That sort of attitude. *I'm a prison officer!*'

She eventually let the police in, and TDC Barr searched the flat. He found a Kodak Instamatic camera in Cairns's bedroom, together with fifty-nine photographic transparencies. A box of film was under the bed.

DCS McGuinness took Cairns into the living room to ask her questions. Barr stood in the doorway, taking notes. McGuinness revealed that Maxine had told them about the photo session in Hindley's cell. Whether or not this was a significant part of the escape plan, it was an important point to the chief superintendent, because it established that Cairns and Hindley had a closer relationship than a prison officer should have with an inmate. He asked if she had supplied the Kodak camera to Croft to photograph Hindley.

'No, I most certainly did not,' Trisha replied.

McGuinness warned her that he would know if she was lying when the negatives were developed. 'If there are photos of her [Hindley] I will know.'

'I can assure you there are certainly not any.'

'If there's anything you do know, now is the time to tell me.'

'There's nothing I can tell you. I just don't know what it is about.' That made Paul Barr smile. 'She was an inveterate liar,' he says. 'She lied about everything.'

'I may have to see you again, and the situation could well be different,' said the chief superintendent. 'Get in touch with me if you change your mind.'

'What is your name?' asked Trisha. 'I've forgotten it.'

'McGuinness. That is Mc, and the same as the drink.'

The policemen left the flat around half past ten, having formed a poor opinion of the former nun. 'I think we all thought she was an arrogant bitch, who thought she could walk away from this,' says Barr. 'That was my view of her. I think Frank McGuinness [agreed]: that she was a manipulative and conniving woman, [and] it was terrible that we thought she could get up to anything like this.'

But it was too soon for the police to congratulate themselves. They had missed vital evidence.

21

GRASSING

While the police turned Holloway upside down, and prisoners and staff found themselves in deep trouble, Myra remained calm. She had sat through her murder trial with barely a flicker of emotion, while those around her suffered agonies, and likewise she seemed unaffected by what was going on now. She got up as normal at half past six each morning, cleaned her cell, slopped out, ate breakfast, did her tapestry work, came back to the wing for lunch, kept up her correspondence, and prepared for her Open University course, as if nothing was out of the ordinary. Meanwhile, having done what she did to help Myra, Trisha Cairns struggled to save herself.

It was the Saturday after the police had visited Trisha's flat, and she was back on duty at Holloway. The prisoners cleaned D Wing on Saturday mornings, and had their weekly bath, after which there were visits and association time, when the inmates watched television and played music, ping-pong and other games. As in the outside world, there was a more relaxed atmosphere in Holloway at the weekend. Trisha spoke to her colleague Miss Taylor during the Saturday shift, confiding in her once again. '[Cairns] saw me and told me that she had been questioned by the police the night before, and that her camera had been taken away, and her room had been searched,'

Taylor said. 'She said she thought they were looking for the photographs. She said she had taken everything to a friend's.'

Taylor had known for months about Trisha's infatuation with Myra Hindley, since she told her that it was her destiny to be with Myra, and she had passed messages for them. Now the police were involved, Taylor began to worry about her position.

Then the press got a sniff of the story. The next day, there was a report of an escape plot in the *Sunday Telegraph*, under the headline POLICE PROBE 'PLOT TO FREE MYRA HINDLEY'. Reporter Peter Gladstone Smith wrote that a woman serving time for forgery in Holloway had been 'asked to use her skill' to make key moulds from prison keys, which had been sent to Scotland Yard's forensic laboratory for tests. The journalist, who clearly had an excellent source, also wrote that some prisoners and members of staff had developed sympathy for Hindley since the furore over last year's walk on Hampstead Heath. The story was picked up by the *Sunday Express* and *News of the World* that weekend, who also ran it in later editions. An indignant Lord Longford thought that these press reports suggesting Myra was part of an escape plot defamed the good woman he knew and he threatened to help her sue the papers, to the annoyance of the police. 'Lord Longford stuck his nose in,' recalls TDC Paul Barr. 'I've got a feeling Longford came to see Frank McGuinness.'

Prison officers Cairns, Harber and Taylor were all at work on Sunday when the story broke in the press. Even more worried now that it was in the papers, Taylor asked Trisha if they could have another chat. 'I was concerned whether my knowledge of the relationship between Pat [Cairns] and Myra, and the message I had passed to Janet [Harber], had involved me in the matter,' Taylor later explained. 'The fact that Maxine had mentioned key impressions to me also worried me.' She and Trisha arranged to meet after work.

Taylor left the prison at half-past four, as it was getting dark. It was the Sunday before bonfire night, and early fireworks were swooshing up into the sky as she walked down to the Wimpy bar near the Nag's Head, not far from the camera shop that Trisha used. Fifteen minutes later Trisha and Janet walked down the road to join her. Over coffee in the Wimpy, Trisha admitted to Taylor that the police were investigating a crime, but she assured Taylor that she wouldn't be involved. Taylor was nonetheless anxious that the police might speak to her. '[Cairns] said if I was questioned about her relationship with Myra I could deny all knowledge of it, or speak as my conscience dictated.' After their confab, the women walked back up Parkhurst Road together, parting company outside the Holloway Castle pub, opposite the prison gate. Taylor caught a bus to Camden Town. Trisha and Janet took the Tube to Finsbury Park.

Lyn Summers and her friend Kath Moores had both left Holloway in recent months, but they still shared a flat in Lancaster Road, Finsbury Park. Lyn had now been convicted of theft, fined £50 plus costs, which she was paying in weekly instalments, something that Kath didn't know about. Although they had both known Trisha at Holloway, it was a great surprise when she rang the flat that Sunday evening from a pay phone, saying that she and Janet were in the area, and asking if they could pop in. 'I thought to myself, *What are they doing here?*' says Kath.

Lyn was in the kitchen having a wash when Trisha and Janet arrived. Kath showed them into the living room, while Lyn put some clothes on. 'Have you seen the papers?' Trisha asked

Kath while they waited. No, Kath hadn't seen the Sunday papers. Trisha was shifting about nervously. 'I have got some news,' she announced.

'Why, what's the matter?'

Lyn entered the room at this point. She didn't seem pleased to see Trisha. 'We can't stay long, we are going out,' Lyn told her.

'We won't be long,' said Trisha. Then she gave them her news. 'The police have been to see me, something to do with key impressions. They were apprehended somewhere. Maxine is involved, and she has told the police I made them.'

'The stupid cow!' swore Lyn. 'What did she give your name for?'

'I can't imagine . . . You met Maxine on the day she had parole, and I thought I had better warn you that the police might want to see you, if Maxine mentioned meeting you.'

'What can I say? I did meet her.'

Janet tried to reassure Lyn that she wasn't in trouble. But Lyn wasn't happy. 'I will have to tell the police about meeting Maxine,' she said, claiming to her friends that she left Holloway because Maxine had a crush on her.

Trisha said that the police had taken prison keys for tests, but they wouldn't find anything on them 'because the keys they had taken were not hers. She told me she had changed them with Janet Harber's keys . . . and then later changed them with [another set],' said Kath, who thought that Trisha might have used Lyn's keys. Trisha also spoke about letters and photographs she had exchanged with Myra, saying that she had sent these to the USA, by which she meant the parcel she posted to Joan Kleinert in California. 'She also said she had sent a parcel to Janet Harber's uncle in Maidstone . . . addressed to Janet,' said Kath. Janet was present when this was discussed. Despite her jealousy over Trisha's friendship with Myra, she seemingly now knew a lot about what had been going on, but had decided to stand by Trisha.

Lyn went back to the kitchen. Trisha followed her. 'You saw Max,' she reminded Lyn when they were alone. 'What are you going to do about it?'

'I don't know,' replied Lyn. Then she added: 'You're crazy, or bloody mad.'

'Yes, that's beside the point,' replied Trisha. 'Are you going to the police? If so, would you tell me first?'

Lyn agreed to warn her if she decided to speak to the police, but as soon as Trisha and Janet had left the flat Kath confronted her friend and told her they had to act now. 'I said to Lyn, "Right, we've got to go to the prison. I'll ring them up straight away." It was just too much for me. I thought, *I can't keep this in my head, I've got to offload it*, and the best place to offload it was to the people at the prison.' Kath was 'gobsmacked' about what she had just heard about an escape plot, and alarmed to learn that the police and the press were investigating. She was amazed that Trisha, a woman she had admired as 'a very strong character', might have been manipulated into helping Myra Hindley, of all people, escape; while the idea of Hindley and Cairns running off to be missionaries in Brazil sounded barmy. 'There was not a chance in China that Myra Hindley would be a missionary. She was too vicious, vindictive, nasty . . . She was a manipulator, and she did nothing except for her own ends. As soon as she got out of those gates, and got wherever she wanted [to be], she would have ditched [Cairns]. I've absolutely no doubt in my mind . . . Because it was all about her.'

Kath was also upset to think that former colleagues might have been injured in an escape attempt. Even with copies of prison keys, Myra would have to get past the night watch officer guarding her wing, plus the officer who sat in the Centre overnight. 'It was a mad plan, [but] in an escape attempt they would have to knock a few people over . . . They would have to really hurt people to do this escape.'

They had to tell the governor at once. 'Lyn, this is just too much. We've got to go to the prison and talk to them about it, tell them what [Cairns] has just said,' Kath told her flatmate.

It was a big decision for Lyn. 'She was probably cacking herself,' says Kath. She says that Lyn agreed to go to the prison, and that they went together that same evening. The record shows, however, that Lyn did not go to Holloway that Sunday night. Like others, she still held back from doing the right thing – for fear of getting in trouble herself, or because she didn't want to grass on a mate.

Out in Essex on Monday morning, DCI Phil Thomas returned to George Stephens's scrap yard to tell him that CID at King's Cross were investigating the key impressions, and the senior investigating officer needed more information. DCS McGuinness wanted to see the letter that came with the impressions, which Thomas had neglected to pass on, and he wanted the packaging the impressions came in. Fortunately, George still had all that material, but he was not pleased to be told that he was also wanted in person to give a witness statement.

'It's got nothing to do with me,' George protested, but Phil Thomas insisted. Reluctantly, he agreed to accompany Phil to London.

Divisional headquarters at King's Cross was a large nick with the Royal crest and motto carved in stone over the entrance. There was a magistrate's court next door, cells in back, and a yard full of suped-up Jaguar Mark III squad cars for detectives to chase after dodgy geezers like George Stephens. King's Cross wasn't a comfortable place for the scrap dealer. He didn't have friends here, as he did in Essex. He only had Uncle Phil on his side as he gave a statement to Hamlet man, Ron Peace.

'I have known a girl named Maxine Croft for about five years. She used to come into my yard and office [with] a friend of mine,' George began his statement. 'As far as I knew Maxine Croft was serving [a] sentence for something in connection with five-pound notes . . . On Monday, 29 October 1973, around lunchtime . . . I received a phone call at my office from a woman who said she was Maxine Croft. I was very surprised and asked her how she could make a phone call from prison. She said she was out for the day, and that she had some personal effects she would like me to take care of.' Maxine explained that she was going to leave these items at Paddington Station, and she proposed to post the luggage receipt to George. 'She asked me for my address, which I gave her.' George went on to explain how he came to work the next day to find a parcel on his desk, rather than a letter with a receipt. He claimed he didn't recognise the handwriting, and he didn't open the parcel immediately because he was distracted by business. 'Some time around 3:30PM to 4:00PM Detective Chief Inspector Thomas came into the yard. I know him reasonably well, and it turned out that he came to see me about the repair of his car. He came into my office, and when we were chatting he asked me what the parcel was. I said, jokingly, "I think it's a bomb."' Phil Thomas then opened the parcel and found the impressions.

'I have been worried about it ever since,' George concluded. 'I bitterly resent being brought here today because I have no involvement in this matter at all. If I am not charged in the matter I don't want to be involved in it in any way.'

That last part of his statement felt tagged on. A few months later, TDC John Dixon was sent back to see Stephens to give him a retyped statement to sign, omitting the last two sentences. Dixon didn't twig at the time, and senior officers didn't enlighten him. 'It's a cover story he's looking for,' he says now, a retired officer with a wealth of experience. The wording of the statement was probably agreed to protect Stephens, but the last part in which he protested his innocence may have been thought too obvious. 'He probably didn't like the idea he was basically grassing somebody.'

It was Maxine who suggested that Trisha send the key impressions to George, though George was no more a forger than she was. 'He couldn't make a rice pudding, let alone keys,' she says. There is no evidence that Maxine and Trisha were offering to pay George, and he had no other reason to help the women. He didn't know Myra Hindley personally. George could do himself some good, though, by betraying the conspirators to the police, especially if he felt they had compromised him by posting the impressions to him direct, contrary to the plan. 'A scrap-yard bloke does a lot of under the counter deals, and often they pass on the appropriate titbits to whoever their police contact is,' says retired constable Trevor Scoble, who played a small part in the investigation. 'They could [be paid for information]. It could also be you turn a blind eye to a particular thing. It's life. It's what goes on.'

George's cover story about Phil Thomas bringing his car into the yard to get it fixed didn't withstand scrutiny. 'Obviously, that story of me dad's statement is not right. It can not be truthful,' says his son, Ian. 'It's quite ridiculous that Phil Thomas [happened to be] in his yard at the time.' George was a police informant who gave DCI Thomas information. 'I know he was. I know that for sure, 100 per cent,' says Ian.

'I would tend to believe the police had a sniff about what was going on, and they got in on it undercover.'

Maxine Croft says that George the Liar was also known, just as unflatteringly, as 'the biggest grass in the East End', and she says that she suggested Trisha Cairns send the impressions to him as part of her secret plan with prison staff to get Myra and Trisha in trouble. 'Everyone knew that George Stephens was not someone you could trust. He was a grass [and] grassed me straight up. I knew he would do it . . . That's why I put his address up.'

The true nature of George Stephens's relationship with the police is confirmed in a document buried in Home Office files, an indiscreet remark by a senior member of staff in the prison division who wrote that, on 31 October, the Home Office was told that the police had come into possession 'through an informer' of prison key moulds. George was the 'informer', and he and DCI Thomas concocted a story to stop that becoming public. By Maxine's account, the subterfuge went deeper still, and some people think she could be right. 'Do you know what? It wouldn't surprise me if it was all a set-up . . . a plot, a fit-up,' says George's daughter, Julie. 'Maybe she was in with it.'

Back at Holloway, during their tea break in the Ivory Tower, Trisha was talking to Miss Taylor again. She told her that she and Janet had been to see Lyn Summers on Sunday night, after their chat in the Wimpy bar. 'Pat [Cairns] said she didn't worry about herself, but she did not want to get innocent people involved.' Sister Therese the nun seemed to be reasserting herself here, but almost in her next breath Trisha revealed a devious streak not generally associated with nuns. She told Taylor, as she had told Kath Moores, that though the police had taken her prison keys she had swapped them over with the keys of other officers, so the keys they were testing weren't the ones that had been copied. She was essentially bragging of criminal prowess. Taylor had heard enough. After the tea break she went downstairs and requested permission to see the governor. She was ready to talk.

The next morning, Detective Chief Superintendent McGuinness returned to Holloway where he interviewed Maxine Croft under caution, while Ron Peace took notes. Maxine took all day to tell her story, holding details back at first, and showing signs of being scared of Myra Hindley. Still, she revealed that the escape conspiracy went back months, and she described the photo sessions that preceded the key copying. As the interview wore on, the interview room filled with so much smoke they could hardly see each other. It was a relief to break for lunch.

During the afternoon session, Maxine described meeting Trisha on her day out of Holloway, and said that George Stephens had agreed to receive a package from them. 'You realise that to get involved in making prison keys with a view to assisting a prisoner to escape is a very serious matter,' McGuinness reminded her. 'Would you like to tell me why you became involved in this?'

'I was pressured. A lot of pressures which affected me to the extent there was no getting out of it. No refusing.'

'Can you tell me about these pressures?'

'I can not explain the pressures . . . because of my family being on the outside. I have reason to believe that there are people who could cause damage to them.'

'Do you know the names of these people?'

'I know certain names, but I am too frightened to tell.'

'Have you ever discussed this matter with Myra Hindley?'

'I don't wish to answer that.' Maxine didn't tell McGuinness, as she now claims, that she was put up to the job by prison staff; but she indicated that she felt cornered, and she hinted at other forces.

At the end of her interview, she agreed to give a statement to DS Peace, who wrote it down in longhand for her to sign. She recalled more now, including Trisha's reaction to her neighbour and colleague Angela Glynn making a complaint against her to the governor. 'Miss Cairns said to me at the time, "Now you see that even statements from officers making complaints are laughed at. Can you imagine if an inmate should make one?"' Maxine's statement became so long that Ron Peace had to come back and finish it later in the week.

In her statement, Maxine spoke about asking her brother to post her address book, containing George's phone number. The police now knew that there had been some correspondence with Dennis Croft, and another detective sergeant, Mike Pearce, was sent to see Dennis at his flat in Dagenham. Dennis told DS Pearce about a letter he had received from a friend of Maxine's asking him to post her address book to London. He still had the letter, which he handed over to the sergeant. It was the one signed 'Marie', asking him to send the book to Susan the hairdresser. When he didn't act fast enough, he received a telegram reminder. 'I showed the telegram to my wife and she tore it up.' Jackie Croft knew Maxine of old and, as Dennis says, 'there was no love lost between them'. Then another letter arrived from 'Marie', which Dennis threw away. It might still be in the bin downstairs. So, DS Pearce rootled through Dennis's garbage, a lovely job for an experienced detective such as himself who, until recently, had served with the Flying Squad. 'I can remember searching a skip of rotten vegetables.' In this mess he found the torn up letter which, when reassembled, read:

> *Dear Dennis,*
>
> *Please burn this letter, the telegram and the letter giving the address of where to send that address book, in case there are any enquiries. Nothing to worry about.*
>
> *Thanks*
> *Marie*

On the contrary, there was now a lot to worry about. Tuesday night Lyn Summers finally went to Holloway to tell the prison staff what she knew about Trisha, Myra and Maxine. Like others she had waited a long time before doing the right thing. With evidence piling up, it was time for Detective Chief Superintendent McGuinness to speak to Trisha Cairns again, and to confront Myra Hindley herself.

22

COME ALONG, PLEASE

Trisha was questioned by DCS McGuinness at Caledonian Road, where she gave him her bank book, supplied samples of her handwriting and had her fingerprints taken. She was shown the note received by George Stephens with the key impressions, and various items the police had recovered from Holloway prison, with Maxine's help. She denied using these to copy prison keys. She denied hiding things in the clock, or writing to Dennis Croft. She denied everything. 'Did you meet Maxine Croft outside prison at Speaker's Corner at Hyde Park on Monday, 29 October?' asked McGuinness, while Ron Peace took notes.

'No.'

'Did you go with her and drink vodka and lime in a nearby bar?'

'No,' said Trisha, though she declined to say what she did that day.

That afternoon McGuinness and Temporary Detective Constable Paul Barr accompanied Trisha home to Earl's Court where they searched her flat again. This time they found something else. 'Is this your driving licence?' asked McGuinness, holding up a piece of card.

'No, it's a friend in Manchester.'

The name on the licence was Myra Spencer. 'Where is she living now?' asked the chief superintendent

'I don't know.'

McGuinness read aloud the name and address on the licence: 'Myra Spencer, 1 Parkhurst Road, London N7.' That was the address of the prison, as they both knew. Trisha didn't comment. The chief superintendent picked up a pad of writing paper. 'Is that your handwriting?'

'I don't know.'

'Come on, please.'

McGuinness now had ample evidence of a clandestine relationship between the prison officer and Myra Hindley, including Trisha's possession of Myra's driving licence, in a changed name, which the police missed on their first visit to her flat, but which Cairns had failed to destroy or hide in the meantime. It was almost as if she wanted them to catch her. There was more. The chief superintendent now found an envelope in the flat addressed to Mrs N. Moulton of West Gorton, Manchester. Nellie Moulton was Myra's mother, having divorced Bob Hindley and remarried a lorry driver named Bill Moulton. Trisha admitted that she knew Nellie.

The next day, Thursday, 8 November, Trisha returned to Caledonian Road where McGuinness pressed her for the truth. 'Who is Myra Spencer?'

'I don't wish to comment on this.'

Cairns continued to play games with the police, but McGuinness had the advantage over her. Lyn Summers had been into the station to tell detectives that she had met Maxine on her day out of Holloway; also that Maxine had told her that she and Trisha were trying to break Myra out; and Trisha had come to her flat to ask if she meant to tell the police. This was powerful evidence. Cairns still denied it all, but McGuinness had heard enough. Shortly before lunch on Thursday he charged her with 'conspiring to effect the escape of Myra Hindley'. Trisha wasn't held in custody. She was allowed to go home, but she was suspended from duty and she was put under police surveillance.

That Sunday, Trisha and Janet Harber took the Tube to Camden to meet Mary McIntosh, a thirty-seven-year-old sociologist with an interest in criminology. Mary had been visiting Myra for almost a year, and was due to see her again in Holloway that afternoon. Before her visit, the women went for coffee at the Wimpy on Parkway, unaware that they were being watched by a female undercover police officer. Trisha told Mary about the trouble she was in, and asked her to give Myra her love when she saw her, and tell her that she was all right. She also gave Mary flowers for Myra. They talked for some time. The coffee they had ordered failed to arrive so they finally got up and left, grumbling about the service.

McGuinness was deeply interested in the undercover officer's report of this meeting, because of 'security services' intelligence passed to him, probably by DCI Hoggarth at the Home Office, suggesting that Mary McIntosh not only knew Cairns and Hindley but somebody linked to the Angry Brigade who had supposedly been in contact with the IRA. The prisons department of the Home Office further noted that Cairns 'is believed to be of Irish parentage', which created even more suspicion, if not paranoia, though in fact both Trisha's parents were born in England, making one wonder about the general quality of their intelligence. Meanwhile, Mary McIntosh was brought in for questioning because of her meeting with Cairns.

The chief superintendent thought that all this was significant. 'Had it not been for this enquiry the Price sisters, recently convicted for their part in the London bomb outrages, when sentenced would have been imprisoned at Holloway,' he wrote to the Director of Public Prosecutions (DPP), referring to Marian and Dolours Price, who had just been convicted of planting car bombs in London, including the bomb at the Old Bailey where a man died. Although the Price sisters would normally have been returned to Holloway to serve their life sentences, they were sent to HMP Brixton on conviction because of doubts about security at Holloway due to the Hindley keys. 'Although there is no direct evidence to connect this [escape] conspiracy with the Angry Brigade or the IRA, it is felt the above facts should be borne in mind when considering any further action to be taken,' McGuinness told the DPP.

Mary McIntosh is remembered today as a feminist and gay-rights leader, one of the early members of the Gay Liberation Front, described in her *Guardian* obituary as a kind and inspiring person whose 'work on gender and sexuality played a significant role in influencing a generation of sociologists'. In the 1970s, she was viewed with great suspicion by old-fashioned coppers like Frank McGuinness, who was a conventional public servant of his generation. The chief superintendent got his news from *The Times*, and wore a tie at the weekend. Regarding gay women, his daughter Catherine thinks that her father 'might have been a bit mystified'. In his report into the Holloway conspiracy, McGuinness refers to several women in the case as having 'lesbian tendencies', or 'strong lesbian tendencies', as if this made them in his mind rare, mysterious and suspect.

A couple of days later, on Tuesday, 20 November, there was a breakthrough in the case. Trisha Cairns came back to the police station with her solicitor. She declined to be interviewed, but she wrote a statement in which she changed her story dramatically.

In this statement, she described Myra's hopes for release, which seemed dashed by the reaction to her 1972 trip to Hampstead Heath. 'She has already spent over eight years in prison, without even a glimmer of light at the end of the long tunnel leading to freedom.' So she decided to free Myra, though she suggested that the escape plan was cooked up with Maxine, who she described as 'a friend of Myra Hindley's', rather than an impressionable young inmate whom they coerced. She admitted making the key impressions with Maxine, meeting her in Hyde Park, and posting the impressions to George Stephens. She conceded virtually everything she had denied. 'It was as if she had never ever said anything that was untrue,' comments Paul Barr. 'It was an admission that was carefully admitted to, according to the evidence, the stuff that we could prove, I would imagine. Her solicitor had gone through it with her and decided how they could minimise [the damage]. I don't think it was a heartfelt hands-up job.'

At the end of her statement, Trisha wrote, 'It is only in recent days that I have come to realise that I have been indulging in criminal activities.' She paraphrased Thomas Hardy from his novel, *Tess of the D'Urbervilles:* 'I was aware only of the "end" and paid no heed to the "means". A case of "our impulses are too strong for our judgement sometimes." I sincerely apologise for all the inconvenience, embarrassment and distress that my stupidity has caused, especially to Dr Bull the governor of Holloway.'

Despite his conscientiousness, Detective Chief Superintendent McGuinness tended to leave things to the last minute. That included getting ready for work in the morning. He often had to run from home in Enfield to the station to catch his train, and, on Thursday, 29 November, he had to be at work early because he had an important appointment at Holloway.

McGuinness read Myra Hindley's record in preparation for interviewing her that day – the whole grisly tale. The woman who emerged from police files lied when it suited her, and lied as though she was speaking the Gospel truth. She appeared affronted by any suggestion that she might be anything but honest and respectable. She had lied to the police from the moment that Superintendent Talbot came to her door in 1965, following a report of murder: telling him untruthfully that there was no man in the house. When Talbot pushed past her into the living room Ian Brady was there. When Talbot told the couple that the police had information about an act of violence being committed in the house, Hindley denied it. Moments later they found Edward Evans's corpse in her bedroom.

Hindley was also shameless enough to cast false blame onto others. Informed that her brother-in-law had told detectives about Evans's murder, she said that David Smith was the liar, and she did her best to frame Smith for murder. 'All I am saying is Ian didn't do it, I didn't do it.'

Questioned about the disappearance of John Kilbride from Ashton-under-Lyne market, Hindley said that she had never been to the market. On the contrary, her sister told police that Myra shopped there every Saturday. Myra still insisted: '[Ian] didn't kill Kilbride and I didn't kill Kilbride. I've never set eyes on Kilbride before.'

The original investigating team gave Myra a chance when they suggested to her that she had changed since she met Brady, and maybe she had fallen under his evil influence. That was how she liked to portray herself in 1973, but she rejected that narrative in 1965. 'I made all my own decisions,' she said stoutly. 'Ian never made me do anything I didn't want to do.'

One crack appeared in her adamantine façade. It came when the police quizzed her about Lesley Ann Downey. First, they showed her the photographs of the child gagged and nude. Hindley sat with her head in her hands, a handkerchief over her mouth. Then the police played the tape recording of Hindley and Brady tormenting the child. Myra started to sob. An artery in her neck pulsated rapidly.

'Did you hear that recording?'

Hindley nodded. 'I am ashamed,' she said. It was a glimmer of feeling. But she soon pulled herself together. 'As far as Lesley Ann Downey is concerned, Ian didn't kill her, I didn't kill her. I suggest you see Smith.' By that time the child's bones had been found protruding, like sticks, from boggy ground at Hollin Brown Knoll. The police found John Kilbride's remains nearby on the moors a few days later, in October 1965, guided to the precise spot by the photo Brady had taken of Hindley posing on the grave with her dog.

That December, Hindley and Brady were brought to Hyde Magistrates Court for a committal hearing, to test the evidence against them. Brady was charged with the murders of Kilbride, Downey and Evans; Hindley was charged with the same three murders, plus harbouring Brady knowing that he had killed Kilbride. They continued to deny everything, and gave the appearance of being at their ease in court. Lesley Ann Downey's mother couldn't remain composed in front of Hindley, who sat twelve feet away from her at the committal hearing. She turned to Hindley in a fury. 'I'll kill you . . . . I'll kill you . . . an innocent baby!' she screamed. An officer tried to calm her. 'She can sit staring at me, and she took a little baby's life . . . the beast . . . Tramp!' This stirred Hindley, but only inasmuch as she felt offended. She turned to Brady and told him that she wasn't a tramp. He said that he knew she wasn't.

Myra continued to maintain her innocence during the subsequent murder trial, and she rarely showed emotion after conviction, save for when she was alone with sympathetic people such as Assistant Governor Joanna Kozubska. The police had come to Holloway in the past to try to talk to Myra about the two missing children, Pauline Reade and Keith Bennett, but she had turned them away without answers, claiming to know nothing. That was in many ways her cruellest lie, for the families were left in purgatory not knowing for sure what had happened. Meanwhile, Myra persuaded Trisha Cairns, Joanna Kozubska, Lord Longford, Dorothy Wing, among others, that she was a decent person who, in her virginal innocence, was caught up in a boyfriend's wickedness, as if she was a victim; on top of which she was now a devout Christian.

This was the woman DCS McGuinness prepared to interview about the escape conspiracy, knowing that he had a fundamental problem. Although he had abundant evidence against Cairns and Croft, he had much less evidence against Hindley. Yet she was the focus and surely the instigator of the whole plot.

McGuinness began by telling Myra his name and rank, and explaining his investigation. She stopped him at once.

'Am I allowed to ask for a solicitor before I answer any questions?'

The chief superintendent said, yes, that was her right.

In that case she wanted a lawyer.

At the time, detectives did not always tell suspects that it was their right to have legal representation during police interviews, only summoning a solicitor if one was requested. This issue arose when the police first questioned Hindley over the murders. They did not tell her that it was her right to have a lawyer. 'It has been my experience that if a solicitor had been present we would have been less likely to get at the truth,' DCI Joe Mounsey, one of the senior officers in the case, admitted at the 1966 murder trial. McGuinness probably thought like Mounsey, but having been through this process before Myra knew her rights. McGuinness had to postpone their interview until legal representation was arranged. Myra was too sharp for him.

Five days later McGuinness returned to Holloway to try again, this time with Myra's lawyer present. Her answers were monosyllabic at first, giving away nothing of consequence. For example, yes, of course she said that she knew Trisha and Maxine. Everybody in Holloway knew everyone else. That didn't mean they had done anything illegal.

'Have you ever discussed with either of these people plans for your escape from this prison?'

'No.'

Paul Barr says that Myra behaved differently to most criminals under questioning. She was clearly intelligent, thoughtful, and she was slow to answer. 'Every question you put to her was consumed before it was answered. She didn't just come out with an answer. She'd think about it . . . She listened to the question and [McGuinness] might have to ask it again, because she might not answer. Then she would come out with something, [having] thought about it. Most criminals when you are talking to them [are] eager to deny it, or throw you off course. But she was not eager to open her mouth at all . . . She said very little.' Barr was also struck by Hindley's disdain for the police. 'She oozed hatred when she looked at me.'

She didn't seem to care as much if she incriminated others. She casually agreed that she owned photographs of Trisha. Maxine had told the police that Myra carried these in a leather pouch under her clothes. 'Not in a leather pouch, but in a material pouch,' Myra clarified. That admission wouldn't send her back to court, but it was further evidence of Trisha's illicit relationship with the prisoner. In the same way, Myra admitted receiving letters from Trisha who, she agreed, wrote to her as Glenis Moores. She said that Trisha had given her clothes, too. Also, Maxine passed messages for them.

'What is the nature of the messages?'

Myra's answer to this question was unexpectedly candid. 'Miss Cairns and I have been having a relationship,' she admitted, 'and messages were just messages of sending my love and receiving hers.' This was a sudden and bold declaration of love. It showed another side to a woman who, despite all her lies, was capable of surprising McGuinness with a glimpse of what might be her true feelings. It was as if Myra had pulled the blind up.

Having admitted her love for Trisha she went further, agreeing that Maxine had taken photographs of her in her cell for Trisha; that she and Trisha conversed through a gap in a wall where she did her tapestry; and they met in the prison chapel, when she was supposed to be practicing the piano. But she denied that they had plotted an escape.

'Did you tell Maxine Croft there was a lot of outside help for your escape?'

'I have never discussed an escape with Maxine Croft or anybody . . . I have never discussed key impressions with Maxine Croft. I don't know anything about key impressions.' Myra agreed that she had destroyed photographs she had of Trisha. 'I was very frightened and paranoid,' she explained. 'I got so frightened that people might find out about our relationship. By people, I mean staff.'

McGuinness asked about the driving licence the police had found. Myra agreed that it was hers, and that she had changed her surname to Spencer, though she didn't explain why. She was asked why her driving licence was at Trisha Cairns's flat. 'I wanted Miss Cairns to keep it. Because we were going to live together when I got out of prison. That is when I was released.'

'When do you expect to be released?'

'I don't know.'

'Do you expect to be released before 8 February 1976, which is the date the licence expires?'

'I doubt it.'

The chief superintendent then delivered what he hoped would come as surprising news. 'Miss Cairns has admitted to planning your escape from this prison,' McGuinness told Myra, thinking that this might force a confession from her. 'Can you think of any reason why she would plan your escape?'

'I had no idea she was planning my escape,' Myra replied, pulling her blind back down. 'I didn't know anything about it.'

23

THE FACE OF 1974

Myra's true feelings erupted after DCS McGuinness left the prison. She made frantic attempts to contact Trisha and, as staff reported, tried to 'subvert both officers and other prisoners in the hope that they would convey messages [to Cairns]'. Separated from her beloved, her hopes of freedom dashed, Myra exhibited frustration, anger and depression.

She stared mournfully out of her window at the huge London plane trees that had been growing in the yard since the jail was built, the same trees that Ruth Ellis, the suffragettes, Oscar Wilde and Diana Mitford had known in their time in Holloway. The branches were bare as winter approached, and the yard was littered with dead leaves. One tree was known as the Hanging Tree, though no prisoner ever hanged from this or any other tree at Holloway. The misnomer grew from the prisoners' morbid fascination with the history of judicial execution in the jail. Myra went out and hugged the bare tree. 'It makes me feel so sad to see it like this,' she wrote to Quaker prison visitor Dr Rachel Pinney, a woman described as being 'eccentric to the point of instability' by DCS McGuinness who was studying everybody who had contact with Hindley. 'I went over to it and wrapped my coat around the trunk, and tried to rub some warmth into it.'

One day, a budgie escaped from the prison aviary, and hopped about among the plane trees, before perching on the perimeter wall, watched by inmates who variously tried to coax it down, or urge it to fly to freedom. Myra identified with the bird, as she did with the tree, though she doubted that the budgie would survive long in the outside world. Here were two examples of Myra's yearning for freedom, and her tendency to sentimentality at low moments. 'She was very self-indulgent,' says Maxine Croft, scornfully.

The governor became so concerned about Myra and her attempts to contact Trisha, and the danger of her corrupting other women, that she confined her to her cell. 'Myra Hindley is trying to exert pressure in quite a sinister way on at least one member of staff and one inmate, both of whom have kept us informed of the situation,' Dr Bull reported to Joanna Kelley, Assistant Director of prisons at the Home Office (and herself a former Holloway governor). Locked up with her tapestry and her books, Myra grew resentful and bitter. Staff started to see a new side to the woman.

Everybody agreed that Myra was the likely instigator and architect of the escape plot, and DCS McGuinness wanted the Director of Public Prosecutions to prosecute her, along with Cairns and Croft. Unlike the other two, Myra denied any knowledge of the plot, and there wasn't nearly as much evidence against her. So, McGuinness had to argue the case for prosecution.

Puffing on his pipe as he worked at his desk at King's Cross, the chief superintendent wrote a lengthy report for the DPP, complete with descriptions of the main characters in the case; noting for example that Hindley 'has formed a close relationship with Cairns. She has lesbian tendencies'; and '[Janet] Harber is not a particularly bright individual and she

Trisha Cairns shared a flat with Janet Harber at the top of this prison service hostel at 18 Collingham Gardens, Earl's Court, west London.

Trisha Cairns and Maxine Croft mixed up modelling powder to copy prison keys in the Ivory Tower kitchen, where trusties made the staff teas. Towels cover the tea things to protect against the vermin that infested Holloway.

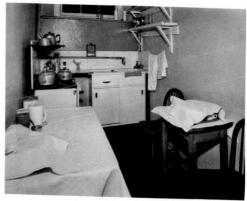

Trisha Cairns hid her Kodak camera and key impressions in an old clock, here in the staff lounge at the top of the Ivory Tower.

The key copying kit, including Cairns's prison keys, soap, modelling powder, the teapot they mixed the powder in, the Kodak Pocket Instamatic and the broken clock. These items were labelled by TDC Barr as evidence.

Salvage man George Stephens is seen having fun with DCI Phil Thomas and their wives. George is the third man from the right at the table, hugging Mary Thomas. Next to him, DCI Thomas has an arm around Joyce Stephens. 'As you can see, they are very close friends,' writes George's daughter Julie.

George Stephens with Mary Thomas, wife of DCI Thomas.

A recent picture of what was George Stephens's scrap yard in east London.

Detective Chief Inspector Phil Thomas, who supposedly took his car into George Stephens's yard to be repaired the day the key impressions arrived.

Detective Chief Superintendent Frank McGuinness, known as Gentleman Frank.

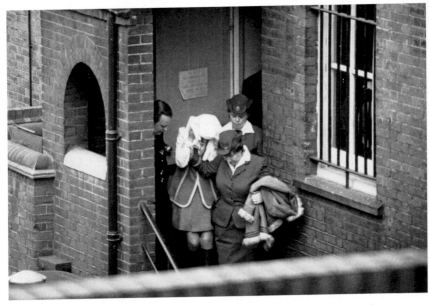

Myra Hindley, with her head covered, leaves Old Street Magistrates Court in London, in 1974, having been remanded for trial.

Trisha Cairns (second from left, in the furry coat) tried to hide from press photographers outside Old Street Magistrates Court, in 1974, but one photographer caught her looking directly at him.

Myra's jail affair with ex-nun who plotted her freedom

By Richard Wright

LOVE MESSAGES were passed from Myra Hindley, the Moors killer, to a 30-year-old prison officer who was a former nun, an Old Bailey judge "heard" yesterday.

Hindley carried photos of the other woman next to her body and hoped they could live together when she was free.

But the prison officer, Patricia Cairns, was jailed herself yesterday, for six years. She and Hindley, and Maxine Croft — another prisoner they used as a go-between—all admitted conspiring to effect Hindley's escape from Holloway.

Sentencing the former nun, Mr. Justice Melford Stevenson said: "The most sinister feature of this case is that you exercised pressure on an inmate of the prison who was subject to your control.

"These things you did with calculated deliberation and cunning.

"I can find no extenuating circumstance to explain your conduct and you have not improved your position in my eyes by putting before the court a facade of piety which proved to be very brittle.

A 'facade of piety' hiding the prison officer's sinister cunning

future, he hoped—the facts behind this case should be remembered and taken into account.

Cairns was a Carmelite nun for six years but left her convent because of illness. Later she went to Holloway and became a prison officer, said Mr. Brian Leary, prosecuting.

He read out a statement in which Hindley said she was very friendly with Pat Cairns and carried her photos next to her body.

They had been having a relationship and met in the prison chapel, and she had sent messages of her love to Cairns.

'We were going to live together when I got out of prison or when I was released,' she added.

Plaster cast plotters

The plot was to make plaster casts of the five keys necessary for Hindley to escape from Holloway. She and Cairns had talked of fleeing together to Brazil.

three pleading guilty lasted only three and a half hours.

Hindley looked wan and listless, her face framed by lank, fair hair falling to her shoulders. Her voice was barely audible as she pleaded guilty.

She was wearing white trousers with a pink shirt under her beige, sleeveless jacket.

Mr. Flack read a letter written, he said, by Hindley about Cairns.

"During the course of several conversations she awakened in me a beautiful thing in my soul, and it was due to her influence and encouragement that I made my first confession in 12 years," it said.

A beautiful bond developed between them and they shared many mutual interests.

Mr. Flack read a statement from Hindley claiming responsibility for the "whole thing" and pleading for leniency for Croft.

"She has involved herself in this out of concern for me. She was sympathetic about my predicament and often said 'I don't know how you have endured eight years,'" said Hindley.

Also pleading for Cairns,

Hindley said she came from a background, above reproach and was a good officer. She had passed for teams to become senior officer but refused promotion because it would have meant moving away.

"Neither of us could bear the thought of her being moved away," said Hindley.

"She felt as deeply as I did when I talked to her about escape. Her mixed emotions were stronger then her black principles and duty as an officer," said Hindley.

"Her motives were good. She was prepared to mend the rest of her life on the run."

As for herself, Hindley said: "I want to say I maintain my innocence of the charges against me in the Moors murder trial.

"There are things of which I am guilty and of which I am deeply, bitterly ashamed."

Of the escape plot Mr. Leary said Cairns and Croft made casts of four keys, and the idea was that Hindley would eventually leave by a door in the perimeter wall.

Eventually—after a rehabilitation "day out" of prison, which was used to further the escape plot—Croft blurted out to a probation officer: "I am frightened. Cairns is going to break Myra Hindley out."

Croft said she had been asked by the two if she knew anyone who made keys. After being threatened, she agreed to help.

Cairns's flat was searched and a driving licence was found in the name of Myra Spencer. Olympia Moors. It was for use, by Hindley.

The letters between them

Hindley told Croft, she and Cairns used to correspond by using the address of Hindley's mother. Cairns used the name Olympia Moors. In a three-month period Hindley sent Olympia Moors 74 letters—and received 83 back.

Mr. Nicholas Freeman, for Croft, said of Hindley, serving a life sentence on two murder charges: "She is clearly able to persuade those about her that she is a reformed character. I observe that as a result of contact with her the governor of Holloway has resigned.

Mr. Flack said it was quite wrong to say that Mrs. Wing, former Governor of Holloway, had fallen under Hindley's influence and had to resign.

Myra Hindley..."A beautiful bond between us"

Maxine Croft

Patricia Cairns ... secret meetings in chapel

Victim of a wicked woman

Croft was jailed for a further 18 months to start next June, at the end of a three-year sentence for possessing forged five pound notes.

But the judge told her: "You were undoubtedly the victim of a very wicked woman. She practised something approaching blackmail and took advantage of her position to make you do things which you would not have done otherwise.

Hindley, aged 31, who is already serving a life sentence, was sentenced to a token 12 months and the judge said if she was considered for parole in the future—the remote

Divers' find may be lost couple

By John Christopher

POLICE FROGMEN on a routine diving exercise may have solved the three-year-old riddle of the disappearing lovers. Thirty feet down in the depths of Barry Docks in Glamorgan, the divers found a rusting Morris Oxford saloon.

DAILY EXPRESS ENTERPRISE

Maxine Croft is seen in the middle of this *Daily Express* report of the 1974 Old Bailey trial, with Cairns on the right (appearing to poke her tongue out), Hindley's 1965 mug shot on the left.

In the 1990s, Hindley dropped Trisha Cairns for Dutch criminologist Nina Wilde.

Lord Longford was Hindley's loyal supporter, arguing that she was
a 'good religious woman'.

Few mourners attended Myra Hindley's funeral, which was held on a freezing cold evening in November 2002 at Cambridge Crematorium.

Trisha Cairns in a recent photograph.

After her death, in 2002, Hindley's ashes were scattered at Walkerwood Reservoir in Stalybridge Country Park, approximately six miles from where the children were buried on the moors, which can be seen on the horizon.

Flowers and stuffed toys are still left on Saddleworth Moor in memory of Keith Bennett, whose remains have never been found.

has undoubtedly been hood-winked by Cairns.' As half-baked as the escape plan might appear, McGuinness believed that it could have worked. 'It should be appreciated . . . that had the keys been made it would have been possible to release any of the prisoners in D Wing at Holloway prison.' That would include terrorists. McGuinness concluded that all three women should be charged with conspiracy to break Hindley out – including Hindley herself.

Legal advice within the DPP was that the case against Hindley was circumstantial, and the Crown would have to rely on Maxine Croft's evidence to have a hope of a conviction. Proceeding on such a basis was not recommend, but the Director of Public Prosecutions decided that it would be wrong not to charge Hindley.

When criminal charges are serious enough to be tried in a crown court the accused is brought before a magistrate initially to be remanded for trial. Remand hearings are among the briefest of criminal court proceedings, and they are not usually attended by reporters unless someone special is in the dock. The remand appearance at Old Street Magistrates in Shoreditch, east London, on Thursday, 17 January 1974, was such an exception.

A large press pack gathered at Old Street to witness Myra Hindley's first public appearance in eight years. She had dressed up for the occasion, wearing high heel shoes; a brown pleated skirt, cut above the knee; a yellow blouse; and the same sleeveless tunic she had worn for her illicit photoshoot with Maxine. 'The face is long, slim, the hair a natural brown resting on the collar of the brown suede jacket. A face of the '70s,' noted a fascinated *Daily Mail* journalist, writing a colour report more in keeping with the fashion pages than the front of the newspaper. This florid description was complemented by an artist's impression of Hindley's new look, in comparison to what Myra called her 'monster' mug shot from 1965, which she felt gave the public the wrong idea about her. 'Now that has all gone, the face of 1974 is thinner, more sophisticated,' wrote the *Mail* journalist, who agreed that Myra looked much nicer, 'she has slimmed down. Her face is more relaxed.'

Maxine Croft was brought into the dock to stand with Myra, but hardly anybody looked at Little Max. The two women were on view for no more than five minutes, just enough time for the magistrate to be told that they were charged, along with a third person, who was not in court, of conspiring to effect Hindley's escape, upon which the magistrate remanded them into custody. It was a 'straight up and down', reporters told their news desks when they phoned in their copy. Picture editors were crying out for a new image of Hindley to illustrate the story, but to their frustration none of the photographers outside court got a shot of Myra coming or going.

Thirteen days later, Myra and Maxine were brought back to Old Street for another remand appearance, and this time Trisha joined her alleged co-conspirators in the dock. Having failed to get a picture at their first attempt, press photographers found a vantage point that allowed them to shoot down into the yard at the side of the court, and they managed to snatch a shot of Myra from the back as she was taken in. The snappers waited in expectation of getting a face shot when she came out. In court, all three women were remanded to stand trial at the Old Bailey, not far away in the City of London. With Hindley expected to plead not guilty, the trial was scheduled to last for two weeks. DCS McGuinness made a note in his diary. Myra emerged from the building with a towel over her head, again denying the press a front page picture of the Moors murderer now. The photographers cursed her.

Trisha was less successful at avoiding the press, less wily than Myra and more vulnerable because she had to use the front entrance. She still did her best not to be identified. She came to court wearing a hooded coat and dark glasses, but was caught by photographers outside the building. As they banged off their photos, she covered her face with a newspaper and buried her head in the shoulder of a protective female companion.

Janet Harber stood by Trisha during her ordeal, and she guaranteed one third of the £3,000 surety that meant Trisha left court that day on bail. To the dismay of former colleagues, Trisha was allowed to stay at their Prison Service flat in Earl's Court, where she spent her time working on her case. Unable to talk to Myra or Maxine, Trisha told her flatmate details she hadn't previously shared with her. Despite their long friendship, Janet started to see that Trisha had betrayed and compromised her, as she had other friends and colleagues.

Finally, the worm turned. Janet had already given the police two statements − both brief and guarded. She now returned to Caledonian Road to give Ron Peace a third statement, which was fuller, franker and much more damaging to Trisha and Myra. She described the visit she and Trisha paid on Lyn Summers the weekend the story broke in the press, reporting everything Trisha said that night, and subsequent conversations in which she described trying to break Hindley out. 'I asked her how on Earth did she think she could get anyone out of Holloway. I can hardly imagine Myra jumping over the wall,' Janet told DS Peace. Trisha replied that they now hoped to use the secret back gate, rather than having Myra climb the wall. 'I took this remark with a pinch of salt,' said Janet, who doubted the existence of a secret gate. 'I also asked her how anyone in D Wing could possibly escape after being locked in. She said, "It's simple, one has only to walk through [the] reception door and [down] the stairs."' Janet couldn't believe this either. 'I said, "But D Wing is right near the Centre and if anyone came from their room they would be heard." Miss Cairns replied, "Not necessarily." I said, "It would be a bit of risk, and you would be stupid if you tried it." Miss Cairns just shrugged.' Trisha also apparently told Janet that Maxine knew somebody who could forge passports.

Janet told the police that it was plain to her that Trisha was planning nothing less than a prison escape. 'I sincerely believe that Miss Cairns's sole intention in all this was to get Myra Hindley out of prison.' But she also continued to support and help her flatmate, listening to her, posting bail for her, and shielding her from the press by answering phone calls at the hostel.

Most of these calls were from members of Trisha's Manchester family, who were astounded to read in the papers what had been going on in London. 'It's unbelievable to think what she has actually done, or got involved with,' says her brother-in-law, Stan Ball, who was married to Trisha's sister, Kath, in Ashton-under-Lyne, in the heart of the area where the Moors murders had taken place, and where Hindley's name was an obscenity. 'She has been very, very naughty, Trish has . . . We all told her. It was wrong, definitely wrong, especially being a Catholic Christian and everything that goes with it,' says Stan. 'Myra Hindley was a figure that no one even wanted to speak of here. She was that disliked.' But Trisha 'pulled the shutters down' when her family tried to talk to her about Hindley, and she wouldn't listen to reason. Relatives stood by Trisha, though, despite their belief that she had behaved wrongly and foolishly.

Colleagues were less forgiving. Trisha was shunned by the sisterhood of prison officers, who were appalled by what she had done and continued to do. One Thursday afternoon around this time, Heather Sanders was shopping near Bond Street Tube station in London when she saw people protesting about 'Torture in British Prisons' and handing out leaflets. 'If you do not believe that torture takes place in British prisons, consider what is happening EVERY DAY to four young people on hunger strike,' one pamphlet read. It was illustrated with pictures of the Price sisters, Gerry Kelly and Hugh Feeney, all four on hunger strike in prison having been convicted of bombing the Old Bailey and Scotland Yard. It was claimed that they were being force fed. 'Forcible Feeding is Torture.' Sanders was surprised to see Trisha at the demo, a woman she had worked with at HMP Bullwood Hall. 'I recognised and almost spoke to her but I suddenly thought of the trouble she was in and stopped myself.' Sanders reported Trisha to the police, though, and the police considered whether as a suspended prison officer Cairns had committed an offence against the Prison Discipline Code by apparently joining such a demonstration. They didn't pursue the matter, but this incident showed how far Trisha had drifted from the behaviour of a conventional jailer.

Former Assistant Governor Judy Gibbons read about the Holloway arrests in her newspaper while travelling on the Tube to her new job at a central London hospital. She spoke to Dr Bull by phone when she got to her office, and agreed to meet her for lunch at the prison where, until recently, she had been a senior member of staff. Judy wasn't too surprised by what had happened, having warned the governor before she left that Cairns, Croft and Hindley were up to something, but she hadn't been able to stop it, and neither had Dr Bull. 'You see, unless you have [proof], you can't go around accusing staff,' she says.

Another former member of staff, who rose to be a governor, says that Trisha Cairns was the only prison officer she knew in her whole career who behaved like this. 'We were absolutely horrified. We couldn't believe that one of us, a prison officer, could stoop so low and plot an escape,' says Veronica Bird. But she also saw tragedy in Cairns's situation. 'I think she did have that caring instinct, and that's what got her in trouble.' As Trisha cared for Myra she cared about IRA bombers, but she forgot that her primary duty was to keep prisoners locked up. Colleagues had said from the start that she wasn't suited to work in the Prison Service. 'Whether Patricia felt she was a misfit, I don't know – going to be a nun and [then] into the Prison Service is such a weird scenario,' says Veronica Bird. 'I think she must have been totally obsessed with Myra.'

Staff morale fell in Holloway, especially on D Wing where officers felt that Hindley and Cairns had made fools of them. At the same time Myra became overtly troublesome for the first time. She started to lodge complaints, which became a feature of the rest of her prison life. She complained about being on Rule 43, and announced that she was fed up with D Wing, which was too noisy for her to concentrate on her studies. She made so many complaints that Dr Bull moved her to F Wing, where she wouldn't have to be segregated. The governor was then embarrassed to be asked by Hindley's solicitor to be a character witness at her forthcoming trial, a cheeky request which was turned down flat.

Arriving on F Wing was like joining a new class, with a new group of girls to get used to. Many of these women disliked Myra on principle, and one inmate in particular seemed determined to pick a fight with her. 'On the night I arrived on F Wing, and for several days afterwards, she reacted to my presence on the wing in an hysterical and abusive manner, screaming that she would refuse to live on the same wing as myself,' Myra complained to the governor, saying that this woman was inciting other inmates. She tried to ignore her initially, and when that didn't work she spoke to her to try and reach an understanding that would allow them to rub along together. 'During this conversation she told me she had nothing against me personally, it was what I was in here for . . . She added that she has a child who is dying from an incurable disease, and that whenever she sees me she can't help thinking about what I'm in here for.' The woman then started to come to Myra's cell to read aloud from letters she had received about her dying son, 'saying that she thought they might help me to understand why she felt about me as she did.'

Myra continued to make requests and lodge complaints, as if she was staying in a second rate hotel with poor service. She wanted the prison electrician to look at her radio, which wasn't picking up FM. She wanted to see her solicitor to discuss taking out an injunction to stop ITV transmitting a drama she thought was based on her case. She requested private meetings with the governor. She needed new shoes, wanting to look her best when she appeared at the Old Bailey in what would be her biggest public appearance since she was convicted of the Moors murders. Myra was about to step back into the limelight.

24

THE CRUCIBLE OF SUFFERING

Myra, Trisha and Maxine were reunited in the dock at the Old Bailey, the Central Criminal Court of England and Wales, on 1 April 1974. With a limited wardrobe to choose from, Myra wore the same tunic she wore for her photo session and her remand appearances. She wasn't the same defiant woman, however. She appeared downcast to the reporters who crowded into Number One court. 'Myra Hindley looked wan and listless . . . her face framed by lank [brown] hair falling to her shoulders,' George Glenton wrote in the *Daily Mirror*.

An acerbic judge in his seventies, Sir Melford Stevenson was known for his conservative views (he once ran for Parliament as a Conservative Party candidate) and for making sarcastic remarks. His court gaffes included calling bookmakers 'a bunch of crooks', a barrister a 'fat slob', and saying that nobody sane would choose to live in Slough, Birmingham or Manchester. A law and order judge, Justice Stevenson resided in a house named Truncheons. He wanted the death penalty brought back for murder, and he wasn't inclined towards gay rights, dismissing law reform for homosexuals as a 'buggers' charter'; all of which may have coloured his view of the defendants before him this April Fool's Day.

The first news was that all three women were pleading guilty to 'conspiracy to effect the escape of a prisoner from lawful custody'. Myra had decided at the last minute not to fight the case, and capitulation seemed to have demoralised her. 'Her voice was barely audible as she pleaded guilty to the escape-plot charge,' reported Glenton. Proceedings would therefore be short – the hearing wrapped up in a day – and most of the witnesses would not have to give evidence in person, though their statements were before the court.

The prosecutor, Brian Leary, outlined the escape plan for the judge. He said that Hindley and Cairns had formed a 'close relationship' in Holloway, explaining Cairns's background as a novice nun. He said that they had secret meetings, and whispered through a gap in a wall; they also exchanged illicit letters, with Cairns writing to Hindley under a false name; while Hindley carried photographs of Cairns under her clothes. Leary described the prison cell photo sessions, and how impressions of keys were made and smuggled to George Stephens. A senior police officer who had gone to see Stephens to get his car fixed happened to see the parcel, he said. Thinking it might be a bomb, he opened it to discover the impressions. Reporters wrote this down on trust. Fleet Street would print it overnight for millions to read the next day, and it would go unchallenged for almost half a century. In light of research for this book, it now seems clear that this was in fact a cover story.

Mr Leary read from police statements, including Maxine's confession statement in which she described how it all started for her when she was asked to pass notes and gifts between Cairns and Hindley; how she feared she would be 'fitted up' unless she co-operated; and how Trisha Cairns tried to persuade her to lie to the prison governor after their key impressions were intercepted.

The prosecutor also read Trisha's confession, giving the court an insight into the depth of her feelings for Myra. In this statement Trisha said: 'I have tried to be a source of consolation and encouragement to her, for just being Myra Hindley is penance enough without the added rigours of long years in prison which this deeply sensitive person has endured.'

Myra Hindley, a 'deeply sensitive person'? The journalists reporting the trial glanced at each other and smirked.

Detective Chief Superintendent McGuinness gave evidence in person, providing the court with further detail about the escape plot and the conspirators. Cross-examined by Aubrey Myerson, QC for Cairns, McGuinness mentioned the Violet Ali case, which was the start of it all. 'There was an incident in 1971, in which she [Cairns] gave evidence before a Visiting Committee, which in light of this inquiry shows this to be manifestly untrue,' said the chief superintendent.

The judge asked McGuinness to clarify: 'Sorry, shows what to be manifestly untrue?'

'The evidence given at the Visiting Committee inquiry.'

The judge still wasn't clear. 'Shows what to be manifestly untrue?'

'Well, the allegation was that an inmate of the prison had reported an association between Hindley and Cairns, and this inmate was, in fact, taken before a Visiting Committee and lost a hundred and eighty days' remission for making a false statement. In light of this inquiry, it would appear that the evidence given by Hindley and Cairns at that inquiry was false.'

'Let's not mince words. This was obviously a close lesbian association?' said the judge.

'That is so, yes.'

Cairns's barrister rose to object, telling the judge that his characterisation of the relationship between Cairns and

Hindley, as having a lesbian association, 'is not accepted by [Cairns]. The relationship was not physical in any sense whatsoever. It was a bond based more upon mutual respect and admiration for the Roman Catholic religion they both shared.'

More smirking from the journalists as they took notes.

'She [Cairns] was living in a cloud-capped tower,' Aubrey Myerson continued in Cairns's defence, 'unable to exercise the objectivity she should have shown.'

Speaking up for Maxine Croft, barrister Nicholas Freeman said that his client found herself caught between Hindley and Cairns, and was understandably scared of getting in trouble with a prison officer. As the court had heard, when a previous go-between tried to tell the governor what was going on in Holloway she hadn't been believed. 'That fact was well known to Miss Croft and she was terrified – and it would be no exaggeration to use that expression – that that would be her fate if she were to make a complaint.' As a result, Maxine didn't inform when she should have done, but 'was drawn into this conspiracy and went along with it'. Maxine had been of considerable help to the police since then, though, with DCS McGuinness describing her confession as 'the backbone' of his case. 'Croft was certainly under very considerable pressure from the combination of Miss Hindley and Miss Cairns. She had an anxiety to please,' Freeman told the judge, hoping to soften his cold heart towards the youngest defendant in court. '[Hindley] has persuaded some of the highest in the land that she is a reformed character. Such is the woman who brought Croft into her thrall.'

The reference to 'some of the highest in the land' pointed to the Seventh Earl of Longford, who appeared in court as a character witness for Myra. Lord Longford explained in his lisping voice that he had been visiting Myra *wegularly* for years, and they also corresponded, pointing out that all their letters were read by prison staff. 'I hope that will satisfy anyone who thinks I have come under her *thwall*,' he said, apparently unable to comprehend that this *is* what many people thought. For the popular press in particular Longford was a bit of a fool, though tabloid editors valued him in the role of Britain's Pottiest Peer, as they hugged Hindley to their breasts as Britain's Wickedest Woman. Both were useful stock characters in the pantomime of public life. Others felt that Longford made a valid point when he argued that Myra should not be treated differently to any less infamous life prisoner, while a smaller number of people felt as he did that she was a reformed character who, in fact, may not have murdered anybody. 'I offer my own strong opinion that she is not a bad woman, but a woman with much good in her, making a determined effort to make amends for her past and to do good in the future,' Longford told the Old Bailey. 'Only the Almighty can tell us whether to try to escape, when there is no hope of being let out, is a sin, although it is illegal and wrong.'

Myra was the star of the trial, and her words were the highlight of the day, giving the court an insight into a fascinatingly enigmatic personality. Some if not most people in court looking at Hindley in the dock saw a shameless twisting liar who had manipulated the emotions of an eccentric prison officer, in Trisha Cairns. But could it be true that their love – even if platonic, and conflated with religious delusions – was genuine and mutual? Robert Flach for Hindley told the court that though his client's relationship with Cairns had been 'purely spiritual', it was 'very intense'. He then read a statement written by Myra. Like her letters it was long, verbose and over-stuffed with quotations that showed off her prison education. She quoted from Saint Augustine, Emily Brontë, Socrates and, of course, the Bible. But her affection for Cairns shone through the verbiage.

'Life in prison, with the stigma attached to me, has not been easy,' Myra began. 'Although I have made many good and loyal friends, the majority of the prison population has been hostile and antagonistic towards me, and though I managed to cope with all this and take it in my stride, I know that without Patricia [Cairns's] unswerving support and consolation I would have been crushed with despair . . . During the course of several conversations, she awakened many beautiful things in my soul, and it was due to her influence and encouragement that I made my first confession in twelve years.' From this beginning a 'beautiful bond' developed. 'She has transformed my life completely and has been an unfailing source of strength and encouragement.'

Myra described being depressed in 1973, after her application to take an Open University degree had been referred to the Home Office, interpreting this as a sign that she had no realistic hope of parole. That was when she told Trisha that she must escape from Holloway. She also discussed this with Maxine Croft, ultimately deciding to flee to Brazil with Trisha. 'I want to claim responsibility for the *whole* thing . . . I am responsible and culpable. I want to ask for leniency for Maxine, because she is young and has already spent over three years in prison. She involved herself in this out of concern for me.' (That was not what Maxine said.) 'I beg for leniency for Patricia [Cairns] on many more grounds. She would *never* have done what she has done if it wasn't for me . . . She took and passed a [Principal] Officer exam, but declined promotion because it might have included a transfer to another prison [and] neither of us could bear the thought of her being moved away. She knew I was terribly dependent on her and she was a tower of strength to me. She was acutely aware of all the antagonism and hostile threats I was exposed to, and was often present when I was subjected to verbal abuse. This was a source of much distress to her and she could also see, during the last year, that my morale had greatly deteriorated, and that I was becoming more and more depressed.'

Myra said that Trisha's sympathy outweighed her sense of duty, insisting that 'her motives however misguided were pure. She was prepared to sacrifice everything and commit herself to a life "on the run," to being as implacably hunted as I would have been had I escaped on my own'. This evoked a romantic if absurd image of Myra and Trisha running across the Brazilian pampas, perhaps disguised as nuns, pursued by police.

She explained her sense of despair in prison with an extended metaphor about life in custody being like 'an endless black tunnel' at the end of which was the light of 'faith and love'. Mixing her metaphors, she saw hands reaching out to her through this light. 'God's hands, Patricia's, my mother's, Lord Longford's . . .' Most reporters didn't bother writing down this metaphorical stuff. It would only get cut from their copy.

Myra argued that she would not be a danger to the public if she was released. She was reluctant to revisit the Moors case, but she restated her innocence for the court. 'I maintained my innocence of the charges laid against me at my arrest, during my trial and throughout my imprisonment, and I will continue to do so until my dying day.' She admitted, vaguely, that she had done some wrong. 'There are many things in my past of which I am deeply and bitterly ashamed.'

Instead of saying what exactly she had done, Myra veered off into a rhetorical crescendo worthy of a church sermon, borrowing a phrase associated with the suffering of Job in the Old Testament: 'I have caused suffering by my sins but I have suffered, too, both for the suffering I have caused and from the suffering inflicted upon me by others. I believe that sin can be atoned for and purified in the crucible of suffering.'

Again, the journalists smiled and shook their heads.

Continuing to skate over the details of her crimes, Myra said that she had renounced the 'repugnant and odious' parts of her past. 'That "person" I was then no longer exists.' This brought her to Ian Brady. Even now, Myra couldn't denounce Ian totally. 'Up to the time of my involvement with the man I came into prison with – and by saying this I do not seek to do him down, his is an unenviable and sad existence – my character and background were free from criminal stain.' She described herself pre-Brady as 'an ordinary decent citizen' and claimed to be so again. 'Patricia [Cairns] would not have been aiding the escape of an "evil, sadistic monster", to use but one of the terms by which I have often been described, but of someone who strove only to be like she is. She is good and kind, with a rare honesty and integrity, and has a beautiful soul and equally beautiful heart, and I implore you once again to judge her with compassion and forgiveness.'

As the defendants had entered guilty pleas, Justice Melford Stevenson only had to sentence the women. He had background reports before him. Holloway probation officer Valerie Haig-Brown had written a constructive appraisal of Maxine, suggesting that a further prison sentence would only harm her chance of rehabilitation. If she could be released on parole, she would have the benefit of a supervised reintroduction to society. Trisha's probation officer was of the opinion that she acted in good faith in helping Myra; about whom a third officer wrote: 'She is now tragically aware of the negative elements in the relationship [with Cairns] and her part in the destruction of Miss Cairns's career in the Prison Service.'

The judge asked the defendants to stand. All eyes were on the three women, including those of Detective Sergeant Alec Edwards of the Flying Squad who was at the Old Bailey for another case, and had slipped into court to watch the sentencing. He was standing at the back of the room, behind the dock, which gave him a unique view of Myra and Trisha. 'And they were holding hands,' he recalls. 'I thought it was intriguing to see that. Even at that stage they were still committed to each other.'

Justice Melford Stevenson gave Myra Hindley a token additional year on her life sentence, warning her that if she was ever considered for parole her escape attempt would count against her.

The judge told Maxine Croft more kindly, 'You were undoubtedly the victim of a very wicked woman who practised upon you something approaching blackmail, and took advantage of your position to make you do things which I do not think you would have done left on your own.' He gave Little Max eighteen months to follow her current sentence. Maxine says that she expected this, and had been given the nod by her contacts that she would soon be released. Had she not got involved with the escape plot, however, she would have been free months ago.

The judge turned a face like thunder on Trisha Cairns. 'You were in a position of trust and great responsibility in a valuable social service. That trust you have betrayed.' As Melford Stevenson prepared to throw the book at the disgraced guard, a dock officer noticed that Myra and Trisha were holding hands. She administered a karate chop, separating the women.

'The most sinister feature of this case is that you exercised pressure on an inmate of the prison [Croft] who was subject to your control and influence. These things you did with calculated deliberation and cunning.' Trisha's Christian talk, and her background as a novice nun, hadn't impressed the judge. 'I can find no extenuating circumstances to explain your conduct and you have not improved your position in my eyes by your façade of piety, which proved to be very brittle.' He sent Trisha Cairns to prison for six years.

Myra and Trisha looked lovingly at each other for the last time in a long time, before being taken down to the cells.

25

LOVE STORY

Reports of the Old Bailey trial filled the newspapers the next day. The story made ideal copy for the *Sun*, whose editor gave the court case a screaming front-page headline:

JAIL LOVE AFFAIR

OF MYRA HINDLEY

AND AN EX-NUN

Journalists contacted the former Holloway governor Dorothy Wing for a comment on the case. Mrs Wing expressed regret about Myra's conviction, and blamed herself for starting a chain of events: 'If I hadn't taken her for that walk in the park, I don't think an escape would have entered her mind . . . What was meant to be a kindly act, and what she regarded as a kindly act, resulted in her being crucified by a public outcry.' Mrs Wing agreed with Trisha Cairns's QC that the love between Myra and Trisha probably wasn't physical. She suggested that it was more like a 'schoolgirl crush . . . They used to exchange love letters and whisper softly to each other through a gap in the cell wall.' It was difficult for staff to prevent that. 'I feel very sorry for Myra . . . She will never have the chance of walking out in the park again. She's lost all that, and everything else, too.'

In the short-term, the consequences for Trisha were worse. Having been a prison guard, she now found herself locked up as a criminal. Normally, a woman handed a jail sentence at the Old Bailey would be sent to Holloway, at least initially, but Myra was there, and the women couldn't be together, so Trisha was sent to HMP Styal in Cheshire, which was also nearer to her Manchester family.

Styal was a 'semi-secure' prison, where women lived in houses, originally built for orphaned children, in an enclosed prison village surrounded by fields; it was very different to Holloway but not a soft prison. Officer Cairns became Prisoner 774989, and her colleagues became her jailers. 'And of course that made things difficult, initially, because she knew all the prison rules,' says Veronica Bird, who having worked at Holloway was now a principal officer at Styal. There was also the issue of how fellow prisoners would treat Trisha, who was put to work in the sewing shop. 'We were very concerned that she may be ill-treated.' But she held her own. That led to another fear: that she might teach the prisoners how to beat the system.

Then Trisha got into trouble again. Dormitory doors at Styal were not locked, but they had alarms to make sure the prisoners stayed put overnight. Principal Officer Bird was on duty one evening when she caught Trisha in the wrong dormitory after eleven o'clock. 'What are you doing here?' Bird asked. 'You should be in your dormitory.' She put the prisoner on report. As a result, Trisha was sent to the punishment block, Bleak House, where Maxine Croft once kicked her heels. 'She just took it,' says Bird. 'She knew she was out of order.' News of Cairns's punishment was phoned through to Holloway, where the screws rejoiced. 'The Holloway staff apparently cheered when they knew she'd been found misbehaving, because they felt so let down by her.'

Myra heard the cheers in Holloway and begged to see the governor, beseeching Dr Bull's permission to be allowed to contact Trisha, saying that their relationship was of 'vital importance' to her. When Dr Bull denied her petition, Myra reacted badly. 'Since her recent trial her abiding passion has been to obtain permission to correspond with [name redacted].[1] She becomes very angry with me when I remind her that she is using the same arguments she used some years ago to justify her correspondence with Brady,' an officer wrote in the prison files. 'Her feelings for [redacted] is of comparable quality and intensity to what her feelings for Brady was [sic], though she denies this and takes great pains to stress its intensely spiritual nature.'

Myra lost her temper completely. She went crazy, showing the staff, 'behaviour we had never seen from her before – lying on the floor and kicking and screaming and threatening suicide'. Was this an expression of genuine feelings for Trisha?

Myra was partly on edge because of the F Wing inmate who was spoiling for a fight with her, a simmering problem that came to the boil during film night at Holloway. One Sunday each month, a film was screened for the prisoners. Women competed for seats, and tried to reserve places next to their friends. The films were well past their release date, but they came as new to long-term inmates like Myra who hadn't been to the cinema since 1965. On Sunday, 14 April, 1974, the staff screened *Love Story,* in which Ryan O'Neal's character, Oliver, falls in love with a student named Jenny, played by Ali MacGraw, who contracts cancer. 'What can you say about a twenty-five-year-old girl who died?' Oliver asks in an

---

[1] Although the name is redacted, it is obvious from the context and from subsequent events that this is Cairns.

emotive voice over. For ninety-five minutes the prisoners were distracted from their wretched existence by this tear-jerker.

During the crucial part of the film, when Oliver is told that Jenny has leukaemia, Myra heard her name called. It was that woman from F Wing, telling Myra that her child was dying, like the pretty girl in the film.

'Do you know what it is like to have someone dying?'

'Shut up!' someone shouted.

The woman called out again to Hindley.

'Can't we just watch the film, please?'

Myra passed her enemy as they returned to the wing, and told her that if she ever did anything like that again she would tell the governor. The woman said that it was nothing personal. Myra stormed back to her cell in a fury. An officer found her there, crying. 'If that [woman] makes another crack at me I will kill her,' she said. That was a threat from a murderer, and the officer wrote it down. Later, Myra rang her bell for the officer to return. 'I didn't mean it when I said I would kill [her], but I am fed up with her making snide remarks about me.'

The attitude of Holloway staff towards Myra hardened after her escape attempt. All the time she had presented herself as being compliant she had been plotting against them, proving that she was two-faced; and it seemed that she may have been willing to hurt members of staff to escape. Her depression was noted, but it won her little sympathy. Myra was described as 'devious and untrustworthy' by the assistant governor in charge of F Wing, who wrote: 'She has lost the trust that people in Holloway once had in her. She is aware of this, and regrets the fact that the governor particularly can no longer trust her . . . Apart from her religion, Myra has little else to give her hope. The possibility of further escape attempts cannot be ruled out.'

The escape plot also shone a spotlight on the character of a woman who had killed, highlighting the vital issue of whether she remained a danger to society. The assistant governor's tone became sarcastic when she addressed this: 'I find it impossible to assess the likelihood of her reoffending should she be released. Whatever she attempts, whether it were to be missionary work, studying, writing or even murder, I suspect that she would be thorough, precise, efficient and probably successful.'

When the old lag Violet Ali heard that Hindley and Cairns had been prosecuted, she contacted her local MP, in Birmingham, to tell him that when she was in Holloway, in 1971, she told the governor that those women were up to no good, but she wasn't believed. In fact, she was punished for making a false allegation. William Wilson, MP, raised this issue with the Home Office, and he arranged for Violet to speak to journalists to publicise her claim for compensation. 'No one likes to be called a liar, let alone be punished for it as well. Now at last the truth is out in the open,' Violet told the *Sun*, adding a new allegation: she said that Holloway staff had intercepted a note she had been carrying between Cairns and Hindley, which indicated a cover-up at the time, for despite asking repeatedly Mrs Wing had been unable to obtain examples of the notes. 'Then before my eyes the letter was torn into pieces.'

After reading Violet's story, Justice Melford Stevenson wrote to the Court of Appeal to let his colleagues know that had he been fully aware of Ali's case when Cairns, Croft and Hindley came before him at the Old Bailey, he would have given Maxine Croft a lighter sentence. The Home Office subsequently decided that the 1971 ruling by the Visiting Committee was unsafe, and Ali would receive a pay-out from the government.

The judge's intervention paved the way for an appeal by Maxine Croft. Since being sentenced in April, Little Max had been at East Sutton Park open prison near the pretty village of Sutton Valence in Kent, where she worked in the prison garden. 'I was told I would get eighteen months as a thank you, and three or four months later I would probably walk out,' she says, claiming this was part of the deal she was offered to entrap Myra, 'and sure enough when I went to the Appeal Court [the] judge said, *You are going home today.*' There is no proof that Maxine was given a lighter sentence in exchange for help with trapping Myra. In fact, she was in prison longer because of the conspiracy. She had now been in custody for three years, a long time for a woman of twenty-two, but she seemed to have turned a corner. She was back in touch with her family, and she told her probation worker that she would get a job and go straight if she was released.

Maxine came before Lord Justice Roskill at the Court of Appeal in London on 9 July 1974, when it was decided that she had served long enough. A place had been found for her in a hostel for ex-offenders. 'You can go there today,' the judge told her, effectively cutting her eighteen month sentence for the Holloway conspiracy to three. He explained to her the importance of seizing this opportunity. 'It is not easy for you, but we hope it is going to be the end of what happened before, and the beginning of something very much better.'

'Thank you, sir.'

Maxine walked out of court into the Strand, with the sun on her face – a free woman at last. She says that the judge asked her not to talk to the press. But when a journalist took her drinking up the road in Fleet Street she told him her story. It ran in the tabloid magazine *Titbits* under the headline 'WHAT MYRA HINDLEY DID TO ME (by the girl forced to aid her prison escape)'. *Titbits* got two weeks out of it. At the end of the second instalment, Little Max was quoted in philosophical mood: 'As I look back on my life I think my problem was boredom, lack of money and coming under the influence of the wrong sort of people,' she said. 'Now it's a matter of rebuilding my life. It will be a struggle, but that's far better than going in and out of prison.'

The fact that Myra was denied permission to correspond with Trisha didn't stop them from communicating. If Myra couldn't write to her beloved legally, she would do so illegally. Myra started to write to another prisoner who had been transferred to HMP Styal, and this go-between – the latest in a succession of messengers, stretching all the way back to Carole Callaghan – passed her letters to Trisha. 'She did send me letters, got them smuggled through. I read them, then destroyed them straight away,' Cairns later admitted to journalist Duncan Staff. 'It was dangerous, though, and we used a code right from the start.' In doing so, Trisha was again repeating what Hindley did with Brady; they had also exchanged coded prison letters. At least one of the women's missives was intercepted, which may have been the reason for Trisha being moved to HMP Durham.

Judging by prison records, further illicit letters reached Trisha in Durham, and though some names are redacted in the files it seems that she sent at least one reply. Then their go-between threatened to inform, which jeopardised Trisha's hopes for parole.

'Agitated and shaking', an unnamed prisoner (who, once again, by context, and by what she later said herself, is clearly Cairns) is described as approaching a senior member of staff at Durham, in 1976, on the pretext of asking for nail scissors. She then said that she had received letters from Myra

Hindley when she was at Styal. She had considered reporting it but hadn't. Now the letters were starting again. She was sick with worry and couldn't sleep. 'I asked her if she had received any letters since her transfer to Durham,' reported the prison officer. 'She said she had. I asked her where had inmates been [concealing] the letters.'

'Internally.'

Four days later, this same prisoner wrote to the governor of Durham saying that she had received several 'written and verbal illegal communications from Myra Hindley' in Styal and Durham. 'I experienced a mixture of reactions on receiving these various communications. They were principally annoyance and distress. Annoyance, because Myra was showing no consideration for the messengers and the punishment they would have to endure had they been caught. Distress, because I was still struggling to extricate myself from my emotional attachment to Myra.' She asked the governor to take steps to prevent Myra sending her further letters.

When Myra was told that her sweetheart didn't want to hear from her, she was devastated. Holloway staff reported that she was 'ill for several days' and grew 'thin and haggard'. The screws were more concerned about her causing further trouble in her obsessive desire to reach Trisha. 'During the past year she has spent a considerable time in cultivating the friendship of various inmates who might be able to contact [name redacted],' wrote a member of staff. 'She has shown herself to be quite a successful manipulator in this matter. Unfortunately, to accomplish this she has had to develop control of the inmate sub-culture and impose her personality on others. She has used two methods in this, either to present herself as a poor wronged and misjudged person, or by using her knowledge of the internal trafficking, and backing this with threats of violence from her group of admirers. She has also used the sub-culture to protect herself from the open hostility which she still gets from some of the inmates.'

Aggressive young inmates sometimes tried to make their mark by assaulting the Moors murderess. One such prisoner was Josephine 'Josie' O'Dwyer, who had followed a similar crooked path in life to Maxine Croft, from approved school via Bullwood Hall to Holloway, where O'Dwyer encountered Hindley in 1976, when O'Dwyer was still only nineteen. Despite her youth, Josie O'Dwyer had convictions for assaulting a probation officer, damage to property and possession of an offensive weapon, which added up to three years in custody, and she was notoriously troublesome and dangerous. Veronica Bird once had to restrain her. 'It took six of us . . . She was extremely violent.' O'Dwyer was being held on D Wing, which Myra had recently moved back to. The two women were on collision course.

O'Dwyer was a child when the Moors murder case was first reported, too young to have followed the story. It was now ten years since Hindley and Brady had been convicted, and some members of Holloway staff thought that Josie might benefit from a history lesson. On Sunday 26 September 1976, a couple of screws invited her into their office, so she said, to show her that morning's *News of the World*. The newspaper had reprinted the transcript of the infamous Lesley Ann Downey tape to remind its readers why 'these two monsters [Hindley and Brady] must never be free'. The Deputy Governor had already spoken to Myra about the article, and had ordered that the *News of the World* should not be available in the prison that weekend in case it provoked trouble. Myra knew that inmates would probably see the paper, anyway, and tried to carry on as normal, which meant walking about the wing with her head held high, which some women interpreted as her arrogance.

Having read the paper, an enraged Josie O'Dwyer went looking for Myra, who considered Josie to be unbalanced. Myra's friends blocked O'Dwyer's way while Myra pleaded with the duty officer for sanctuary, saying that she was 'so uptight I'm going to freak out'. But since her escape attempt, and the departure of Assistant Governor Kozubska, staff were disinclined to grant Myra favours. They told her to go to her cell.

Myra climbed the stairs to the fours. To get to her cell she had to pass the recess where prisoners slopped out. O'Dwyer was there, washing her hands after carrying lunch trays back to the kitchen. 'Child-murdering bastard,' she said as Myra walked by. Myra made a gesture, tutted, and carried on walking. She may have clicked her teeth or hissed at Josie, which was a prison insult. O'Dwyer followed her and told her not to 'suck her teeth' at her. 'Who do you think you are *tutting* at?'

'Shut up and mind your own business,' Myra shouted, loud enough for staff to hear.

'You don't talk to me like that, you cunt!'

Josie flew at Myra, grabbed her, swung her around by her hair, got her down on the floor and kicked her in the face. 'She proceeded to kick me in the mouth repeatedly with large heavy boots.' Myra felt her blood wet on her chin. She put an arm across her face to protect herself and clutched the railing with her free hand to stop O'Dwyer pushing her over.

'*Stop it! Stop it!*' staff shouted. The emergency bell rang, and officers blew their whistles.

'You bastard of a child-killer,' O'Dwyer screamed at Myra, as she put the boot in. 'Cry for mercy, you bastard, like those little children did.'

Myra later described the assault, and her injuries, in a vivid statement: 'I was punched repeatedly about the head and shoulders and kicked in the stomach and both legs. When the officers arrived, they had difficulty in dragging her away from me, but before they were able to do so she had dislocated [a] few of my front teeth, one of which had almost embedded itself in my inside bottom lip, causing a deep cut which bled profusely . . .' She didn't retaliate, whereas O'Dwyer exerted herself to such an extent during the assault that stitches she'd had to a wound in her arm burst open, causing her to bleed.

When staff had dragged her off, O'Dwyer was taken to the clinic to have her wounds attended, while Myra received attention on the wing and was confined to her cell for her safety. A few days later she was taken to the nearby Royal Northern Hospital to have corrective surgery to her nose. Years later Josie O'Dwyer claimed that prison officers set her up to attack Myra, and they rewarded her with tobacco. Her claim was reminiscent of Maxine Croft's story that prison staff incited her to entrap Myra in an escape plot that could not work, but would get her and Trisha Cairns in serious trouble. They had succeeded in this, and in breaking the women apart, but Myra and Trisha had not forgotten each other.

26

BACK TO THE MOORS

New prison blocks had been built around the decrepit core of the old Holloway castle, modern brick buildings with flat roofs and gardens between the wings, like the campus of a polytechnic. Myra had watched the construction work for years, but she wasn't allowed to move with the other inmates into the new dormitories, which had the luxury of bathrooms. She was told at the last minute that she was being transferred to HMP Durham in the morning. 'She was absolutely shattered by the news,' wrote prison officer Valerie Haig-Brown, for Holloway had been Myra's home as well as her dungeon for more than ten years. Early the next day, 29 January 1977, she left Holloway for good. With a police escort she was driven north at high speed in a prison van to another grim fortress.

Most of the inmates at Durham were male, but there was a female wing, H Wing, sometimes known as Hell Wing, which held some of the highest security women in the country, and until recently this was where Trisha Cairns was imprisoned. The women inmates could see but not mix with the male prisoners, who shouted at them from their cells, and exposed themselves to the women. Myra hated Durham. She complained that she had been given one of the nastiest cells, 'with two great holes in the wall where the plaster has cracked and fallen off', and Trisha was no longer there, so there was no reunion. Staff assessed Myra on arrival as a 'self-aware, self-possessed, cunning and devious woman' who was also 'rather neurotic'. She didn't like them, and they didn't like her.

The campaign for Myra's release began in earnest after she moved to Durham, with Lord Longford arguing in the *Brass Tacks* television debate on BBC 2, in July 1977, that it was time to consider Myra for parole. He was supported on the programme by Dr Sara Trevelyan, a family friend who believed Myra when she told her that she hadn't killed anyone, and found her to be a 'sensitive . . . very nice person'. They were joined by a hard-faced former prisoner, Janie Jones, who met Myra in Holloway while serving time for controlling prostitutes. Myra, who still denied taking part in murder, gave the BBC a statement in which she insisted that her only crimes were to be in the same room when Ian Brady photographed Lesley Ann Downey, and as an accessory after Edward Evans's murder. 'I can't show remorse for things I haven't done.'

Ranged against her supporters were what Myra called 'the anti-brigade', foremost amongst whom was Ann West, the mother of Lesley Ann Downey. 'Lord Longford is talking about parole for Myra Hindley. When will I get parole? I am serving a life sentence for that monster,' said Mrs West on air, recalling the horrific recording of her daughter's ordeal, which she had to listen to. She characterised Myra's supporters as 'misguided do-gooders' and threatened that Hindley would be 'one dead woman' if she was released. This chimed with the feelings of other parents and John Kilbride's father, Patrick, rang in to say that he would kill Hindley, if Mrs West didn't get her first. Countless members of the public rang the BBC, and the newspapers, to express their vehement opposition to the suggestion that Hindley might be considered for parole.

Far from persuading the public that Myra deserved parole, the TV debate reminded viewers of the terrible nature of her crimes, and brought scorn upon her supporters. Myra felt that Lord Longford had been an unimpressive advocate. She asked him not to do anything like this for her again. But she developed a loathing bordering on hatred for Mrs West, who won the debate with her heartfelt contribution. Myra began to accuse Mrs West of 'exploit[ing] her poor daughter's tragic death'.

Two years passed without a glimmer of a parole hearing. When the Labour Home Secretary, Merlyn Rees, decided, in 1979, that Hindley's case wouldn't be revisited for another three years, she wrote to him to say that she had been society's 'scapegoat and whipping boy for far too many years'.

'What must I do to get out?' she railed at her jailers. 'What do they want – blood?'

As her letter to the Home Secretary showed, Myra was more outspoken as she entered middle age, and increasingly prone to displays of frustration. The picture of her that emerges in her prison files is mixed, however, showing a woman with many sides. To her credit, Myra had educated herself to a high standard, obtaining a Bachelor of Arts degree. She was regarded in prison as cultured and articulate. She had maintained her faith, which most staff and chaplains considered to be genuine, though others thought it was affected. The trashy image of the young murderess had been shed. 'Many of those who met her were struck by the change in image from the hard, brassy blonde of some sixteen years ago to an intelligent, well-educated woman who had taste, and whose views seemed culturally more attuned to middle-class values,' wrote one officer. Another noted that Hindley 'showed sorrow and regret for the harm she has caused others, which the cynic would perhaps describe as self-pity, but the more generous observer might accept as evidence of real change.' But one adjective was used repeatedly to describe Hindley. 'She is an arch manipulator,' wrote one officer speaking for many colleagues. 'I admire the way that she refuses to allow herself to become a cabbage, but I do not trust her. She often appears to be a scheming woman building up contacts with anyone she thinks has influence.'

Myra was determined not to stay in Durham, and threatened to go on hunger strike unless she was moved. This was a crude example of her manipulation: plain emotional blackmail. Fearing that Hindley might indeed kill herself, the authorities gave in to her demand and, in 1983, she was transferred to HMP Cookham Wood near Rochester in Kent. This was a smaller, more modern prison, but Myra was hardly any happier.

When the Parole Board ruled, in 1985, that her case wouldn't be reviewed again for a further five years, Myra wrote an indignant letter to Conservative Home Secretary, Leon Brittan, accusing him of being another 'political careerist', too frightened of the press to face up to granting her parole, which almost any other life prisoner who was not a danger to society might have expected by now. 'I was just twenty-three years old when I stood trial: I am now almost forty-three,' she reminded the Home Secretary. 'How much retribution do you want?'

As horrendous as the Moors murders were, some people thought that Myra had a valid argument. The former editor of the *Observer*, David Astor, decided that Hindley was being treated differently to other prisoners because of her notoriety, which was unjust. Astor was the multi-millionaire son of the late press baron and sometime Member of Parliament, Waldorf Astor, and his wife, Nancy Astor, MP; a liberal toff who felt drawn to unpopular causes, and a friend of Lord Longford. Astor began to correspond with Myra, sharing Longford's interest in her case, but he agreed that Longford's public statements on her behalf were not helpful, because the public didn't take the peer seriously. Astor persuaded Longford to step aside, and allow a more charming friend to lead what became a well-organised and generously endowed public relations campaign for Myra's release, bankrolled by Astor. The individual chosen as frontman, Reverend Peter Timms, was a former governor of Maidstone prison, a Methodist minister and therapist. He wore a dog collar and large white metal cross, giving what Astor called their 'marketing job' the imprimatur of the Lord. Astor saw the tabloid press as the enemy, and he considered the emollient Timms to be 'skilled at fobbing off the press'.

While Myra's team began her PR campaign, Ian Brady was talking to a journalist at HMP Gartree in Leicestershire, where he was in poor mental health. Brady told Fred Harrison of the *Sunday People* that there had been other murders. This story broke in the *People* in June 1985, when Harrison reported that Brady had indicated that he had killed the two missing children, Pauline Reade and Keith Bennett, and that Hindley was implicated. 'If I revealed what really happened, she would never get out in one hundred years,' Brady told Harrison. Myra denied it, and suggested that Brady should talk to the police if he had something new to say. The love she once felt for Ian had faded in custody. Now it curdled into animosity.

A new policeman entered the story at this stage. Detective Chief Superintendent Peter Topping of Greater Manchester Police, an earnest officer from the same part of Manchester as Myra, visited Brady to see if he would say more. DCS Topping didn't get anywhere initially, finding Brady agitated, emaciated and only semi-coherent. Brady was declared insane shortly afterwards and moved to the Park Lane secure psychiatric hospital near Liverpool. Recruiting Detective Inspector Geoff Knupfer as his number two, Topping continued to investigate the possibility of reopening the Moors case, anyhow, and decided to try to talk to Hindley. In preparation for a challenging encounter with a woman who had never favoured the police with help, the detectives spoke firstly to people who had known her in prison to get a better sense of the woman they were to come up against.

Twelve years had passed since Maxine Croft had been convicted of her part in the Holloway escape plot. Since being released on appeal, in 1974, she had returned to Essex where she had married, in 1982, and had children. She had, as she says, 'moved on'. It was a surprise therefore to receive a visit from DCS Topping and DI Knupfer in 1986, when Maxine was thirty-five years old. 'Could I give them any advice, did I know anything about the [missing] children? Did she say anything about them? I said to them, "She's very manipulative, you have to be careful. And the only way you are going to get any information from her is [to] promise her parole!" Say she'll get parole, if she helps you out, and she'll tell you anything you need to know. Because that's all she was ever after.' The officers thanked Maxine, but they couldn't offer Myra a deal.

Topping and Knupfer also sought out Trisha Cairns, who had been paroled after four years of her sentence, and had returned to Greater Manchester where she applied for a job as a bus driver. One day her former Holloway colleague Kath Moores received a letter regarding Trisha. 'She had applied for a job, and they asked me to give her a reference.' Kath reflected on all the trouble Trisha caused at Holloway, but she also remembered her good points. 'She's paid the price for what she's done. So I wrote the reference for her.' Trisha got the job, which she held for many years. Driving a bus in Greater Manchester meant coming into contact with members of the public who remembered the Moors case, including people who had been directly affected by the crimes. 'I got on the bus one weekend to go to Ashton and she [Cairns] was the driver. I just stood there and said, "Oh, my God,"' John Kilbride's brother Danny told Hindley biographer Carol Ann Lee. 'I turned round and told everyone on the bus who she was, and she had a tough time of it.'

Trisha was still working as a bus driver when Topping and Knupfer tracked her down to an address east of Manchester, not far from the moors, where she was using a new pseudonym, Trisha Forrester. 'Peter and I went to see her one afternoon,' recalls DI Knupfer. 'She was charming. I remember thinking what a nice lady.' Nevertheless, at the age of forty-two, she also seemed to be a lonely woman, who kept a dog for company. '[She] struck me as rather a sad figure . . . obviously fell for Myra and paid the price . . . I'm sure she bitterly regretted what she had done.' But Trisha's feelings for Myra were more complex than the police realised. There would be another dramatic chapter in the story of Trisha's love for Myra Hindley.

An unexpected letter arrived at HMP Cookham Wood from Mrs Winnie Johnson, the mother of Keith Bennett. It was a humble letter from a woman who had lived for years not knowing for certain what had happened to her son, after she saw him across the road on his way to his grandma's house in 1964, 'not knowing whether my son is alive or dead, whether he ran away or was taken away'. She now wrote to Myra in the hope that she would give her the answer. 'Please I beg of you tell me what happened to Keith. My heart tells me you know and I am begging you on bended knees, begging you to end this torture and finally put my mind at rest.'

Myra was troubled by the letter, the first she had received from Mrs Johnson, though not the last. Many such letters followed, seemingly written for Mrs Johnson by journalists, but this first one read as if it came from a mother's heart. 'She became extremely upset and tearful whilst reading it, and it took a very long time for Myra to compose herself sufficiently to talk (this is unusual as Myra is normally very controlled),' wrote a prison officer. Myra told the officer that she knew nothing about Keith Bennett. 'I wish I did know something – I could at least then put the poor woman out of her misery.' But she now had the problem of how to respond to Mrs Johnson. If she didn't reply, she would appear callous. If she wrote back, she felt sure that Mrs Johnson would share her letter with the press. And she didn't know what to say.

Myra discussed her dilemma with an inmate who was serving time in Cookham Wood for a drugs offence. 'I remember in prison her saying, "What do you think I should do?"' says Bernadette (not her real name). 'I said to her, "For fuck's sake, Myra, if you know where her son is, tell her."' The fact that Brady had been talking to a journalist was an added pressure. He might talk in detail about Keith Bennett before she had a chance to explain things her way.

Two weeks after Mrs Johnson's letter, the Manchester detectives Topping and Knupfer came to HMP Cookham Wood to see Myra, assuming that she wouldn't help them. 'We had been told *ad nauseam* by everybody we had spoken to who had met her, and I'm talking primarily about former prisoners and prison staff, that she was very, very manipulative and we wouldn't get the time of day out of her,' says Geoff Knupfer.

They decided to cold call anyway, only alerting the governor that they were coming. Whatever Hindley said, they would then tell the press that they would revisit the moors, to put pressure on Brady, thinking he was more likely to crack. But the woman who walked into the interview room surprised the detectives.

Myra in her forties looked very different to the police officers' expectations, based on old photographs. Her hair was now dark with a reddish tint. Her nose was broken, her figure had thickened in middle age, and her voice was deep and husky. She rolled her own cigarettes and she chain-smoked as they talked.

'What do you want to know?' she asked the policemen.

In recent months, Myra had been having visits from David Astor's friend, Reverend Peter Timms, for counselling sessions, though the Prison Service grew uneasy about her receiving special treatment and thought that Timms had a wider agenda. 'Although the Rev. Timms describes his involvement with Miss Hindley as being that of a counsellor, it is nevertheless true to say that the role which he wishes to play goes beyond the normal counselling role. He is acting as a public relations agent for her.' Timms felt compassion for Myra, and believed she'd had a tough life, starting with her childhood. They talked about her family background as a starting point to encourage her to open up. Timms took the interviews slowly, assuming that they might talk for years before Hindley felt able to discuss her offences, but she reached that stage soon after they started talking, and after she received Mrs Johnson's letter. By the time the detectives came to see Myra, she had decided to alter her long held strategy of blanket denial. 'She was very polite,' says Knupfer. 'She listened to what we had to say, and very quickly we arrived at this accommodation where she was prepared to point out "areas of interest" on Saddleworth Moor, of interest to Ian Brady, which was code really for, *Yeah, I'll point you in the right direction.'*

Early on a cold day in December 1986, Myra was flown by police helicopter over two hundred miles north from Kent Police headquarters in Maidstone to Saddleworth Moor, as part of a huge operation involving 135 officers. Most of these officers were deployed on the moors to keep the public and the press at bay. Another pack of journalists had staked out HMP Cookham Wood in Kent for days in advance to be sure of knowing when Hindley left, her return to the moors having been announced by her team as part of the PR campaign, but the date of the operation had been kept secret.

It had snowed overnight, and cloud cover made landing the helicopter on the moors a perilous operation. When she finally set foot on the ground, Myra had trouble orientating herself in a landscape she had not visited since 1965, and which was covered in snow. An added factor was that Myra was physically unfit, a wheezy middle-aged chain smoker who lived behind bars, so out of shape that DCS Topping and DI Knupfer had to take her by the arms to support her as they stumbled together over the bumpy moorland.

They went first to Shiny Brook, where Myra said they should search for Keith Bennett's remains, but she could not identify the spot. It soon started to snow again, making the operation even more difficult. After lunch, they looked at Hoe Grain, a stream that runs into Shiny Brook. Then they went to Hollin Brown Knoll, where Myra pointed out where they might look for Pauline Reade's grave. On the way back up the road she showed the police where she used to park her car. There was a scare when John Kilbride's father, Patrick, arrived with a knife, which he showed to journalists in a pub. 'I came prepared to kill her,' he said. Although he didn't get near to Myra, this was a reminder of the bitter personal feelings involved in the case. At the end of a challenging day, during which little progress was made, Myra was flown back to Kent. The search was then suspended for the rest of the winter.

The reopening of the Moors investigation was a huge news story, so big that Prime Minister Margaret Thatcher was briefed about progress before taking part in a radio phone-in programme. She was told that Hindley had not been offered immunity from prosecution, and 'has not admitted to any knowledge of the murders which the police suspect have been committed'. But Myra was about to surprise everybody again.

The detectives returned to HMP Cookham Wood in February 1987. They met Myra and Rev. Peter Timms, who held her hand as she started to confess to her involvement in all five Moors murders, including those of the missing children, Reade and Bennett, talking off the record initially. 'It was a very long, drawn-out process with lots of cigarettes, an atmosphere you could cut with a knife because of the cigarette smoke,' says Knupfer, who was developing respect for Myra. 'My goodness me she was bright.'

Having been cautioned that anything she said could be used against her in a trial, Myra started to talk on tape the next day, Friday, 20 February. Going through the five murders in order she admitted to picking up the first victim, Pauline Reade, and taking her to the moors, saying that she had waited in the van while Brady abused and killed the girl behind Hollin Brown Knoll. Brady brought her to the scene while Pauline was dying. 'I asked her if she could see that Pauline's throat had been cut. She said she heard a gurgling noise and saw lots of blood, and that she felt sick,' Topping wrote of her confession. Here for the first time was direct evidence that Brady killed Pauline, whom Hindley procured, something she had always denied, and a crime they had not been charged with because the body had not been found.

Likewise, Myra finally admitted to picking up the second victim, John Kilbride, from Ashton-under-Lyne market. She said that she watched the boy go 'willingly' with Brady onto the moor while she waited behind in the hire car. Brady came back after burying the body. She said that she knew what he'd done. 'In her mind she believed Brady had sexually assaulted the boy,' wrote Topping.

She also admitted to picking up the third victim, Keith Bennett, having said only recently, when his mother wrote to her, that she knew nothing about his disappearance. Suddenly, she remembered: Brady took Keith to Shiny Brook; she followed at a distance and kept watch while Brady murdered him.

On Monday, they discussed Lesley Ann Downey. Myra was already heavily implicated in this crime, with her voice on the tape. It may not have been coincidental that she found this murder the most difficult to discuss. She gave a fractured account of what happened, pausing frequently. She appeared to cry, and she digressed, making DCS Topping doubt that she was telling the whole truth when, for example, she said that she was in the bathroom at Wardle Brook Avenue, running a bath, when Brady raped and killed the girl in the adjoining bedroom. Having falsely implicated David Smith in this and the Evans murder for years, Myra finally admitted that her former brother-in-law took no part in any of the murders.

After lunch, she explained how Edward Evans came back to Wardle Brook Avenue willingly, saying that Brady planned to mug the teenager when they got him home. Topping didn't believe that. It didn't make sense, as he explained: 'You don't bring someone back to your house if you are going to rob them; you do it on the street.' All hell had broken loose when Myra was out of the living room, but she admitted to helping Brady clean up the mess after he killed the lad.

Then, Myra read a long statement that put her in the best possible light. The detectives grew impatient as she rambled on, quoting Flaubert pretentiously, and referring repeatedly to God. When they thought she had finished, she read from the manuscript of a book she proposed to write. She only stopped talking when the tape ran out.

Topping and Knupfer came away from the prison feeling drained but elated at having secured confessions to Hindley's part in five murders – a remarkable breakthrough in a case of historic importance. Still, Myra insisted throughout the interviews that she was not on the spot when any of the victims were killed by Brady alone. She was waiting in the vehicle, she was over the hill, or in the next room. 'I think the chances are that she was at all of them,' says Knupfer, though he believed that Myra had been 'absolutely genuine in trying to help us with our inquiry.' His boss was more sceptical. 'All the way through her confession she admitted she was as guilty as Brady, but in a subtle way she was trying to make out that she was not,' concluded Topping. 'I believe she told me just as much as she wanted me to know, and no more.'

She continued to help the police, though, returning to the moors undercover in March 1987, and speaking with officers by telephone from Cookham Wood as they searched for the remains of Pauline and Keith into the summer. Brady was also brought back to the moors, eventually, but he appeared confused. In hospital interviews with DCS Topping, Brady admitted in a roundabout way to killing Pauline and Keith, but Myra was much more helpful to the police. During one phone call she made a remark that caused the search team to look at an area of the moor behind Hollin Brown Knoll. On 1 July 1987, Detective Inspector Geoff Knupfer was a member of a party of three officers doing a line search at this spot, working backwards over the ground, when he made a discovery. 'All of a sudden, we realised there was something there.' Knupfer got down on his hands and knees and moved the earth with his trowel, exposing a white object. 'It was a white plastic stiletto shoe.' It was one of Pauline Reade's shoes, looking as new as the day she bought them. 'And then as we gingerly scraped away a bit more, we realised there was still a foot in it.' Pauline's body had been preserved in the peat for twenty-four years, as if it had been mummified.

They continued to search for Keith Bennett. Myra said that Brady buried the boy in a shallow grave in the soft peat side of a gulley, in or around Shiny Brook. Every time it rained, however, rain water gushed through those gullies in torrents. Knupfer thought it was likely that Keith's body had been washed out of its grave in a storm surge soon after burial in 1964, 'and the moment it becomes exposed it will be predated by foxes and alike'. That was probably why they couldn't find his remains more than twenty years later, despite an exhaustive search. 'All those gullies have been tipped out, from top to bottom, and it's simply not there.'

The police called off the operation. Then Myra got back in touch with Trisha.

27

OLD LOVE, NEW LOVE

When she confessed to her part in the Moors murders Myra risked being charged with the additional crimes, though that also presented her with an opportunity. When the Attorney General decided that it would not be in the public interest to put Brady and Hindley on trial again, for murdering Pauline Reade and Keith Bennett, Detective Chief Superintendent Peter Topping felt that Hindley may have been disappointed not to be able to use a trial as a platform to show the world she had changed. 'When I broke the news to Myra Hindley that there would be no criminal prosecution, she took it calmly and quietly. She was relieved, she said, but I sensed that she was also slightly disappointed . . . I think she secretly hankered after the opportunity to put her case in public.'

By confessing, Myra had alienated some supporters who believed her when she said she knew nothing about the murders. Sara Trevelyan, who spoke up for Myra in the *Brass Tacks* debate, was one friend who felt that her trust had been misplaced. 'When this came to light, I was gutted, sick,' she said. Others saw Myra's belated confession as cynical, even cruel. 'A long, long time later to say, *I'll take you to the moors and show you where the bodies are*, my God, what kind of evil is that?' asks former Holloway guard, Kath Moores, who had never had any time for Myra.

With people turning against her again, Myra reached out to one woman who might forgive her anything, and Trisha Cairns was delighted to hear from her old flame. 'About nine months ago, Myra renewed a relationship with an ex-Holloway officer who was involved in her last court appearance. They have formed a deep relationship. They correspond several times a week, and one visit has taken place between them so far,' a Cookham Wood prison officer reported in April 1990.

Ex-prisoner Janie Jones, another former supporter who had lost faith in Myra since her confession, asked Trisha how she could forgive Myra all the lies she had told. 'At least she's had the guts to admit it after all that time,' Trisha replied, according to Jones's memoir, *The Devil and Miss Jones*. Jones asked Trisha what their reunion had been like. 'I thought she looked older, and I'm sure I do, too. She looked less strong . . . I always looked upon her as a really strong character. It really shocked me.' Jones suggested that Trisha couldn't have the same feelings for Myra. 'Well, in a different way . . . It's not the same as when you first fall in love, is it? Time changes people.' Jones now saw Myra as a manipulative and cruel woman, but Trisha thought this was simplistic. 'I agree with you that there is an amount of cruelness in her, and there is a kind of naïveté as well. A very complex person.'

Trisha's relationship with Myra had always been wrapped up in faith, and Myra showed renewed interest in Roman Catholicism now that they were reunited. A Jesuit priest gave her a course in Ignatian spiritual exercises (named for Ignatius of Loyola, a sixteenth-century saint) which brought her to an audacious conclusion. 'No words of mine could express the deep remorse and regret I feel for what I was involved in over a quarter of century ago, and for the unpardonable length of time it took me to find the courage and the decency to confess my part in these crimes,' she told her Parole Board in 1990. 'I shall forever carry the scars I sustained through the wounds I inflicted, whether in prison or outside. But I believe God has forgiven me, and I try not so much to look at the past, but to the present and the future.'

Despite having said at the time of her 1987 confession that she would not be applying for parole in 1990, not wanting people to think that was her motive, fortified by God's forgiveness Myra did make an application that year, giving an excuse for not confessing sooner. 'She said that she had served many years in prison believing/hoping that denial of the extra offences would be the best policy, and that this served as a shield. Lurid media attention and fabrication added to her resolve, because it also created anguish and anxiety for her gran and her mother,' reported a Parole Board member. The board concluded, however, that Myra's confession was a factor 'against her release not a positive one', partly because it wasn't clear whether she had told the whole truth. Her case would be reviewed in another four years. Behind the scenes, Conservative Home Secretary David Waddington decided that Hindley was one of a small number of egregious offenders in the prison system who would in fact serve a whole-life tariff, meaning that life for her would mean life. But Myra wasn't told that she would never be released.

Trisha was soon introduced to Myra's rich supporter, David Astor, and his wife Bridget, who took her under their wing. Trisha was off work from the buses, having hurt her back, and was no longer enjoying her job. She came to London to be nearer Myra, and the Astors gave her the use of a room in their London home, in Cavendish Avenue, St John's Wood, where their next door neighbour was Paul McCartney. The Astors owned other fabulous houses in Oxfordshire and Cornwall.

Trisha and her dog, Jacob, became part of the family at St John's Wood. A love of dogs was something Trisha shared with Myra, as well as their passion for Wimbledon, which was the one event Myra made a point of watching on television each year. In the summer of 1992, Trisha watched the tennis tournament at Cavendish Avenue with the Astors, who were hospitable and unstintingly generous. They arranged for Trisha to have a telephone and a parking permit, among many favours. Trisha joined campaign meetings with David Astor and Reverend Peter Timms where they discussed furthering Myra's case for parole. Myra wrote to thank the Astors, saying how happy Trisha was with them. She wrote that she and Trisha had started to think of David as a second father, a better man than the drunkard fathers they had.

Myra and Trisha appeared closer than ever during prison visits. Some of the coyness of the past was gone. Myra declared herself to be a lesbian now, and Trisha referred to Myra and herself as lovers.

When Myra's American friend Joan Kleinert visited Britain around this time, it was Trisha who took her and her girlfriend to see Myra. They found her in bed in the health care unit at Cookham Wood. Myra wasn't ill. The governor allowed her to stay in the unit to give her a break from younger inmates who bothered her. The governor, Christine 'Chris' Ellis, was the latest in a series of senior prison officers to see the best in Myra. Ellis had grown up near Myra in Manchester, around the same time. 'We had a lot in common . . . We went to the same swimming baths, complete with cockroaches.' She appreciated Myra's sense of humour, and didn't consider her to be the worst female criminal in the country. 'She didn't actually commit any murders . . . She didn't actually strike the blow,' she says, sharing Myra's belief that the media demonised her and distorted her case. 'There were so many other female prisoners who had committed really bad offences who the media had never heard of, and they got paroled and went trotting off into the blue yonder. But that name Myra Hindley was enough to turn heads, and media companies would pay fortunes for any dirt on Myra.' The governor was sure that Myra was not a danger to society. If the prison had been populated with Myras, running Cookham Wood would have been easy. 'You could go away for a week and leave her to sort herself out.' So she did her best to make Myra's time in Cookham Wood tolerable. She made her a trusty, which meant that Myra spent her days in the kitchen opposite the governor's office. She made the tea, watered the plants and cleaned up.

Governor Ellis met David Astor and Trisha Cairns when they visited Myra, but the women didn't take to one another. Ellis thought Cairns 'a very insignificant person . . . a bit mousy'; while Trisha thought that Myra was obsessed with Ellis, a handsome woman with a commanding personality. 'She had at one point, interestingly, a suspicion that Myra might have been having an affair with Chris Ellis, which is absolutely ridiculous,' says Joe Chapman, who started to work with Myra in 1993. 'Myra and Chris were always together and Myra was always talking about Chris . . . Trish, I wouldn't say she was jealous, but she was always suspicious that something was going on. I said, "If you love Myra, you will trust her and know her governor has taken an interest in her, and is doing more than people have done for many years."'

Joe Chapman was a prison officer from Aylesbury who left the service to work in the charity sector around this time and, with David Astor's financial support, became Myra's private counsellor. This was after Reverend Peter Timms stopped visiting Myra, following what some members of her campaign team now considered to be the disaster of her 1987 confession, which had not worked to her advantage, though Timms was still active behind the scenes. Trisha was soon in touch with Chapman. 'I immediately warmed to her. She was a kind, sensitive, empathic person . . . It was clear that she'd rekindled her relationship with Myra and was back possibly where she was at the very beginning, in terms of loving her and wanting to spend her life with her.'

Myra made her personal situation clear to her counsellor. 'I am a lesbian now and I am happy with that,' she told Chapman. 'However, I am a lesbian through the circumstances of my sentence, so without this I might have settled into a heterosexual relationship with a husband and kids.' She led Chapman to believe that she had never stopped loving Trisha, saying that their love was stronger than ever. 'Clearly, they loved each other. They were happy to see each other,' says Chapman. Myra said she regretted their Holloway escape plan. 'She always said it should never have happened, and Trish should never have involved herself with it, and the plotting and planning that had gone on had been naïve to say the least. And she wished she could turn the clock back, and Trish hadn't had to suffer . . . She was really upset and terribly depressed about the fact that Trisha had ended up [as a prisoner].'

That was behind them, but Myra was just as determined to be a free woman. The new plan was for her and Trisha to live together after she was paroled. Myra had no doubt that she would be paroled, though others thought it less likely. 'Trisha wasn't overly convinced that she was going to get a release, but what she did feel was that while Myra was planning for the future that was keeping her positive,' says Chapman.

The decision was made to buy a property for the couple to live in when parole came, with David Astor's help. Astor wanted a house in London, where Myra would benefit from the anonymity of metropolitan life, and he would be close at hand. A plain, three-bedroom house was purchased in Kinveachy Gardens, Charlton, south east London. Trisha let out her house in the north and moved into the London house under the surname Forrester, giving local people to believe that she was a retired nun. She consulted Myra about the refurbishments. They decided to do the house up like a Tudor cottage, with dark faux beams, plus pink wallpaper with a panic button in the master bedroom. (Myra feared assassination.) Trisha brought catalogues into Cookham Wood for Myra to choose the carpets and curtains.

While the couple planned their future, they couldn't escape the past. Myra had lied to Trisha, who believed her when she said that she was innocent. 'There were things that Trisha wanted to understand about Myra that she never would, because Myra was never going to tell her. As far as [Myra] was concerned, time had moved on. Her words to me were, "I don't need to continuously keep going back into the past and I'm not that woman now, therefore it is irrelevant." To Trish it was very relevant that she didn't know and couldn't clearly state what Myra's involvement in the crimes were,' says Chapman, who discussed this with Trisha over coffee. 'She said, "There's part of me that can't believe what happened, can't believe she had any part in it at all, part of me wants to believe the story she told me about Brady is true: he tortured her into taking part. She took part not of her own volition." But [then] she said, "There's also part of me, knowing Myra, that thinks she would have done [it]." Because Myra was an all or nothing type of person . . . She doubted, really, Myra's sincerity.'

249

★

One day, a Dutch criminologist named Nina Wilde, a boyish woman in her thirties, came to Cookham Wood on work placement, recommended to Governor Ellis by a colleague. Ellis showed Nina around Cookham Wood. It was a small prison, with only 140 inmates, so it wasn't long before they met the governor's trusty.

'Myra, have you met Nina?' asked Ellis, introducing them.

Despite being a criminologist, Nina claimed to have only a vague idea who Myra Hindley was when they met – which had also been Trisha Cairns's story. 'When the governor told me that Myra had been in prison for almost thirty years, I thought there must have been some mistake.' Nina interviewed many inmates in Cookham Wood during her work in the prison, but increasingly she spent her time with Myra, often playing board games with her. Myra loved playing games. She was a fiend at *Scrabble*, and a terror at *Trivial Pursuit*. On Christmas Day 1993, Myra and Nina played *Trivial Pursuit* with Governor Ellis. Myra and Nina also played tennis in the gym, and Nina tried to teach her Dutch. Staff watched the women growing close as they spent so much time together, and Nina became part of the prison community.

Joe Chapman was surprised, however, when Nina was given a bunch of prison keys. 'I said to Chris [Ellis], "Is this a wise move?" Immediately it put the backs of the security department up. [But Nina] thought she had every right to have keys.' There were obvious security concerns, bearing in mind Myra's history with prison keys, and Nina appeared to Joe to be unworldly. 'She was vulnerable. She could have been taken hostage. She didn't have a lot of training,' he says, '[but] she felt she had a right to do what she did, and that the system was all wrong.'

Stories about Nina's friendship with Myra started to leak to the *Sun* newspaper, appearing under the byline of its senior reporter John Kay. In May 1994, Kay reported that Myra had the run of HMP Cookham Wood because of a 'girl on work experience' who had been given keys, and that this Nina Wilde was living in the prison hostel, which was causing disquiet among staff. Myra and Governor Ellis were furious to see stories leaked to the *Sun*. This wasn't the first, and more followed. Ellis thought that they were being targeted. 'Fuck the *Sun*!' she says, still angry about it. They developed a particular loathing for the reporter John Kay, who Myra denounced as an imbecile. The fact that he was getting inside information drove Myra and Nina to distraction, and created paranoia in the prison. Meanwhile, Governor Ellis looked into John Kay's background and discovered that he had a colourful past. Myra started telling people that Kay was a murderer, and that he was projecting his guilty conscience onto her. The truth was slightly different. Kay drowned his wife in the bath in 1977, during a nervous breakdown, then tried to kill himself. The police found him naked and covered in blood. He pleaded guilty to manslaughter due to diminished responsibility and, after a spell in a psychiatric hospital, returned to the *Sun*, where he was made chief reporter but did not go out of the office on stories.

While John Kay focussed his attention on Myra's burgeoning friendship with Nina, Trisha started to feel sidelined. She was receiving fewer visiting orders from Myra, but didn't know the reason. 'Why all of a sudden does she not want visits this weekend?' Trisha asked Joe Chapman, who found himself in an awkward position. 'And of course she didn't want a visit because Nina was [with] her,' he explains. Previously, Myra would also have long telephone conversations with Trisha, talking about their new house. Suddenly she was spending all her phone time talking with Nina, even though she saw her almost every day in the prison. Trisha told Joe that Myra liked to 'collect people'. She had now collected Nina. Myra lost interest in the London house and started to fantasise about going to live in Holland with Nina after she was paroled. That August, Myra and Trisha had a terrible row on the telephone, after which Trisha told friends that Myra had dumped her.

'I am the injured party,' she told Joe. 'I wish I hadn't stepped back into her life.'

Trisha retreated, heartbroken, to Manchester and the London house was put up for sale. The people who bought it thought that the decor Myra had chosen was hideous. Myra couldn't even remember the address of the house, and pretended not to know where Trisha was currently living in order to write to her. Her mind was focussed on Nina, who was now receiving a charitable grant from David Astor. As soon as one grant was spent, Myra pressed Astor to renew it, singing Nina's praises. In September 1994, Astor released a further £4,000 to Nina.

Then the *Sun* ran a story claiming that Nina had been found with Myra in her cell. Nina Wilde said the story was fabricated, and that an investigation cleared her. Nevertheless, the Home Office told Governor Ellis that Nina could not work in the prison any more.

Nina fled to her sister's cottage in Cornwall, pursued by a team from the *Sun*, which then splashed with MYRA'S LESBIAN LOVER SACKED. A week later, the paper was still on Nina's case in Cornwall, one of its photographers snatching a picture of her in the street. As the paper reported, 'She screamed: "I've got nothing to say – Myra Hindley's the one you should be talking to."'

There was an investigation at Cookham Wood into who had been leaking stories, and Governor Ellis came under suspicion. 'I was exonerated finally.' She suspects that somebody high up in the prison department was selling information about Myra to John Kay. 'I didn't trust headquarters.' Once more Hindley was at the centre of chaos and upset. While presenting herself to Governor Ellis as a model prisoner, she had disrupted life in HMP Cookham Wood, just as she did in Holloway, and Trisha had been hurt again. But Myra and Trisha were still not finished with each other.

28

I NEVER CAME TO TERMS WITH IT

It was getting towards Christmas, 1994, when Chris Ellis received a telephone call from the Home Office to inform her that an important, confidential letter was being couriered to HMP Cookham Wood for Myra. She was to stay late to receive it. 'No specifics. But absolute secrecy. Say nothing to anybody.' Such was the distrust between the prison and headquarters by this time, over press leaks, Ellis asked one of her assistant governors, Peter Macklen, to stay behind as her witness.

When the letter arrived, the governor asked Myra to step into her office to receive the news. Myra asked Ellis to open and read the letter to her aloud. It informed Myra that she would never be released from prison. 'She immediately burst into tears,' says Ellis. 'She was pretty distressed.' Although the decision to impose a whole life tariff had been made five years previously, the authorities didn't inform Myra, or the other prisoners affected, until the House of Lords ruled that inmates had to be told. The reason given to Myra for her tariff was expressed in the bland language of the civil service: a whole life tariff was being imposed in her case due to the 'circumstances of the offences in question'.

★

That Christmas, Myra didn't even send Trisha a card. She told their friend, David Astor, that there had been a 'breakdown in communication' between her and Trisha who, she grumbled, never told her what was on her mind. In February, Myra wrote to Trisha to break it off, saying that they should just be friends. She insisted that the breakup had nothing to do with Nina, though her letters to other people were full of references to the Dutch criminologist.

When Myra asked Trisha to return a cassette tape of herself, singing and playing the guitar in Holloway in the 1970s, Trisha wrote an anguished letter to Myra, and shared her feelings with the prison counsellor, Joe Chapman. Trisha said that she knew that Myra gave this cassette tape 'to other lovers beside me'. She accused Myra of betraying her with Nina, and noted how painful it was to have her fears confirmed by reading about the couple in the press. 'Perhaps because she has been out of the real world for so long, she [Myra] can't see that to use me in this way is a pretty low down thing to do,' she complained, as Chapman later reported in his prison memoir, *For the Love of Myra*. 'I was being duped.' Trisha also felt that Myra had misused their friend, David Astor, which was 'unforgivable'. Yet Myra seemed angry with her. If everybody judged Myra as she judged others, she would have no support. 'She has a strange way of showing love, after all that she has put me through for the past sixteen months,' she said, referring to their reunion. So she decided to 'terminate' her relationship with Myra.

When David Astor visited Myra in prison in March she gave him two parcels. When he got home he discovered that Myra had given him the letters that Trisha had written to her.

Embarrassed to be put in such a position, he wrote to ask Myra what he was supposed to do with these letters: destroy them, or pass them to Trisha? Either way Trisha would be 'terribly hurt'. He told Myra that Trisha still asked after her. There is no record that Myra even replied.

Having caused so much discord at Cookham Wood, Myra was transferred back to HMP Durham in 1995, where she almost immediately broke her left leg falling down in the prison yard. 'We heard *snap! snap!* and all went, "What was that?"' says fellow inmate, Linda Calvey, 'looked round, and Myra was really sweating.'

'My leg's just broken.'

Myra was diagnosed with osteoporosis (brittle bones), and spent two weeks in hospital, during which time she had pins and plates inserted in her broken leg. Nina Wilde moved to Durham, with David Astor's financial support. Astor was also now sending Myra £50-a-month pocket money, a sum which would rise as she took increasing advantage of his generosity.

When she started to hobble about H Wing again, Myra needed to lean on a walking stick. She heard that press photographers – 'disgusting creatures', she called them – were competing for a picture of her as a feeble older woman with her broken leg and stick, which would fetch a high price on Fleet Street. Together with angina and hypertension, Myra's health was now poor and it got worse. 'I think she was in constant pain,' says Linda Calvey, who had first met Hindley ten years earlier in Cookham Wood, when Linda was serving a sentence for armed robbery. Linda was now in Durham for murder, and Myra was in her early fifties. 'She looked *twenty* years older,' says Linda. Chain-smoking didn't help. Myra reeked of cigarettes.

Another notorious woman, Rose West, joined H Wing in 1995, following her conviction for ten murders committed at home at 25 Cromwell Street, Gloucester, and a previous address. Myra and Rose struck up a brief friendship in Durham. There was a big age gap – Rose West was eleven years younger than Myra – and they were very different characters. West is a crude woman of limited intelligence, who is quick to lose her temper; whereas Myra was clever, subtle and generally calm. Their cases were strikingly similar, though, and equally unusual. Female serial killers are rare. Furthermore, West and Hindley had taken part in serial murder in cahoots with older male partners, as part of their relationships, committing sadistic sex crimes against young people, whose remains were buried in places of significance to the couples. This very unusual pattern of behaviour put West and Hindley in a criminal class of their own. If Hindley and Brady had married, like Fred and Rose West, and continued killing for twenty years, they might have rivalled the Wests' toll of twelve known victims.

In terms of criminal celebrity, West was the only woman in the prison system to approach Myra Hindley's level of infamy, and fellow inmates treated both women with the deference shown to the famous, mixed with fear and scorn for 'nonces'. 'There is that sort of hierarchy. Myra was It. Until Rose came on the scene,' says Pearl Davison, a Durham restaurateur who voluntarily visited the women on H Wing to monitor conditions for the Home Office. To help win their trust, Pearl would offer the women a cigarette when she came to their cells, and for years she had a regular smoke with Myra in her cell in Durham.

'Do you believe you will ever get out?' Pearl asked her one day.

'Oh, yes, you've got to have something to hang onto,' Myra replied, telling Pearl that she hadn't forgotten how to drive. She believed that she could pick up her life almost where she left it in 1965. Despite the whole life tariff, David Astor and sympathetic lawyers were still agitating for her parole, and she had convinced herself that they would get her out eventually.

Pearl Davison didn't argue. She avoided confrontation with the prisoners. Privately, she agreed with Astor that Myra should be treated the same as any other life sentence prisoner, and given parole if she was no longer a danger to society, after so many years inside; but she didn't believe Myra when she said that Brady had controlled her. She felt that Myra probably derived a sexual thrill from the Moors murders, like Rose West did in Gloucester. Personally, however, Myra remained an enigma even to someone who met her frequently. 'She was hard to read because she was hard,' says Pearl. 'She was a hard-faced person, and I think every question that could have been asked of her had been asked over the years. She was used to it, and she was used to batting them off. She was on her mettle all the time.'

Nina Wilde was also a frequent prison visitor. She and Myra described themselves as 'partners' now, but after Myra got back on her feet they had to meet in the public visits room at HMP Durham with everybody else, and Nina was reduced to tears by people staring at them and making snide comments. Myra wrote to the Chief Inspector of Prisons saying that open visits were making her and Nina miserable, and they required privacy. The stress became too much for Nina. 'Myra saw I was on the edge of a nervous breakdown and suggested we stop the visits,' she wrote in her book, *The Monstering of Myra Hindley*.

Nina then clashed with David Astor and Reverend Peter Timms over Myra's campaign, which caused Myra to turn on Astor, criticising him for talking about her to the media. Astor was stung, reminding Myra that he and his friends had worked tirelessly for her release. 'So we have not done nothing . . . May I suggest one word to you on your future dealings with the public? I think I know how very deeply you feel remorse, and I have greatly admired your struggle to face the truth. My one word is to say that you should find some way of communicating that remorse directly to the public.' Astor was too valuable an ally to alienate for long, and he and Myra were soon reconciled, while Nina faded from the scene.

Myra was moved again, in 1997, to HMP Highpoint, a relatively modern prison that had been built on a former RAF base in rural Suffolk, and she was happier here. 'I love my room. It's much bigger than the average cell, it's a room not a cell with an ordinary door,' she wrote to Pearl Davison, who says that Myra usually wrote to her when she wanted something: in this case Myra needed ink cartridges for her printer, which Pearl was kind enough to post to her. Myra was writing her autobiography on a word processor. She wrote fluently about her childhood, but got stuck when she came to her life with Ian Brady. She still could not deal with their crimes, the memories of which kept her awake at night, as they had for decades. Myra listened to pop music to distract herself. She had Fleetwood Mac playing in her cell when she wrote to Pearl, in 1998, describing an idea she had to arrange the stones in the prison yard into a Japanese-style garden, which she wanted to complement with climbing plants. The governor vetoed that. 'I can't plant anything against the fence or walls that might grow high – for security reasons,' she explained to Pearl. It would be too embarrassing if Myra was to escape finally by climbing a beanstalk.

Life in Highpoint was made more comfortable by the Astors, whom Myra milked for cash and gifts. Astor raised her allowance to £200-a-month in 1998, and paid for curtains for her cell, also buying a duvet for Myra when she said she felt cold at night.

With Nina Wilde less evident, Myra reached out to Trisha Cairns again and asked if they could be friends. Trisha wanted to know first why Myra had treated her so badly when she was at Cookham Wood. Myra struggled to be honest about her infatuation with Nina, but she hoped that she and Trisha could make it up. 'I care deeply about her, and bitterly regret the pain I've caused her in the past,' she told the Astors, adding however that she was sometimes irritated by Trisha's superior attitude. The former nun spoke to her, she grumbled, 'as though I were a naughty child . . . I could never live up to her expectations of me, and her often inflexible high standards.'

Trisha did allow herself to get drawn back into Myra's world, and she was soon running errands for her. She visited Myra's mother, Nellie, now in her seventies, and became Myra's personal shopper, buying comforts and treats for Myra, her mother, and Myra's niece and her children. This became such a financial burden that Trisha told David Astor, in 1999, that she couldn't afford everything that Myra requested. Astor told Trisha to send him the bills. He would pay for whatever Myra wanted. The first monthly bill for items including stamps, a tapestry frame, Easter eggs, a dressing gown for Myra and whisky for her mother, totalled £175. Many more bills followed.

Myra's uncanny ability to persuade people to do things for her was one of her primary personality traits. It was a skill she used to pick up the children who were murdered, but she was just as skilled at manipulating adults in everyday life. She had managed to twist all sorts of people around her finger over the decades she had been behind bars. She had won over powerful men, like David Astor and Lord Longford; also senior prison staff, including Dorothy Wing, Joanna Kozubska and Chris Ellis; not to mention prisoners including Violet Ali, Joan Kleinert and Maxine Croft. Linda Calvey was a former armed robber from east London with a conviction for murdering a man with a shotgun, a formidable and indeed an intelligent woman, but Myra was even able to persuade a tough character like Linda to do things for her. Linda was also in Highpoint now, the third prison she and Myra had shared. Myra convinced Linda that she was too feeble to wash and tint her own hair. Myra said that she 'looked and felt like Basil Brush gone wrong' when white hair showed through at her roots. So Linda agreed to do Myra's hair for her once a month, which meant she was able to study Myra up close in her last years. 'She got very thin and she had high cheek bones. She got quite boney and witchy looking' says Linda, who noticed a marked deterioration since Durham.

One day, when Linda was doing Myra's hair, a call came through from Nellie. Myra asked Linda to talk to her mother. The old woman said that she was pleased that Myra had a friend in Highpoint. Linda shuddered at the thought of being considered 'Myra's friend', but she felt sorry for Nellie, as she explained to the other inmates. 'Can you imagine having to live your life carrying the knowledge you were Myra's mother?'

Myra suffered a brain aneurysm in January 2000, soon after which she revised her will and David Astor increased her allowance to £250-a-month. He also continued to pay for the shopping Trisha did for Myra, and more. There seemed to be no end to Myra's requests, including copious amounts of Old Holborn tobacco, Moonberry Musk body spray and a *Friends* video for herself; also a new sofa for her mother. At the end of the year Myra wrote to Bridget Astor asking her to simply buy Nellie whatever she wanted from a shopping catalogue. The money was not significant to the Astors, but Myra's demands were relentless. David Astor was in his late eighties now. Realising that he would not be able to help Myra much longer, he looked into the possibility of his charitable trust buying a house in Kent where Trisha would be Myra's 'resident guardian' if she was paroled after his death. Despite everything that had happened, Trisha remained the fixed star in Myra's world, as she had been ever since they met in 1970. David hadn't heard from Nina in ages.

David Astor died in 2001, but his death seemed to make little impact on Myra who carried on fighting for her release, now planning with her lawyers to take her case to the European courts. 'It was still going on when she died,' says former Detective Inspector Geoff Knupfer, who had stayed in touch with Myra since the reopening of the Moors investigation in the 1980s. 'She was a one-off. She was a unique personality. She was so manipulative, so intelligent.'

Myra complained of feeling unwell in late 2002 and was taken to the West Suffolk Hospital in Bury St Edmunds, under the name Christine Carlton, her final alias. Security was intense, with prison officers disguised in hospital gowns guarding her death bed. She was visited by the Highpoint chaplain, Father Michael Teader, who gave Myra the last rites. 'She was repentant. Finally, she reached a point of complete confession and acknowledgement of her sin.' Myra died in hospital of pneumonia on 15 November 2002, aged sixty.

Her personal effects were meagre and prosaic, including a plastic rosary, a box of Christmas cards, a pink baseball cap, £501 in cash, and a Westlife CD. Also found in her room was a short note, apparently intended as a forward to her unpublished memoir. 'A major criticism is that I've never publicly expressed remorse for the past. This is partly because I could never come to terms with what I'd done . . .' she wrote, which may have been as close to the truth as she ever got.

The funeral at Cambridge Crematorium was a strange affair. It was held in the dark of the early evening. Uniform police guarded the building, while the press were penned behind crowd barriers, hired by Cambridge City Council. The council also hired floodlights, which allowed photographers to get good pictures of the hearse arriving, in the rain, with Myra's casket visible through the glass side panels. It was greeted with an excited flurry of camera clicks, like the star at a film premiere. While this was going on outside, few mourners were inside the chapel – less than a dozen. Most of the people who had been invited to the funeral chose not to come, including Trisha Cairns, and those who did attend did their best not to be identified.

One year later, Myra's ashes were scattered at Stalybridge Country Park, within sight of the moors that she and Brady had made sinister, and close to where Trisha now lived alone in a neat bungalow with her memories. Meeting Myra in Holloway had shaped and defined Trisha's life. 'She was a good prison officer up to her meeting Myra Hindley,' says her brother-in-law, Stan Ball, shaking his head as if he still can't believe what Trisha did. 'Like anyone who is in love, they are ruled by their heart, aren't they?'

★

Crime, especially murder, is a secret business, and it remains impossible to know for sure the full extent of Myra Hindley's involvement in what happened to the five children and teenagers who were murdered. It is unclear whether she was on the spot with Ian Brady when some or all of their victims were killed, and what if any part she took in the sexual abuse and final snuffing out of their lives. She insisted, perhaps implausibly, that she was never there. He suggested that she was alongside him, and she enjoyed the abuse and murder as he did. The Lesley Ann Downey tape indicates that Hindley may well have been a full participant in every aspect of their crimes, but only Brady and Hindley knew the whole truth. At the very least she was his child catcher, and without her the murders would not have happened.

After Brady and her family, Hindley's friendship with Trisha Cairns may have been the most significant of her life, and it certainly lasted longer than her relationship with Brady, though it was not as intense. Whatever awful things Myra did in her youth, she spent thirty-seven of her sixty years in custody, and she matured as she aged in jail. It is tempting to interpret the story of Myra and Trisha, and their escape plan, as a prime example of Hindley's essential cunning in targeting, deceiving and then using a vulnerable person, as she targeted murder victims. Yet there are intriguing glimpses in this prison story of love for Cairns, who was one of several bright people who, having got to know Hindley in custody, sincerely believed that she was remorseful and deserving of parole, though her view was muddled by her infatuation and by religion. Religious people are shown in this story to be gullible and prone to self-delusion, a weakness Hindley was able to exploit.

Ultimately, Myra Hindley remains a conundrum. There were many sides to this complicated woman, and it is possible that she was capable of enjoying child adduction and murder with Brady in her twenties, but came to regret what they did; and that she loved Trisha Cairns, who loved her back and wanted to think the best of her. Yet Hindley struggled throughout her years in prison to face the truth about her part in the Moors murders, knowing that the whole truth was so terrible that nobody, not even her most devoted friend, might feel able to forgive her, and that the only way she was ever going to get out of prison was by escaping.

POSTSCRIPT
MY WORLD IS GONE

The new Holloway prison, built on the same site as the Victorian jail, soon became equally dirty and dysfunctional, and it closed for good in 2016, with plans to redevelop the land for housing. Nothing remains of the Holloway that Myra Hindley knew save for the trees that grew in the prison yard, including the so-called Hanging Tree, and some items of architectural salvage, including the stone dragons that guarded the gate, which have been taken to the Museum of London.

What happened to the women Hindley knew in HMP Holloway, and the other people caught up in this story, after the events described in this book, is set out below.

Violet Ali received compensation from the Home Office in 1974, at which stage she was in her mid-forties and living in Birmingham. She was never heard from again.

David Astor died in 2001, aged eighty-nine. His widow, Bridget, paid for Myra Hindley's funeral, and was one of her few mourners. She died in 2019. David Astor's archive, at the Bodleian Libraries in Oxford, reveals his unstinting support for and financial generosity to Hindley, which she took full advantage of.

Paul Barr went on to serve on the Flying Squad, and with the anti-terrorist branch of the Metropolitan Police. After leaving the police, he worked as a driving instructor, and then retired to France where he keeps cocker spaniels.

Veronica Bird, OBE had an illustrious career in the Prison Service, becoming governor of HMP New Hall. In retirement, she gives talks about her prison experiences, and of all the prisoners she encountered in her career the one she is asked about most often is Myra Hindley. 'They say she should have been hung. I have to explain hanging had finished,' she says. 'Then they say, *Did she ever really apologise? Did she ever confess to what she did?* And they want to know what happened to her ashes . . . People are horrified to think they could be anywhere near the body of that little boy [Keith Bennett], haunting that child.'

Ian Brady spent the rest of his life in secure psychiatric hospitals, having been declared insane. Despite being a chain-smoker, and trying to starve himself to death, he outlived Hindley by many years, finally dying in 2017, aged seventy-nine.

Dr Megan Bull remained the governor of Holloway until 1982, and was awarded an OBE. Her husband, Professor Graham Bull, was an eminent physician and when he was knighted Megan became Lady Bull. She died in 1995.

Patricia 'Trisha' Cairns lives under a different name, not far from Saddleworth Moor. She declines to speak about Myra Hindley, or the escape plot.

Carole Callaghan fell out with Myra after she sold stories about her to the press. Twice married, with three children,

Carole gave up crime in later life, save for some occasional shoplifting. She died in 2016, aged seventy-three.

Linda Calvey's first husband was shot dead by the police in 1978, after which Linda took up armed robbery. In 1991, she was convicted of murdering her boyfriend, Ron Cook, after a contract killer she had hired failed to do the job, and she subsequently became known as the Black Widow. 'I like to think I am actually a nice person.' Since leaving prison, Linda has launched a new career as a crime writer.

Joe Chapman stopped counselling Myra Hindley in 1995, after becoming concerned that she wasn't facing up to her past, and that she was deceiving Trisha Cairns.

Maxine Croft went straight after Holloway, and lives under another name by the sea. Many of the women she knew in prison in her youth are dead, some having died in tragic and bizarre circumstances. 'One got chopped up. One hanged herself, apparently in a telephone box, if you can believe that,' she says. 'My world has diminished. It's gone.' She is estranged from her brother, Dennis.

Pearl Davison was the chairman of the board of visitors at HMP Durham for more than ten years. 'It took over my life.' She no longer visits prisoners, but still enjoys a cigarette.

John Dixon rose to the rank of inspector in the Metropolitan Police, and saw policing change enormously during his career. 'When I joined the police, in 1969, guys were moaning that they had to use a biro to do their notes, because prior to that they [could] do them in pencil. The job will never be the same!'

Chris Ellis (now Duffin) retired from the Prison Service in her fifties, and is currently restoring a branch railway station in Warwickshire.

Angela Glynn remarried and lived latterly in Dorset. She retained a poor opinion of her former neighbour, Trisha Cairns. She died in 2017, aged eighty-nine.

Janet Harber worked for the Prison Service until she retired. She died in 2005, aged sixty-four. She never spoke about Trisha Cairns.

Bob and **Nellie Hindley** divorced in 1966, and Bob became estranged from the family. Their younger daughter, Maureen, died in 1980, aged thirty-three. Bob died soon afterwards. Nellie never stopping loving Myra. 'Myra was a lovely girl, and she is a lovely woman. When they call her a beast, or the Devil, they don't know what they are talking about,' she said in 1985. But she thought it best that her daughter remain in prison. She died not long after Myra.

Winnie Johnson, the mother of Keith Bennett, died in 2012. Keith's remains have never been found.

John Kay was arrested in 2012 as part of Operation Elveden, the police investigation into journalists making payments to public officials in exchange for information. He stood trial at the Old Bailey, accused of paying a civil servant £100,000, and was cleared, but his source went to jail. Kay died in 2021.

Patrick Kilbride, the father of John Kilbride, who threatened to kill Myra Hindley if she was released, died in 1999.

His wife, Sheila, died three years later. Their son, Danny, who confronted Cairns on a bus, died in 2011.

Joan Kleinert changed her name to Sage Mountainfire after she returned to the United States. 'I didn't go back to prison [or] become a drug smuggler again!' She worked instead as a teacher, and at an animal shelter, before retiring to live with her partner in a house they built in a remote part of California.

Geoff Knupfer, MBE retired as a detective chief superintendent and has remained busy, latterly working as a consultant forensic scientist in Northern Ireland with the Independent Commission for the Location of Victims' Remains.

Joanna Kozubska left Holloway in 1973 to work in other prisons. In retirement, she wrote a memoir, *Cries for Help*, which gives an insight into her relationship with Myra Hindley. She was one of a small number of prison officers who continued to visit and correspond with Hindley, and one of very few people invited to her funeral. She died in 2015.

Lord Longford remained Myra Hindley's most high-profile supporter, though she came to consider him as more of a hindrance than a help, and she said she would scream if he ever described her again as a 'good religious woman'. Acknowledging that some sections of the media considered him to be a 'nutter', Longford preferred to be remembered as 'the outcasts' outcast'. He was ninety-five when he died in 2001.

Ellen Maybury lived with her granddaughter Myra up to her arrest, latterly at 16 Wardle Brook Avenue, where she was upstairs in bed on the night that Edward Evans was murdered in the room below. Brady said that Granny Maybury was 'selectively deaf'. She died two years after the murder trial.

Frank McGuinness was promoted to commander and received the Queen's Police Medal. He retired to Seaford, on the coast of East Sussex, where he continued to enjoy his pipe and classical music, but cut back on the whisky. He died in 2013, aged eighty-seven.

Mary McIntosh gave a statement to the police about her Wimpy bar meeting with Trisha Cairns, and said that she spoke to Cairns again afterwards, when she asked after Hindley. No action was taken against her. She later became the head of the sociology department at the University of Exeter, and died in 2013.

Anna Mendleson of the Angry Brigade was released from prison after five years, claiming that her case was a miscarriage of justice. She moved to Cambridge, where she wrote poetry under the pen name Grace Lake. She died in 2009, aged sixty-one.

Kath Moores worked as a telephonist after she left HMP Holloway, and says that she is amazed to learn all that had been going on in the prison during her time there. 'I must have been going round Holloway with me head in the sand.' She lives in retirement in the north of England.

Josephine 'Josie' O'Dwyer was sent to HMP Styal after she attacked Hindley in Holloway. She was paroled in 1977, and diagnosed as paranoid schizophrenic. Imprisoned again for murder, she died in Bullwood Hall in 1997, aged forty-one.

Gail Payne remarried after serving her sentence and moved abroad.

Zoe Progl wrote a book about her life of crime, and her escape from Holloway, *Woman of the Underworld*, published in 1964, which ends with her thanks to the governor for persuading her to go straight. She was never heard from again.

Joan Reade suffered with mental-health issues and spent time in a psychiatric hospital after the Moors murder case, but the police finding her daughter Pauline's remains in 1987 helped her to make a recovery. She died in 2000, five years after her husband, Amos.

Trevor Scoble retired from the police to live in Spain, where he remains garrulous good company. 'Anything I'm involved in is going to be hilarious.'

David Smith was jailed for three years, in 1969, for stabbing a man, after which Myra Hindley's sister Maureen left him. In 1972, he was convicted of manslaughter for the mercy killing of his father, for which he was given a nominal two-day sentence. He lived latterly in Ireland where he died in 2012, aged sixty-four.

George Stephens disappeared shortly after the Holloway conspiracy, later admitting to members of his family that he went to prison (for an unrelated matter). He was soon back to his old tricks, with a spell as a dodgy mini-cab driver. The police seemingly turned a blind eye to the fact that he didn't hold a cab licence. He contracted lung cancer and died in 1985, aged fifty-two.

Sir Melford Stevenson died in 1987, aged eighty-five. 'Regarded as one of the legal profession's most robust characters, the name of his house in Sussex, Truncheons, symbolised his singular blend of judicial toughness and humour,' wrote his *Daily Telegraph* obituarist.

Lyn Summers returned to the west country after her torrid time in London. She trained as a chef, and ran a small catering company near Bristol. 'She had a robust business for some time, but sadly she became unwell with cancer and died young [in 2003],' says her sister Jane.

Phil Thomas retired from the Metropolitan Police soon after finding the Holloway key impressions. He and his wife, Mary, took up bowling in retirement and continued to enjoy a busy social life, but they were not as close as they had been with George Stephens. Uncle Phil died in 1993, aged seventy-four.

Reverend Peter Timms continues to argue, in his nineties, that Myra Hindley should have been treated the same as any other life sentence prisoner, and rejects any suggestion that she manipulated her supporters.

Peter Topping wrote a book about the reopening of the Moors inquiry, but ran into legal problems with the result that *Topping* was withdrawn from circulation. It remains, however, an indispensable account of Hindley's confessions. Topping shunned the media in later life and died in 2020, aged eighty.

Ann West, the mother of Lesley Ann Downey, campaigned tirelessly against Myra Hindley's release, becoming her greatest enemy. She died before Hindley, in 1999, aged sixty-nine, having promised to pursue her if possible even after death. 'I will still be a thorn in her side after I pass on, I will haunt that woman.'

Carol White continued to get in trouble, and was last arrested for being drunk and disorderly in her sixties. 'She was a character,' says her daughter, Louise, who shocked her mother to her core when she told her that she was joining the police force. Carol died in 2015, aged seventy.

Nina Wilde wrote an unrevealing book, *The Monstering of Myra Hindley*, about her partner, in which she is critical of the press, which she has largely avoided.

Dorothy Wing went to live with her sister in Herefordshire after she retired as governor of Holloway prison. 'I always tried to help and rehabilitate the girls, and not prolong the agony of making them pay endlessly for the crime they had committed.' This well-meaning woman died in 1993, aged eighty-four.

ACKNOWLEDGEMENTS

My thanks to the following retired police officers who worked on the Holloway prison investigation: Paul Barr, John Dixon, Mike Pearce and Trevor Scoble. Thanks also to Catherine McGuinness, daughter of the late DCS Frank McGuinness; and to Phil Thomas and Jo Ross, children of the late DCI Phil Thomas; also former Detective Superintendent Alec Edwards, who attended the 1974 conspiracy trial (when he was a DS); and former Detective Chief Superintendent Geoff Knupfer, MBE, number two on the Moors investigation in the 1980s (when he was a DI).

I am grateful to former HMP Holloway prisoners Maxine Croft and Joan Kleinert; also 'Susan' and 'Bernadette'; and Linda Calvey who knew Myra Hindley in three prisons. Thanks also to: Maxine Croft's brother, Dennis; Carole Callaghan's daughter, Laurel; and Carol White's daughter, Louise.

Thanks to former members of Holloway staff: Muriel Allen, MBE, Veronica Bird, OBE, Monica Carden, Judy Gibbons and Kath Moores; also Deirdre 'Dee' Bird, daughter of the late Angela Glynn; the family of the late Janet Harber (her sister-in-law, Maureen Harber, and niece, Susie Forward); and Jane Smith, sister of the late Lyn Summers. Other retired prison staff who spoke to me include: Joe Chapman, Chris Duffin (formerly Ellis), Peter Macklen and Margaret Middlemiss. Thanks also to prison visitor Pearl Davison.

Julie Wilson and Ian Stephens spoke about their late father, George, the Essex salvage man. I am also grateful to: Trisha Cairns's brother-in-law, Stan Ball; Pat Garvey (*née* Cummins), one of the last people to see Pauline Reade alive, and her husband, Ged Garvey; and Trish Gooch, who bought the Charlton house.

Father Vincent Coyne and Anselm Nye helped me with the Carmelites. I also spoke to the late Father Michael Teader, Hindley's priest at HMP Highpoint.

I am grateful to several people whom I met while producing a television documentary about Myra Hindley in 2020: Dr Tom Clark of Sheffield University, who has made a study of Hindley's files in the National Archives; Reverend Peter Timms; producer Melissa Mayne; and Dan Chambers at Blink Films.

For general research, thank you to the staff at the National Archives at Kew; the British Library, London; and Bodleian Libraries in Oxford, which hold David Astor's archive. Thanks also to: Duncan McCormick, local history librarian at Salford Museum; Bob Fenton of the Association of Ex-CID Officers of the Metropolitan Police; and James Hyman of HYMAG, custodian of the Hans Tasiemka Archive since the death of our friend, Edda Tasiemka.

Finally, thank you to Vicky Eribo and her colleagues at Seven Dials; and to Gordon Wise at Curtis Brown.

NOTES

Public records, including police, prison and Home Office files, have been an important resource for this book, complemented by the recollections of surviving witnesses and other sources. Where I use a public record from the National Archives in Kew, I give the file reference in the following source notes (DPP [Director of Public Prosecutions] 2/5366/2, for example, being one important file) and often further information that identifies the relevant document/s in the file. Where I quote someone I have spoken to, I identify the quote as 'to author'. I've changed the names of a couple of living individuals, as marked in the text, and abbreviated their references accordingly. The Archive of David Astor refers to his papers at the Bodleian Libraries in Oxford, used with permission.

Evidence from the 1966 Moors murder trial is from contemporaneous court reports in the press, and/or the trial transcript published as *The Moors Murders: The Trial of Myra Hindley and Ian Brady*, by Jonathan Goodman, which I refer to as 'Goodman' in these notes. 'Topping' refers to Peter Topping's 1989 book, *Topping: The Autobiography of the Police Chief in the Moors Murder Case*, which contains Hindley's belated confessions to the murders. A detailed account of Brady's often contradictory version of events is in *Ian Brady: The Untold Story of the Moors Murders* by Dr Alan Keightley. (Brady's own 2001 book, *The Gates of Janus*, reveals nothing about the murders.)

'McGuinness' is DCS Frank McGuinness, the senior investigating officer in the 1973–74 conspiracy case. Like many of the police officers in this book, McGuinness attained higher rank later in his career, but I stick with the ranks of officers at the time of the events.

Quotations from television programmes, newspapers, books and other publications are individually identified. Full publication details of books I referred to are listed in the bibliography.

MYRA HINDLEY IN LOVE

1 Muriel Clarke reports Violet Ali: Clarke's 26.3.21 statement, DPP 2/5336/2.
1 'full of remorse . . . tell the truth': *ibid*.
1 Ali speaks to Browning: Ali's March 1971 disciplinary case, DPP 2/5366/2.
1 Leissner's background: *Cries for Help* (Kozubska).
2 'Did you know Hitler, Miss?': Maxine Croft to author.
2 'You know it is . . .' and Ali's reply: Leissner's 26.4.71 evidence to governor, DPP 2/5336/2.
2 'About seven months . . .': Ali's 23.3.71 statement, DPP 2/5336/2.

WE'VE ONLY JUST BEGUN

3 'built-in depression': Chris Duffin (formerly Ellis) to author.
3–4 Dorothy Wing background: author interviews; ATS records; *Cries for Help* (Kozubska); and Hindley's profile of Mrs Wing in *Behind the Times* (Issue 2, 1973), in which the governor describes Holloway as 'terribly grim'.
4 HMP Holloway background: thanks to Veronica Bird (quoted).
4 'The place stank . . .': *ibid*.

5 'highly dangerous': *Bad Girls* (Davies).

6 'Though I believe . . . normal sort of girl': Justice Fenton Atkinson letter 8.5.66 to Home Secretary, HO 336/48.

6 'She looked very pale . . .': Veronica Bird to author.

7 'gate fever': Hindley's 5.12.70 letter to Longford, HO 336/44.

7 'Who is that?': Carole Callaghan in *Myra Hindley: The Prison Years* (Granada Productions, 2006).

7 'She's nice': *ibid*.

7 Callaghan background: thanks to her daughter, Laurel Reid; also Callaghan interview, *Sunday People*, 31.10.71.

8 'When you are in prison . . .': Callaghan in *Man Alive* (BBC, 1972).

8 'She stood out . . . in those days as well': Cairns in *The Lost Boy* (Staff).

8 Naked in cell: *ibid*.

9 'Open up . . .': *Myra Hindley: The Prison Years* (Granada Productions, 2006).

9 Friendship formed: various statements and documents, DPP 2/5366/2.

10 'I'm afraid . . .': Veronica Bird to author.

10 Cairns returns to cell, 'I love you . . .': *The Lost Boy* (Staff).

TENDRILS OF POISON

11 Callaghan's prison visits: thanks to Laurel Reid.

11 'A prison officer must . . .': Mrs Wing to the *Daily Express*, 4.4.74.

12 'all that this woman has accused . . . fabricated nonsense': Cairns's 26.3.71 statement, DPP 2/5366/2.

13 Exhuming remains: *Bad Girls* (Davies).

13 'It may be irrelevant . . . to the contrary': Hindley's 23.3.71 statement, DPP 2/5366/2.

14 'considerable spiritual help . . .': *ibid*.

15–16 Gorton background: thanks to former residents, Pat and Ged Garvey.

15 'I disliked him intensely . . .': Hindley in the *Guardian*, 18.12.95.

16 'You get quite shrewd . . .': Chris Duffin (formerly Ellis) to author.

16 'I had a wide circle . . .': Hindley in *Verdict*, Oxford Law Society magazine, Hilary (term) 1986.

16 Cairns's background: thanks to her brother-in-law, Stan Ball.

16-17 'He was always . . .': Ball to author.

17 'Her childhood was marred . . .': Cairns's 29.3.94 social enquiry report: J 267/447.

17 Salford monastery: thanks to Father Coyne, Our Lady of Dolours, Kersal.

17 Cairns claimed little knowledge of Moors case: *The Lost Boy* (Staff).

17 'Sherlock Holmes would . . .': *Life*, 2.11.65.

18 'There would be a grille . . .': Coyne to author.

18 Cairns decides to leave monastery: her Old Bailey barrister (*Evening News*, 1.4.74); and papers in J 267/447.

18 'I was never sure . . .': Margaret Middlemiss to author.

18-19 'A true Christian . . . wrong road here': Ball to author.

THE VISITING COMMITTEE

21 'She was a pretty . . .': Ali to *Daily Mirror*, 3.4.74.

21 'I used to pretend . . .': Ali's initial 1971 interview with Wing, DPP 2/5366/2.

22 'I think you must . . . proved it': *ibid*.

22 Ali background: *Coventry Evening Telegraph*, 11.11.69; *Guardian*, 3.4.97; and *Sun*, 3.4.74.

22 'They came in . . .': Monica Carden to author.

23 'Dear Governor . . .': 1971 letter, DPP 2/5366/2.

24 'Do you remember . . .' etc (VC dialogue): transcript of 11.5.71 VC, DPP 2/5366/2.

26 Hindley requests 'holy pictures' and an interview with the governor: Holloway 'history sheets' entries 18.5.71 and 19.5.71, HO 336/126.

THIS WOMAN

27 Payne murder case: *The Times*, 7.3.69; and *Daily Mirror*, 13.3.69.

27 Cairns seen to pass note, and Payne's dialogue with officers, 'What note?' etc: July 1971 Holloway reports including Briggs's 27.7.71 statement, DPP 2/5266/2.

28 'I was shocked . . .': Payne's 27.7.71 statement to governor, DPP 2/5366/2.

28 'I can only suggest . . .': Cairns's 31.7.71 written denial, DPP 2/5366/2.

28 'I know she [Cairns] was . . .': undated letter from Wing to Joanna Kozubska, *Cries for Help*.

28 'this woman': in prison accident reports, for example, 'This woman stated . . .', HO 336/94.

29 'I was sat . . .' and dialogue with Hindley: Kath Moores to author.

30 'People on her wing . . . bit sharp': *ibid.*

30 Cairns at Bullwood Hall: various prison and DPP files; also author interviews with former colleagues.

30 'We probably had . . .': Margaret Middlemiss to author.

31 'I saw people . . .': Maxine Croft to author.

31 'There was a gay community . . .': Middlemiss to author.

31 'We had one or two . . .': Monica Carden to author.

32 Janet Harber background: family to author; DCS McGuinness's 1974 overview of conspiracy case, DPP 2/5366/2.

32 'She kept herself . . .': Maureen Harber to author.

32 'The governor tried . . .': Carden to author.

32 'I know a lot of . . . ': Middlemiss to author.

32 'I think she was . . .': Judy Gibbons to author.

33 'The above named . . .': governor's memo 4.8.71, HO 336/127.

34 Glenis Moores correspondence: Officer Storrow's 21.1.74 statement (J 267/447) and DCS McGuinness's 1974 overview, DPP 2/5366/2.

IAN AND MYRA

35 'Well, Myra . . .': Brady 12.5.66 letter to Hindley: *Ian Brady* (Keightley).

36 'Wonder if Ian is courting . . .': extracts from Hindley's diary appear in various sources including Topping.

36 Brady a poor kisser: Topping.

37 'Ian is so gentle . . .': Hindley diary entry quoted in *Ian Brady* (Keightley).

37 'I have seen Death . . .': *Brady & Hindley* (Harrison).

38 Hindley intelligent and unlikely to escape: Dorothy Wing memo 2.7.69, HO 336/48.

38 Sex with Brady: Topping.

38 'He did many other . . . over my body': 3.6.98 Hindley letter, Archive of David Astor.

39 'Within months he had . . .': Topping.

39 'We never saw . . .': Pat Garvey (*née* Cummins) to author.

40 Photo album: National Archives, ASSI 84/430.

40 Brady practiced carrying Hindley: 3.6.98 Hindley letter, Archive of David Astor.

41 'Pauline always had . . . grown up with them': Pat Garvey (*née* Cummins) to author.

41–42 Reade murder: *Cause of Death* (Garrett); police overview (HO 336/48); Topping; and the *Criminologist*, August 1968.

42 'You won't need that . . .': Topping.

42 'That's her mother . . .': *ibid.*

43 'I loved him . . .': Hindley trial evidence, 3.5.1966, Goodman.

43 '[She] was designated . . .': Father Kahle, *Daily Express*, 15.9.72.

43 Kahle not a supporter: Cairns's letter 2.9.92 to David Astor, Archive of David Astor.

44 Sisters Eileen and Sophie contact Hindley: visit requests 1972–73, DPP 2/5366/2.

44 'She was desperately anxious . . .': *Avowed Intent* (Longford).

44 'The truth of the matter . . .': Hindley's letter 5.12.70 to Longford, HO 336/44.

44 Brady's repeated reading of *A Christmas Carol*: Ian Brady (Keightley).

45 'It was obvious . . . young person': *Avowed Intent* (Longford).

45 'good religious woman': Longford in the *Sunday People*, 21.8.94, for example.

45 'agonizing' decision: 13.3.72 Hindley letter quoted in *Ian Brady* (Keightley).

45 'Carpe diem' bookmark: Brady prison file HO 336/946.

45 'Ian Brady returned . . .': 1972 Holloway overview, HO 336/120.

45 'I wish . . .': Hindley in *Sunday Times*, 27.7.75.

46 Downgraded: Hindley 'security sheets' including 8.6.72 memo from Mrs Wing to the Home Office, 'She also requested . . .' (HO 336/127).

D WING

47 Hindley moved to D Wing: Storrow's statement 21.1.74, DPP 2/5366/1.

48 Light left on: by the account of several people, including Janie Jones in her book, *The Devil and Miss Jones*.

48 D Wing routine: thanks to Veronica Bird.

48 'It was horrible . . .': Bird to author.

48 'jail rot': *When the Gates Shut* (Kelley).

48 'It was lovely . . . Ugh!': Joan Kleinert to author.

49 Kleinert's case: Kleinert to author.

49 'I remember a time . . . incredible fantasy': *ibid.*

51 John Kilbride's disappearance: witness evidence in murder trial, including Mrs Kilbride on her son's appearance, and John Ryan on last seeing Keith in the market.

51 Firearms: *Criminologist*, August 1968. Trial evidence on 25.4.66 fixed the acquisition of firearms between midsummer and early autumn, 1963, but Brady insisted it was the following year (Goodman).

52 'He often . . .': 3.6.98 Hindley letter, Archive of David Astor, MS 15363/292.

52–54 Murder of Kilbride: trial evidence (Goodman); Hindley's later account in Topping and Brady's version in *Ian Brady* (Keightley). Additional detail: author's local enquiries; and thanks to Geoff Knupfer.

54 'Take that, you bastard!': *Ian Brady* (Keightley).

55 'Not growing up . . .': Kleinert to author.

55 D Wing activities and *Behind the Times*: thanks to Kleinert, who supplied copies of the magazines to the author.

56 'Everyone was aware . . . already been done': *Cries for Help* (Kozubska).

56 'It was delicious!': Kleinert to author.

57 'Why would she . . . that angers me': Maxine Croft to author.

A WALK IN THE PARK

59 'She said, "I want you . . ."': Kozubska, *Inside Holloway: Rebels and Murderers,* Channel 5, 2020.

59 'The problem for Myra . . .': *Cries for Help* (Kozubska).

60 'The door opened . . .': *ibid*.

61 'Doesn't it smell beautiful!' etc: recalled by Mrs Wing to *Daily Express*, 14.9.72.

61 Mrs Wing's other outings: Wing to *Daily Express*, 4.4.74.

62 'I was on holiday . . .': *Daily Express*, 14.9.72.

63 Bennett murder: police files (HO 336/48); author's local enquiries; Hindley's later version in Topping.

63 Hindley's Morris: evidence by Robert Rogers, of the road tax department, at the murder trial, 26.4.66 (Goodman); also photographs of the vehicle, ASSI 84/430.

64 'I couldn't keep her away . . .': *Ian Brady* (Keightley).

64 'It was probably . . .': Topping.

65 'How could she not . . .': Joan Kleinert to author.

ERROR OF JUDGEMENT

67 'MOORS KILLER SENSATION': *Daily Express*, 13.9.72.

67 'This sounds like . . .': *ibid*.

67 'How can . . .': *ibid*.

68 'Hindley enjoyed the walk . . . with her': *Daily Express*, 14.9.72.

68 Kray twins cartoon: *Evening Standard*, 14.9.72.

68 'Myra Hindley has on . . .': *Hansard*, 14.9.72, HO 336/338.

69 Mrs West letter to Home Secretary, 13.9.72, HO 336/191.

69–72 Lesley Ann Downey's abduction and ordeal: police records; tape transcript reported in *The Times*, 27.4.66, and Goodman; plus witness evidence in the murder trial.

73 Hindley's later version of events: Topping.

73 'We all got dressed . . .': 30.4.66 *Daily Express* court report of Brady's evidence. Also Goodman transcript.

73 'flood of light . . .': judge's summing up, Goodman.

74 'I was very tense . . .': Hindley's evidence, 3.5.66, Goodman.

74 'She said, "Do you . . ."': 7.10.65 witness statement of David Smith, *The Medico-Legal Journal*, 1968. NB: it was not

established for certain which crime the police nearly interrupted when they stopped to speak to Hindley on the road, but judging by what Hindley told Smith it seems likely that Brady was digging Downey's grave.

75 'If Myra Hindley leaves . . .': *Daily Mirror*, 14.9.72.

75 'The Home Secretary has no . . .': Home Office to Mrs West, 29.9.72, HO 336/191.

75 'error of judgement': *Daily Express*, 14.9.72.

75 'I think . . .': Kath Moores to author.

75 'Dorothy Wing alone . . .': *Cries for Help* (Kozubska).

76 Christmas 1972 on D Wing: *Behind the Times,* Issue No. 2, 1973.

76 Dr Bull background: *Dictionary of Ulster Biography*; National Portrait Gallery collections; also thanks to Judy Gibbons.

76 'As a prisoner . . . at the least': Mrs Wing 1.12.72 handover report, HO 336/44.

LITTLE MAX

79 'I supported her . . . never be released': *Cries for Help* (Kozubska).

79 'You have this special . . .': *ibid*.

79 Day one: conspiracy indictment, J 267/446.

80 D Wing meeting and quote 'Perhaps due to . . .': *Behind the Times,* Issue No. 2, 1973.

80 Cairns's exam: social report, J 267/447.

80 'Cairns told me . . . Myra had sent her': Taylor (name changed) statement (DPP 2/5366/2 quoted). Background: Storrow's statement 20.11.73, DPP 2/5366/2.

81 'I think in a way . . . speaking to': Judy Gibbons to author.

82 'Although many people . . . pen friend': Dr Bull's response to Hindley's 29.12.72 application to correspond with Kleinert, HO 336/19.

82 'The governor there . . .': Maxine Croft to author.

83 Maxine Croft background: Maxine and Dennis Croft to author; National Archives; 26.3.74 social enquiry report by Valerie Haig Brown (J 267/447 [quoted]); evidence in the 1974 conspiracy trial; Croft's account of her life to *Titbits*, 7.11.74 and 14.11.74. Thanks also to retired prison staff and to Trevor Scoble.

83 'a little devilment . . . bit of an oddball': Dennis Croft to author.

83 '[Grace] got up . . .': *ibid*.

83 'I remember . . . press charges' etc: Maxine Croft to author.

85 'She had just . . .': Dennis Croft to author.

85 'It didn't bother me . . .' etc: Maxine Croft to author.

85 'She lacks . . .': 26.3.74 report by Valerie Haig Brown, J 267/447.

85–86 Croft dialogue with prison officer: Croft to author.

87 Croft made green-band: Storrow's 20.11.73 statement, J 267/446.

87 'I've long believed . . .': Chris Duffin (formerly Ellis) to author.

87 'She was like . . .': Croft to author.

88 'The next day I . . .': Croft's 6.11.73 statement, J 267/447.

88 'She had pictures . . .': Croft to author.

88 'Myra then became very friendly . . .': Croft's 6.11.73 statement, J 267/447.

89 Handkerchief incident (including Croft quote): *Titbits* 14.11.74.

MYRA SPENCER

91–92 Name changes: 27.2.76 Holloway letter to Home Office, HO 336/127.

92 Driving licence application: prosecution exhibits No. 19–21 in the 1974 conspiracy trial, including 3.2.73 letter from

Chronell & Fitzpatrick to the Drivers Licensing Department confirming change of name (Exhibit No. 21, DPP 5366/1).

92 Hindley's new car: murder trial evidence, 25.4.65, Goodman.

93–96 Edward Evans murder: 1966 trial evidence; police records, including case overview (HO 336/48); David Smith's initial police statement as reported by William Mars-Jones, QC in *The Medico-Legal Journal* (Part One, 1968); what Hindley later told Peter Topping (*Topping*), and what Brady later told Dr Keightley (*Ian Brady*).

94 'killing clothes': *Ian Brady* (Keightley).

94 Smith a 'head case': Ged Garvey to author.

94 'people are maggots': Smith cross-examined in court, 22.4.66, Goodman.

95 'I heard . . .': Smith's initial statement, *The Medico-Legal Journal* (Part One, 1968).

95 Brains on floor: attorney general in court 29.4.65, Goodman.

96 'We placed . . . you hit him'": Smith's statement, *The Medico-Legal Journal* (Part One, 1968).

96 'Then she got up . . .' etc: *ibid.*

97 'There is nothing wrong . . . the keys' (dialogue with police): police overview, HO 336/48; and trial evidence.

98 'You fucking murderer!': introduction to *The Moors Murders: The Trial of Myra Hindley and Ian Brady* (Goodman).

98: 'Destroy all Lists': 2.5.66 trial evidence, Goodman.

98 Longford, Hindley and Lord Hunt: Longford's letter 5.7.73, HO 336/19.

99 'politically inspired cautiousness': 28.6.73 letter from Hindley to Longford, HO 336/19.

99 OU application: Hindley's 1.4.74 court statement, *Guardian*, 2.4.74.

99 'absolutely ballistic': Maxine Croft to author.

99 'The fact that . . . I asked her to help': Hindley's 1.4.74

statement, *Guardian*, 2.4.74.

ESCAPE PLANS

101 'The first duty . . .': Joanna Kelley in her book, *When the Gates Shut*.

101 'We were first . . . never be free': Cairns's 20.11.73 statement, J 267/447.

102 'Maxine Croft is a friend . . .': *ibid*.

102 'By this time there was . . .': Croft's 6.11.73 statement, J 267/447.

102 'They're never going to . . . How?': Croft to author.

103 Historical escapes: *Bad Girls* (Davies); *Gangland 2* (Morton); and *Holloway Prison* (Camp).

103 'the wicket-gate . . .': *The Wind in the Willows* (Grahame).

103 'the first woman ever . . .': *Woman of the Underworld* (Progl).

103 The prison wall was eighteen feet high: *When the Gates Shut* (Kelley).

104 'inveterate criminal': *Woman of the Underworld* (Progl).

104 'As I scrambled . . .': Progl's 1960 escape and her quotes: *Woman of the Underworld* (Progl).

105 'Various plans were discussed . . .': Cairns's 20.11.73 statement, J 267/447.

105 Cairns considered the back door: Janet Harber's statement 28.1.74, J 267/446.

105 Security arrangements: 20.11.73 statement by Chief Officer Storrow, J 267/446.

105 'You were locked in . . .': Monica Carden to author.

106 'I said, *It's wide* . . .': Croft to author.

107 'Myra was like . . .': *ibid*.

107 '[Trisha] asked me . . .': Croft's 6.11.73 statement, J 267/447.

107 'You can't prove . . . tough person': Croft to author.

108 'I suggested going . . . missionary work': Cairns's 20.11.73 statement, J 267/447.

108 'I think she had . . .': Croft to author.

108 '[Myra] said she was worried . . .': Croft's 20.11.73 statement, J 267/447.

109 Glenis Moores letters stop: Storrow's 21.1.74 statement, J 267/447.

PHOTOGRAPHING MYRA

111 'I would be given . . .': Croft's 6.11.73 statement, J 267/447.

112 Old prison uniform: thanks to Veronica Bird.

112 Kodak Pocket Instamatic: police exhibit No. 39, DPP 2/5366/1; also advertising material from the time.

112 Croft hides camera in bra, etc: Croft to author; 1974 trial evidence; and *Titbits* 7.11.74.

112 'Miss Cairns picked it up . . . being Myra Hindley': Croft's 6.11.73 statement, J 267/447.

113 'a bad omen': Croft in *Titbits*, 7.11.74.

113 'Wait a while': Croft's 6.11.73 statement, J 267/447.

113 'There was a paper . . .': *ibid.*

113 'I might easily . . .': *Titbits*, 7.1.74.

114 'She wanted them as . . .': Croft to author.

115 False name used by Cairns: Croft in McGuinness 1974 case overview, DPP 2/5366/2.

115 'I was very aware . . . you're happy': Judy Gibbons to author.

115 'In the meantime . . .': Croft's 6.11.73 statement, J 267/447.

116 'It had some photographs . . .': Joan Kleinert to author.

116 Harber's uncle: McGuinness's 1974 case overview, DPP 2/5366/2.

116 'It's amazing no one . . .': Kleinert to author.

KEYS TO THE CASTLE

117 Prison keys: police exhibit photos, police forensic evidence (DPP 2/5366/2); Veronica Bird to author; and *Cries for Help* (Kozubska).

118 'That is why . . .': Bird to author.

118 'I asked her if . . .': Maxine Croft's 6.11.73 statement, J 267/447.

119 'you'll be a little lovelier . . .': Camay advertising campaign.

119 'Soap never . . .': Croft to author.

119 'so that we could . . .': Croft's 6.11.73 statement, J 267/447.

119 'It was like a French . . .': *Titbits*, 7.11.74.

119 'A few days later . . .': Cairns's 20.11.73 statement, J 267/447.

120 'As the escape plan . . . took impressions': *ibid*.

120 Carol White background: thanks to her daughter, Louise; also White's 22.11.73 statement, and previous convictions, DPP 2/5366/2.

121 'As I walked into . . .': White's 22.11.73 statement, DPP 2/5366/2.

121 'You've messed things up . . .': Croft's 6.11.73 statement, J 267/447.

121 'I poured . . . have you nicked': *ibid*.

122 'There is something going on . . . an eye open': Judy Gibbons to author.

122 Soap found on key: *Cries for Help* (Kozubska).

SAYING HER PRAYERS

123 'Do you wish to . . .' etc: Moors trial, 3.5.66, Goodman.

123 'prison religion': phrase used by former Holloway governor Joanna Kelly in *When the Gates Shut*.

123 Percentage of RC inmates: *Holloway Prison* (Camp).

124 'I'm a Catholic . . .': Judy Gibbons to author.

124 'That was where . . .': Kath Moores to author.

125 'These people will . . .': Gibbons to author.

125 'I could not see . . .': Barbara Bates's 21.11.73 statement, J 267/446 2.

126 'very flustered': Taylor statement, DPP 2/5366/2.

126 'The officers stuck together . . .': Veronica Bird to author.

126 Collingham Gardens: thanks to Dee Bird, daughter of the late Angela Glynn; also Glynn 21.11.73 statement, J 267/446.

127 'I showed Pat . . . long time ago': Janet Harber's 28.1.74 statement, DPP 2/5366/2.

127 'not a particularly bright individual': McGuinness's 1974 case overview, DPP 2/ 5366/2.

127 'During October 1973 . . . she hadn't': Harber's 28.1.74 statement, DPP 2/5366/2.

128 'From that time . . . the Prison Service': Harber's 27.11.73 statement, DPP 2/5366/2.

128 'She [Cairns] was frightened . . .': Croft in *Titbits*, 7.11.74.

128 'I asked her . . .': Croft's 6.11.73 statement, J 267 447.

128 'She hadn't a clue . . .': Croft to author.

USING PEOPLE

129 Thompson was acquitted at the Old Bailey of involvement in the 1975 murder of George Brett, part of a gangland murder case: *Daily Mail*, 10.11.80.

129 'just a friend': Maxine Croft to author.

129 Stephens's background: thanks to his children, Ian and Julie.

129 'He used to have . . .': Julie Wilson to author.

129 Stephens's early conviction: DPP 2/5366/2.

130 'My dad wasn't . . .' etc: Ian Stephens to author.

130 'He always had . . .': Julie Wilson to author.

130 'the best dad . . .': Ian Stephens to author.

131 'Maxine said she . . .': Trisha Cairns's 20.11.73 statement, J 267/447.

131 'She told me to . . .': Maxine Croft's 6.11.73 statement, J 267/447.

131 Dennis Croft becomes involved: author's interviews; his 15.11.73 statement, J 267/ 446.

131 'Maxine sat on one . . .': Dennis Croft to author.

131 'This young prisoner . . .': Veronica Bird to author.

132 'She was always . . .': Dennis Croft to author.

132 'She didn't tell . . .': Dennis Croft's 15.11.73 statement, J 267/446.

132 'something I regret . . . of the two': Susan to author (name changed).

132 'She said . . .': Susan's statement, National Archives.

133 Hindley moves cell: 21.1.74 statement by Chief Officer Storrow (DPP 2/5366/2) and 6.12.73 statement of DS Peace, DPP 2/5366/1.

133 Lesbian couple shared a cell: *Cries for Help* (Kozubska).

133 Anna Mendleson and the Angry Brigade: Mendleson's criminal record (DPP 2/53656/1); her obituary, *Guardian* 15.12.09.

134 Longford's communications with Home Office, 'Lord Longford, who seemed . . .': 18.10.73 memo, HO 336/19.

135 'He's useless . . .': Maxine Croft to author.

135 'Dear Dennis' letter: police exhibit No. 2 (DPP 2/5366/1). Croft identified it as being written on prison notepaper: McGuinness's statement 6.12.73, DPP 2/5366/1.

135 'Cairns got a bit annoyed . . .': Croft's 6.11.73 statement, J 267/447.

136 'I wouldn't have . . .': Dennis Croft to author.

136 'PLEASE POST . . .': Dennis Croft's 15.11.73 statement, J 267/446.

136 'As well as . . .': Jane Smith to author.

136 'She was well-liked . . . down the line': Kath Moores to author.

137 'There was very few . . .': Maxine Croft to author.

137 Summers said Croft had crush on her: Summers's 7.11.73 statement, J 267/446.

137 Theft conviction: DPP 2/5366/2.

137 'I thought Lyn was . . .': Moores to author.

137 'She got really upset . . . I don't want to leave': Maxine Croft to author.

138 'She was my friend . . .': Moores to author.

138 'On one of these visits . . .': Summers's 7.11.73 statement, J 267/446.

138 'She said . . . Just get rid of her': Croft's 9.11.73 statement, J 267/447.

IS IT A BOMB?

139 Cairns calls in sick: McGuinness's statement 6.12.73, DPP 2/5366/1.

139 'I noticed . . .': Susan's statement (NB: name changed), National Archives.

140: 'I remember . . .': Susan to author.

140 What Croft wore: Croft's 6.11.73 statement, J 267/447.

140 'a day out for shopping . . .': Maggie Powell's 13.11.73 statement, J 267/446.

141 'I told her . . .': *ibid.*

142 'At twenty to twelve . . . how expensive all this was to her': Croft's 9.11.73 statement, J 267/447.

143 Cairns's savings: McGuinness's statement 6.12.73 (DPP 2/5366/1); and Janet Harber's statement 17.1.74, J 267/446.

143 'I was very surprised . . .': George Stephens's 17.1.74 statement, J 267/446.

143 'He asked what . . .' etc: Croft's 9.11.73 statement, J 267/447.

143 'She said she couldn't . . .' etc: Stephens's 17.1.74 statement, J 267/446.

144 Using Manchester Central Station and finding luggage ticket: murder trial evidence, *The Times* 21.4.66.

144 'When Maxine and I . . .': Cairns's 20.11.73 statement, J 267/447.

145 'Dear George . . .' note: police exhibit No. 7, DPP 2/5366/1.

145 Croft addressed the envelope: her 9.11.73 statement, J 267/447.

145 'because I wanted to go . . .': *ibid*.

146 'I noticed Maxine had been . . .' etc: Lyn Summers's 7.11.73 statement, DPP 2/5366/2.

146 'She never mentioned . . . kind of things': Kath Moores to author.

146 'I liked her a lot . . .': Croft to author.

147 Barking Magistrates Court date: DPP 2/5366/2.

147 'When I heard she . . .' etc: Summers's 7.11.73 statement, DPP 2/5366/2.

147 'I'm frightened . . .': *ibid*.

147 'I know Lyn . . .': Jane Smith to author.

147 'You're a bloody . . . get years': Summers's 7.11.73 statement, DPP 2/5366/2.

147 'Don't worry about it . . .': Croft to author.

148 Cairns adds postscripts: police exhibit No. 17, DPP 2/5366/1; and forensic evidence.

149 Parcel posted: expert witness statement 14.11.73, DPP 2/5366/2.

149 'She was in an emotional . . . calm her down': Powell's 13.11.73 statement, J 267/446.

149 'I ended up knocking . . .': Croft to author.

UNCLE PHIL

151 A package arrives: Stephens's 5.11.73 statement, DPP 2/5366/2.

151 'Mr George': police exhibit No. 17, DPP 2/5366/1.

151–52 Phil Thomas background: thanks to his children, Phillip 'Phil' Thomas and Jo Ross.

152 'My uncle said . . .': Phillip Thomas to author.

152 'He was a good copper . . . murder investigation': *ibid.*

152 'He wouldn't . . .': Julie Wilson (*née* Stephens) to author.

153 'I spent . . . off you go sir': Ian Stephens to author.

153 'They used to . . .': Julie Wilson (*née* Stephens) to author.

153 'I think it's a bomb . . . ordinary way': Stephens's 5.11.73 statement, DPP 2/5366/2.

153 'I'll open it . . . smelt of soap': DCI Thomas's 3.11.73 statement, DPP 2/5366/2.

153 'and looked utterly . . .': Stephens's 5.11.73 statement, DPP 2/5366/2.

154 Handwriting: 4.1.74 statement of police scientific advisor David Ellen, J 267/446.

154 First instructions: police exhibit No. 4, DPP 2/5366/1. Also 23.11.73 statement of Paul Barr, DPP 2/5366/1.

154 Second set of instructions: police exhibit No. 7, DPP 2/5366/1.

154 Third set of instructions: police exhibit No. 10, DPP 2/5366/1.

154 Master key instructions: police exhibit No. 13, DPP 2/5366/1.

154 'My first thought . . .': Thomas's 3.11.73 statement, DPP 2/5366/2.

154 Stephens mentions Croft: Stephens's 5.11.73 statement, DPP 2/5366/2.

154 'He told me . . .': *ibid.*

155 'That's the joke . . . East End girl': Scoble to author. Background: his 8.11.73 statement, DPP 2/5366/1.

155 Hoggarth's handwriting: his 16.11.73 statement, J 267/446.

155-6 'I've got no . . . too slick': Scoble to author.

NOT THE IRA

157 'My principal . . .': Hoggarth's 16.11.73 statement, J 267/446.

157 'an intelligent young woman . . .': social report 26.3.74, J 267/447.

157 Haig-Brown's dismay: *ibid.*

158 'What have you done?': Maxine Croft to author.

158 Haig-Brown didn't believe Croft: her 21.11.73 statement, J 267/446.

158 'She panicked . . . just like Ian Brady.': Croft's 9.11.73 statement, J 267/447.

158 'to tell Pat . . .': Taylor's statement, J 267/446 (NB: name changed).

159 'She then asked . . .': *ibid.*

159 'This is for Patricia . . .': Janet Harber's 27.11.73 statement, J 267/446.

159 'get rid of . . . key impressions': Taylor's statement, J 267/446.

159 'Myra again saw me . . .': *ibid.*

159 'I told her that . . . might be discovered': Haig-Brown's 21.11.73 statement, J 267/446.

160 '[I] was told the police . . .': Croft's 9.11.73 statement, J 267/447.

160 Harber gives Cairns note: Harber's 27.11.73 statement, J 267/446.

160 Hindley speaks to Cairns through door: *The Lost Boy* (Staff); Home Office memo 7.11.73, HO 336/19.

160 'I think that was . . . said *Hmmm*': Dee Bird (*née* Glynn) to author.

161 Two calls from Taylor: Angela Glynn's 21.11.73 statement, J 267/446. Taylor denied calling Cairns on Hindley's behalf on 1.11.73 (J 267/446).

161 'I asked Miss . . . telephone call': Glynn's 21.11.73 statement, J 267/446.

161 'No, I posted it': Croft's 9.11.73 statement, J 267/447.

162 'You'll have to . . . no protection in here': *ibid.*

162 'I'll pray for you . . . God knows why': Croft to author.

163 'He was a good guy . . .': *ibid.*

163 Hoggarth asks governor to leave: *ibid.*

163 Leissner remained: Hoggarth's 16.11.73 statement, J 267/446.

163 'She at first denied . . .': *ibid.*

163 Croft insists now: to author.

164 Price sisters: National Archive, Ireland.

164 'He said . . . It's for Myra Hindley': Croft to author.

McGUINNESS, LIKE THE DRINK

165 'He liked the Bruch . . .': Catherine McGuinness to author.

166 'He did work . . .': *ibid.*

166 'There was no way . . .': Paul Barr to author.

167 'His claim to fame . . .': John Dixon to author.

167 Marwood execution: British Pathé News, 11.5.59.

167 'I used to . . .': Barr to author.

167 'so that somebody . . . any more questions' (McGuinness's initial conversation with Croft): McGuinness statement 6.12.73, DPP 2/5366/1.

168 'Have you ever . . . groundless': *ibid.*

169 'I didn't want . . . knew the villains': Paul Barr to author.

170 Searching the Ivory Tower: Barr to author; and his 23.11.73 statement, DPP 2/5366/1.

170 Cairns destroys evidence: *The Lost Boy* (Staff).

171 'She was indignant . . .': Barr to author.

171 Search of flat: Barr to author; and his 23.11.73 statement, DPP 2/5366/1.

171 'No, I most certainly . . .' (McGuinness questions Cairns): McGuinness's 6.12.73 statement, DPP 2/5366/2.

171 'She was an inveterate liar . . .': Barr to author.

172 'I may have to . . . same as the drink': McGuinness's 6.12.73 statement, DPP 2/5366/2.

172 'I think we all thought . . .': Barr to author.

GRASSING

173 '[Cairns] saw me . . .': Taylor's statement (J 267/446). NB: name changed.

174 POLICE PROBE 'PLOT TO FREE MYRA HINDLEY': *Sunday Telegraph*, 4.11.73. Also *Sunday Express* and *News of the World*, same date.

174 Longford considered articles defamatory: P4 Division Home Office memo 7.11.73, HO 336/19.

174 'Lord Longford stuck . . .': Paul Barr to author.

174 'I was concerned whether my . . . conscience dictated': Taylor's statement, J 267/446.

175 Separated at bus stop: *ibid*.

175 Summers's conviction: Barking Magistrates Court, 30.10.73, DPP 2/5366/2.

175 'I thought to myself . . .': Kath Moores to author.

175 'Have you seen . . .' etc (dialogue with Moores): Janet Harber's statement, 28.1.74, J 267/447.

176 'We can't stay . . .': *ibid*.

176 'The stupid cow!': *ibid.*

176 'I can't imagine . . . meeting Maxine': *ibid.*

176 'because the keys they had . . . addressed to Janet': Moores's 22.1.74 statement, J 267/446.

177 'You saw Max . . .' (dialogue in kitchen): Summers's 7.11.73 statement, DPP 2/5366/1.

177 'I said to Lyn . . . all about her': Moores to author.

178 'It was a mad plan . . .': *ibid.*

178 'Lyn, this is just too much . . .': *ibid.*

178 In her 7.11.73 statement (DPP 2/5366/1), Summers says she went to the prison on 6.11.73.

178 'It's got nothing to do . . .': DCI Thomas's 7.11.73 statement, DPP 2/5366/1.

179 'I have known a girl named Maxine . . . it's a bomb': George Stephens's initial 5.11.73 statement, DPP 2/5366/1.

180 Omitted sentences ("I have been worried . . .'): Stephens's second statement, 17.1.74, J 267/446.

180 'It's a cover story . . .': John Dixon to author.

180 'He couldn't make . . .': Maxine Croft to author.

180 'A scrap-yard bloke . . .': Trevor Scoble to author.

180 'Obviously, that story . . . on it undercover': Ian Stephens to author.

181 'Everyone knew that George . . .': Croft to author.

181 'through an informer': 8.11.73 Home Office document PDG/66 1/177/5, HO 336/19.

181 'Do you know what . . .': Julie Wilson to author.

181 'Pat [Cairns] said she didn't . . .': Taylor's statement, J 267/446.

182 'You realise that to get . . . answer that' (McGuinness interviews Croft): McGuinness 6.12.73 statement, J 267/ 1446.

183 'Miss Cairns said to me . . .': Croft's statement 6.11.73, J 267/447.

183 DS Pearce visits Dennis Croft: Pearce 16.11.73 statement, DPP 2/5366/1; Pearce to author, and Dennis Croft to author.

183 'I showed the telegram . . .': Dennis Croft's 25.11.73 statement, J 267/446.

183 'there was no love lost . . .': Dennis Croft to author.

183 'I can remember . . . rotten vegetables': Pearce to author.

184 'Dear Dennis . . .': Police exhibit No. 3, DPP 2/5366/1.

184 Summers goes to the prison: Summers's 7.11.73 statement, DPP 2/5366/1.

COME ALONG, PLEASE

185 'Did you . . . come on please' (McGuinness interviews Cairns): his 6.12.74 statement, DPP 2/5366/2.

186 Police find envelope addressed to Mrs Moulton: Paul Barr statement 23.11.73, DPP 2/5366/1.

186 'Who is Myra Spencer?' etc: McGuinness's 6.12.74 statement, DPP 2/5366/2.

186 Lyn Summers had spoken to police: her 7.11.73 statement, DPP 2/5366/1.

187 Cairns charged: McGuinness's 6.12.74 statement, DPP 2/5366/2.

187 Cairns watched: undercover officer's statement 23.11.73; and McIntosh's statement 16.2.74 (both DPP 2/5366/1).

187 'security services' intelligence: McGuinness's 1974 report to DPP, DPP 2/5366/2.

187 Cairns's parentage: P4 Division memo 7.11.73, HO 336/19.

187 'Had it not been .. . .': McGuinness's 1974 report, DPP 2/5366/2.

187–88 Price sisters conviction: National Archives of Ireland.

188 'Although there is no . . .': McGuinness's 1974 report, DPP 2/5366/2.

188 McIntosh's 'work on gender . . .': *Guardian*, 24.1.13.

188 'might have been a bit . . .': Catherine McGuinness to author.

188 'lesbian tendencies': McGuinness's 1974 report, DPP 2/5366/2.

189 'She has already spent . . .': Cairns's 20.11.73 confession, J 267/447.

189 'It was as if she . . .': Paul Barr to author.

189 'It is only in recent . . .': Cairns's 20.11.73 confession, J 267/447.

190 Hindley's many lies to police: police case summary P189754, HO 336/48.

190 'All I am saying is . . .': police evidence in her trial, 22.4.66, Goodman.

190 Hindley said in court she had never been to Ashton market, *The Times*, 21.4.66. But her sister Maureen said Myra shopped there weekly: Moors murder trial, 20.4.66, Goodman.

190 '[Ian] didn't . . .': police case summary P189754, HO 336/48.

190 'I made all my own . . .': Hindley police interview, in trial evidence, 28.4.66, Goodman.

191 'Did you hear that . . .': police summary (HO 336/48); and trial evidence, *The Times*, 21.4.66.

191 'As far as Lesley Ann . . .': *ibid*.

191 Finding Downey's remains: forensic evidence in trial 27.4.66, Goodman.

191 Finding Kilbride's remains: the *Criminologist*, August 1968.

191 'I'll kill you . . .': press coverage of committal, including *Daily Express*, 15.12.65.

191 Hindley comforted by Brady: *The Lost Boy* (Staff).

192 Hindley turned police away: Topping.

192 'Am I allowed . . .': McGuinness's statement 6.12.74, DPP 2/5366/2.

192 'It has been . . .': Mounsey in Moors trial 27.4.66, Goodman.

193 'Have you ever . . .' etc (McGuinness's second attempt to interview Hindley): McGuinness statement 6.12.74, DPP 2/5366/2.

193 'Every question you . . . at me': Barr to author.

193-5 'Not in a leather . . . anything about it' (dialogue with McGuinness): McGuinness statement 6.12.74, DPP 2/5366/2.

THE FACE OF 1974

197 'subvert both officers . . .': Home Office memos 14.12.73 and 18.12.73, HO 336/19.

197 'It makes me feel . . .': Hindley to Dr Pinney, *Evening News*, 2.4.74.

197 'eccentric to the . . .': McGuinness's 2.2.74 report, DPP 2/5366/2.

198 Escaped budgie: 'Older and Wiser?' by Myra Hindley and Nina Wilde, *Verdict*, Hilary (term) 1996.

198 'She was very . . .': Maxine Croft to author.

198 'Myra Hindley is trying . . .': 1.12.73 governor memo to Home Office, HO 336/19.

198 'has formed a close . . .': McGuinness's 1974 report to DPP, DPP 2/5366/2.

198 Whether to prosecute Hindley: legal notes in DPP 2/5366/1; and McGuinness's 1974 report, DPP 2/5366/2.

199 'The face is long . . .': *Daily Mail*, 18.1.74.

200 'monster' photo: Hindley in *Evening News*, 2.4.74.

200 Second remand appearance: court reports and photos in daily newspapers, including *Sun*, *Guardian* and *Daily Mirror*, 2.2.74; also case papers, J 267/446.

201 Bail for Cairns: court document 1.2.74, DPP 2/5366/1.

201 Allowed to remain in flat: Holloway memo, 12.11.73, HO 336/127.

201 Harber's initial two statements: 8 and 27.11.73, J 267/446.

201 Third Harber statement ('I asked her . . .' etc): 28.1.74, J 267/447.

202 'It's unbelievable . . . shutters down': Stan Ball to author.

203 Bond St demonstration: police report CR/177/73/144; Sanders quoted from her statement, 15.2.74; and examples of the leaflets, all DPP 2/5366/2.

203 'You see, unless . . .': Judy Gibbons to author.

204 'We were absolutely horrified . . .': Veronica Bird to author.

204-5 Requests and complaints: Holloway 'history sheets' HO 336/126.

204 Hindley moved to F Wing: prison memo 7.3.74, HO 336/19.

204 'On the night . . .': Hindley to Dr Bull, 15.4.74, HO 336/97.

THE CRUCIBLE OF SUFFERING

207 'Myra Hindley looked wan . . .': *Daily Mirror*, 2.4.74.

207 Melford Stevenson background: *The Very Best of the Daily Telegraph Books of Obituaries* (Massingberd).

208 Indictment: Regina vs. Patricia Cairns etc., J 267/446.

208 'Her voice was . . .': *Daily Mirror*, 2.4.74.

208–16 Trial with all quotations, as reported in the *Daily Telegraph*, *Daily Mail*, *Daily Mirror* and *Guardian* (all 2.4.74); *Evening News* 1.4.74; also the July 1974 Court of Appeal judgement; and related legal documents, J 267/447.

211–14 Hindley's statement ('Life in prison . . .' etc) reprinted almost complete in *Guardian*, 2.4.74.

215 'She is now tragically . . .' etc: social reports in mitigation,

J 267/447.

215 'And they were . . .': Alec Edwards to author.

215–16 Sentencing ('You were undoubtedly . . .' etc): *Daily Telegraph*, *Daily Mail*, *Daily Mirror* and *Guardian* (all 2.4.74); also *Evening News* 1.4.74; July 1974 Court of Appeal judgement, and related papers, J 267/447.

LOVE STORY

217 'JAIL LOVE AFFAIR': *Sun*, 2.4.74.

217 'If I hadn't taken her . . .': Dorothy Wing in the *Sun*, *ibid*.

218 Cairns's prison number: appeal papers, J 267/447.

218 'And of course that . . . let down by her': Veronica Bird to author.

219 'vital importance': 8.4.74 document, HO 336/19.

219 'Since her recent . . . spiritual nature': 25.11.74 Holloway report, HO 336/44.

219 'behaviour we had never . . .': *ibid*.

219 Film night incident (and quotes): Hindley letter and staff report, April 1974, HO 336/ 97.

220 'If that [woman] . . .': *ibid*.

220 'devious and untrustworthy . . . probably successful': F Wing AG report 20.11.74, HO 336/44.

221 'No one likes to . . .': Ali in the *Sun*, 3.4.74.

221 Melford Stevenson letter: Croft's 1974 appeal, J 267/447.

221 Compensation for Ali: Home Office document 25.6.74, J 267/446.

222 'I was told I would . . .': Croft to author.

222 Croft appeal: Appeal Court judgement 9.7.74, J 267/447. Also probation report.

222 'You can go there . . .': Appeal Court judgement, J 267/447.

222 'Thank you, sir': *ibid*.

222 'WHAT MYRA HINDLEY DID TO ME': *Titbits*, 7.11.74.

223 'As I look back on . . .': *Titbits*, 14.11.74.

223 'She did send me letters . . .': Cairns to Staff, *The Lost Boy*.

223: Brady told Dr Keightley that he and Hindley exchanged coded messages, and in one of these he claims Hindley told him in advance about the escape plot: *Ian Brady* (Keightley).

223 'Agitated and shaking . . . attachment to Myra': HMP Durham memos, partially redacted, January 1976, HO 336/127.

224 'ill for several . . . some of the inmates': HMP Holloway memo, 29.3.76, HO 336/44.

225 O'Dwyer background: *Criminal Women* (Carlen); Holloway reports and previous convictions, HO 336/127.

225 'It took six of us . . .': Bird to author.

225 Staff showed O'Dwyer the *News of the World*: *Criminal Women* (Carlen).

225 'these two monsters . . .': *News of the World*, 26.9.76.

226 Hindley thought O'Dwyer was unbalanced: Hindley's 26.9.76 statement to the governor re the incident, HO 336/127.

226 'so uptight . . .': Staff witness B, 26.9.76 statement to governor, HO 336/127.

226 'Child-murdering bastard': Hindley's 26.9.76 statement, HO 336/127.

226 'Who do you think . . .': O'Dwyer's undated statement, HO 336/127.

226 'Shut up and mind . . .': Staff witness B, 26.9.76 statement, HO 336/127.

226 'You don't talk to me . . .': O'Dwyer's undated statement, HO 336/127.

226 'She proceeded to . . .': Hindley's 26.9.76 statement, HO

336/127.

226 'Stop it! . . .': Staff witness A, 26.9.76 statement, HO 336/127.

226 'You bastard . . .': Staff witness D, 26.9.76 statement, HO 336/127.

227 'I was punched . . . bled profusely': Hindley's 26.9.76 statement, HO 336/127.

227 Surgery: Holloway memo, 7.12.76, HO 336/127.

227 O'Dwyer later claimed she was set up: in *Criminal Women* (Carlen).

BACK TO THE MOORS

229 'She was absolutely shattered . . .': 1977 Holloway memo, HO 336/126.

229 Driven to Durham: 2.1.77 Holloway memo, HO 336/27.

229 'with two great holes . . .': Hindley letter, *Manchester Evening News*, 4.7.77.

230 'self-aware, self-possessed . . .': Durham assessment, 1990 life sentence review, HO 336/48.

230 'sensitive . . .': Trevelyan in 'Freedom for Myra Hindley?' *Brass Tacks*, BBC, 6.7.77.

230 Jones's background: her book *The Devil and Miss Jones*.

230 'I can't show . . .': Hindley to BBC, 6.7.77.

230 'the anti-brigade': Hindley quoted in 1977 HMP Durham memo HO 336/48.

230 'Lord Longford is talking . . .' etc: Mrs West in *Brass Tacks*, BBC, 6.7.77.

230 Hindley disappointed by programme: H Wing Review Board, HMP Durham, November 1977, HO 336/48.

231 'exploit[ing] her poor daughter's . . .': Hindley to Astor, 15.6.95, Archive of David Astor.

231 'scapegoat and whipping boy. . .': *Evening News*, 26.1.79.

231 'What must I do?': Hindley quotes in prisoner review, HMP Durham, April 1979, HO 336/127.

231 'Many of those who . . .': 1981 prison report, HO 336/ 45.

231 'showed sorrow and regret . . .': *ibid*.

232 'She is an arch manipulator . . .': Durham report 14.3.79, HO 336/120.

232 Threatens hunger strike: 24 ½ year review, HO 336/48.

232 'political careerist . . . do you want?': Hindley's letter 4.6.85, HO 336/45.

233 'marketing job': P4 Division letter 19.9.88, HO 336/30.

233 'skilled at fobbing off . . .': Astor's letter, 7.9.95, Archive of David Astor.

233 'If I revealed what . . .': Brady in *Sunday People*, 23.6.85.

233 Topping's initial meeting with Brady: Topping.

234 'moved on . . . she was ever after': Maxine Croft to author. Thanks also to Geoff Knupfer.

234 'She had applied . . .': Kath Moores to author.

235 'I got on the bus . . .': *One of Your Own* (Lee).

235 'Peter and I went to . . .': Knupfer to author.

235 'not knowing whether my son . . .': Mrs Johnson's 31.10.86 letter, HO 3361/79.

236 'She became extremely upset . . .': 3.11.86 prison memo, HO 336/48.

236 'I wish I did know . . .': *ibid*.

236 'I remember in prison . . .': Bernadette to author (name changed).

236 'We had been told . . .': Knupfer to author.

237 'What do you want . . .': *ibid*.

237 'Although the Rev. Timms describes . . .': Home Office letter 22.4.87, HO 336/104.

237 Timms and Hindley: author's discussions with Timms.

237 'She was very polite . . . right direction': Knupfer to author.

238–39 Police operation: Topping; author's interviews with Knupfer; and author's recollection of staking out HMP Cookham Wood as a reporter in 1986.

239 'I came prepared . . .': News footage of Mr Kilbride, *Modern Times: Myra Hindley* (BBC, 2000).

239 PM briefed ('has not admitted . . .'): Downing Street letter 16.12.86 to Home Office, and reply, HO 336/104.

239 'It was a very long . . .': Knupfer to author.

239 Hindley's confession: Topping, and Knupfer to author.

239 'I asked her . . . she felt sick': Topping.

240 'willingly . . . on the street': *ibid*.

241 'I think the chances are . . . our inquiry': Knupfer to author.

241 'All the way through . . .': Topping.

242 'All of a sudden . . . simply not there': Knupfer to author.

OLD LOVE, NEW LOVE

243 'When I broke the news . . .': Topping.

243 'When this came to light . . .': Sara Trevelyan in *Myra Hindley: The Prison Years* (Granada Productions, 2006).

243 'A long, long time . . .': Kath Moores to author.

244 'About nine months . . . so far': April 1990 Cookham Wood document, HO 336/48.

244 'At least she's . . .': *The Devil and Miss Jones* (Jones).

244 'No words of mine . . .': Hindley's 14.5.90 representation to Parole Board, HO 336/48.

245 'She said that she . . .': Parole committee report, 16.5.90, HO 336/48.

245 Parole Board recommendation 21.8.90, HO 336/48.

245 Whole life tariff imposed in secret: HO 336/154.

245 Cairns not enjoying her job: 1992 Hindley's letter to David Astor, Archive of David Astor.

246 Hindley watched Wimbledon: Chris Duffin (formerly Ellis) to author.

246 Cairns joins meetings at Cavendish Ave, etc: memorandum 27.7.92, and related papers in the Archive of David Astor.

246 Hindley thanks Astors: 1992 card to Astors, Archive of David Astor.

246 Lovers: Chapman quotes Cairns using the word re her and Hindley in his book *For the Love of Myra*.

246 Joan Kleinert visit: Kleinert to author.

246 'We had a lot . . . sort herself out': Chris Duffin (formerly Ellis) to author.

247 'a very insignificant person . . .': *ibid*.

247 'She had at one point . . .': Joe Chapman to author.

248 Confession considered a disaster: *ibid*.

248 'I immediately warmed to her . . .': *ibid*.

248 'I am a lesbian now . . .': *For the Love of Myra* (Chapman).

248 'Clearly, they loved each other . . .': Chapman to author.

248 'She always said . . .': *ibid*.

248 'Trisha wasn't overly . . .': *ibid*.

249 Kinveachy Gardens: Archive of David Astor; electoral register; author's interview with Chapman; thanks also to Trish Gooch, who bought the house next.

249 'There were things that . . . Myra's sincerity': Chapman to author.

250 Hindley meets Wilde: Wilde's book, *The Monstering of Myra Hindley*.

250 'Myra, have you met . . .': *ibid*.

250 'When the governor told me . . .': *ibid*.

250 'I said to Chris . . . all wrong': Chapman to author.

251 First Kay story: *Sun*, 2.5.94.

251 'Fuck the *Sun*': Chris Duffin (formerly Ellis) to author.

251 Hindley said Kay was a murderer: Chapman to author.

251 Kay's background: his obituary, *The Times*, 14.5.21; and *Stick it Up Your Punter!* (Chippindale and Horrie).

251 'Why all of a . . . collect people': Chapman to author.

252 Hindley fantasises: *For the Love of Myra* (Chapman).

252 Cairns says Hindley dumped her: Chapman report, 2.3.95, Archive of David Astor.

252 'I am the injured . . .': *ibid*.

252 'I wish I hadn't . . .': Chapman to author.

252 Decor considered hideous: Trish Gooch to author.

252 Grants for Wilde: Astor to Hindley, 9.9.94, Archive of David Astor.

252 Hindley and Wilde together, claim: *Sun*, 8.10.94.

252 Wilde says *Sun* story fabricated: *The Monstering of Myra Hindley* (Wilde).

252 MYRA'S LESBIAN LOVER SACKED: *Sun*, 8.10.94

252 'She screamed, "I've got . . ."': *Sun*, 14.10.94.

253 'I was exonerated finally . . .': Chris Duffin (formerly Ellis) to author.

I NEVER CAME TO TERMS WITH IT

255 'No specifics . . . pretty distressed': Chris Duffin (formerly Ellis) to author. Thanks also to Peter Macklen.

255 'circumstances of the offences . . .': Home Office letter to Hindley, Dec 1994, HO 336/154.

256 'breakdown in communication': Hindley to Astor, 7.12.94, Archive of David Astor.

256 'to other lovers . . . terminate': *For the Love of Myra* (Chapman).

257 'terribly hurt': Astor's letter, 21.11.95, Archive of David Astor.

257 'We heard . . . broken': Linda Calvey to author.

257 Astor's financial support re Durham: Wilde to Astor, 7.5.95

and Astor to HMP Durham, 29.3.95, Archive of David Astor.

257 'disgusting creatures': Hindley to Astor, 26.4.95, *ibid.*

257 'I think she was in constant . . . years older': Calvey to author.

258 'There is that sort . . . on her mettle all the time': Pearl Davison to author.

259 'partners': various 1996 letters in the Archive of David Astor; also Wilde in *Independent on Sunday*, 9.2.97.

259 Hindley complains to Chief Inspector of Prisons, 1.11.96: Archive of David Astor.

259 'Myra saw I was . . .': *The Monstering of Myra Hindley* (Wilde).

260 Wilde clashes with Astor and Timms: 1997 correspondence, Archive of David Astor.

260 'So we have not done nothing . . .': Astor to Hindley, 1.8.97, Archive of David Astor.

260 'I love my room . . . security reasons': Hindley to Davison, 7.9.98.

261 Raised allowance and gifts: Astor letter, 26.5.98, Archive of David Astor.

261 'I care deeply about her . . . high standards': Hindley to Astors 30.11.98, Archive of David Astor.

261 Astor offers to cover bills: Astor to Cairns, 14.7.99, Archive of David Astor.

261 Stamps etc: June 1999 expenses, Archive of David Astor.

262 'looked and felt like Basil Brush . . .': Hindley to Davison, 7.9.98.

262 'She got very thin . . . Myra's mother': Calvey to author.

262–63 Further expenses: Archive of David Astor.

263 Astor considers buying house in Kent: Astor, 23.10.2000, Archive of David Astor.

263 Astor hasn't heard from Wilde: Astor, 21.2.2001, Archive

of David Astor.

263 'It was still going on . . .': Geoff Knupfer to author.

263 Death bed: 2002 HMP Highpoint files, HO 336/115.

263 'She was repentant . . .': Father Teader to author.

264 Personal effects and last note, 'A major criticism is . . .': 2002 HMP Highpoint files, HO 336/115.

264 Funeral arrangements: *ibid*. Also, author's interviews and contemporaneous press coverage, including BBC News, 21.11.02.

264 Ashes scattered at Stalybridge: *Sun*, 27.2.03.

264 'She was a good prison officer . . .': Stan Ball to author.

BIBLIOGRAPHY

Bird, Veronica and Richard Newman, *Veronica's Bird*, London, Clink Street, 2018

Camp, John, *Holloway Prison: The Place and the People,* Newton Abbot, David & Charles, 1974

Carlen, Pat (ed.), *Criminal Women: Autobiographical Accounts*, Cambridge, Polity Press, 1985

Chapman, Joe, *For the Love of Myra*, privately published, Amazon, 2018

Chippindale, Peter and Chris Horrie, *Stick It Up Your Punter! The Rise and Fall of the Sun*, London, William Heinemann, 1990

Davies, Caitlin, *Bad Girls: A History of Rebels and Renegades*, London, John Murray, 2018

Garrett, Dr Geoffrey and Andrew Nott, *Cause of Death: Memoirs of a Home Office Pathologist,* London, Robinson, 2001

Goodman, Jonathan, *The Moors Murders: The Trial of Myra Hindley and Ian Brady*, London, Magpie Books, 1994

Grahame, Kenneth, *The Wind in the Willows*, London, Methuen (1st pub. 1908)

Harrison, Fred, *Brady & Hindley: Genesis of the Moors Murders*, Bath, Ashgrove Press, 1986

Jones, Janie, *The Devil and Miss Jones: The Twisted Mind of Myra Hindley*, London, Smith Gryphon, 1994

Keightley, Dr Alan, *Ian Brady: The Untold Story of the Moors Murders*, London, Robson Books, 2017

Kelley, Joanna, *When the Gates Shut*, London, Longmans, 1967

Kozubska, Joanna, *Cries for Help: Women Without a Voice, Women's Prisons in the 1970s, Myra Hindley and Her Contemporaries*, Hook, Waterside Press, 2014

Lee, Carol Ann, *One of Your Own: The Life and Death of Myra Hindley*, Edinburgh, Mainstream, 2010

Longford, Lord, *Avowed Intent*, London, Little, Brown & Co, 1994

Massingberd, Hugh (ed.), *The Very Best of the Daily Telegraph Books of Obituaries*, London, Pan Books, 2001

Morton, James, *Gangland* (vol. 1 & 2), London, Warner Books, 1992 and 1994

Mosley, Charlotte (ed.), *The Mitfords: Letters Between Six Sisters*, London, Fourth Estate, 2007

Progl, Zoe, *Woman of the Underworld*, London, Four Square Books, 1964

Ritchie, Jean, *Myra Hindley: Inside the Mind of a Murderess*, London, Angus & Robertson, 1988

Staff, Duncan, *The Lost Boy: The Definitive Story of the Moors Murders*, London, Bantam Books, 2008

Sturgis, Matthew, *Oscar: A Life*, London, Head of Zeus, 2018

Swinnerton, Jo, *The London Companion*, London, Robson Books, 2004

Topping, Peter with Jean Ritchie, *Topping: The Autobiography of the Police Chief in the Moors Murder Case*, London, Angus & Robertson, 1989

Wilde, Nina, *The Monstering of Myra Hindley*, Hook, Waterside Press, 2016

ILLUSTRATIONS LIST

Insert 1
P.1
All images © The National Archives

P.2
All images © The National Archives

P.3
Image 1 © Mirrorpix / Getty Images
Images 2 and 3 © PA Images / Alamy Stock Photo
Image 4 © Evening Standard / Getty Images
Image 5 © PA Images / Alamy Stock Photo

P.4
Above © Mirrorpix / Getty Images
Below © John Donat / RIBA Collections

P.5
Images © ANL / Shutterstock

P.6
Full page © Ken Lennox

P.7
Above © Brian Bould / ANL/ Shutterstock
Centre © Clifford Ling / ANL/ Shutterstock
Below © Mirrorpix / ExpressStar

P.8
Above © The National Archives
Centre © Sage Mountainfire
Below © Howard Sounes

Insert 2
P.1
Above © Howard Sounes

Centre © The National Archives
Below © The National Archives

P.2
Above © The National Archives
Below © Julie Wilson

P.3
Above © Julie Wilson
Centre left © Howard Sounes
Centre right © Joanne Ross
Below © Catherine McGuiness

P.4
Above © Graham Wood / Evening Standard / Hulton Archive / Getty Images
Below © Daily Express/ Mirrorpix

P.5
Full page © Terry Gibson / The Telegraph

P.6
Above © Independent / Alamy Stock Photo

Below © Popperfoto / Getty Images

P.7
Above © PA Images / Alamy Stock Photo
Below © Noble / Draper

P.8
Above © Howard Sounes
Below © Shutterstock / Matthew Talboys

INDEX